READING
AMERICA

READING AMERICA

Essays on American Literature

DENIS DONOGHUE

Alfred A. Knopf *New York 1987*

THIS IS A BORZOI BOOK
PUBLISHED BY ALFRED A. KNOPF, INC.

Owing to limitations of space, all acknowledgments
for permission to reprint previously published
material can be found on page 320.

Library of Congress Cataloging-in-Publication Data

Donoghue, Denis.
Reading America.

1. American literature—History and criticism.
2. United States in literature. I. Title.
PS121.D66   1987   810'.9   87-45125
ISBN 0-394-55939-8

Manufactured in the United States of America
FIRST EDITION

For Frances

TABLE OF CONTENTS

Contents

INTRODUCTION

Near the end of this book I quote a few lines from John Ashbery's poem "Many Wagons Ago":

> *How easily we could spell if we could follow,*
> *Like thread looped through the eye of a needle,*
> *The grooves of light. It resists. But we stay behind, among them,*
> *The injured, the adored.*

The dictionaries say that to spell means to read something slowly and with difficulty, taking first steps in construing. The O.E.D. cites a sentence from Thackeray's *Pendennis:* "He was spelling the paper, with the help of his lips." In Ashbery's poem "spell" is like a zero in mathematics, its force depends upon what goes with it. Presumably it means to make some connections, to establish relations, however tentative, between one person and another, short of defining the relations. Thread looped through the eye of a needle doesn't need to prescribe anything, it trusts to the decisive power of the needle and the hand and mind that direct it. It is a question of how incised a relation should be. Harold Rosenberg remarked, in *The Tradition of the New,* that "lifting up a word and putting a space around it has been the conscious enterprise of serious French poetry since Baudelaire and Rimbaud." Ashbery is French in this attribute: the crucial words in his poetry are only sufficiently assertive to be there, to create a space for the mind's true business, which is to keep going. To spell is to work through the process of reading: the process would end if a meaning were to be prescribed, but Ashbery has an interest in postponing the end and enjoying the freedom the interval provides.

Reading comes after spelling: it moves more quickly, jumps a few gaps, takes some signs for granted. One of the consequences of literary theory in the past ten or fifteen years has been to assign to the reader some of the mystery traditionally vested in the author. Reader-response theory seems to me a tautology: it proposes to give polemical force to the self-evident proposition that a reader reads a poem, say, pretty much as he wishes. So much depends upon the context of interests upon which his reading of this poem intervenes. While the dictionaries say that to read means to decipher, discern, interpret, or construe, and imply that there is something, a document, waiting to be construed, modern theories of reading have dissolved the apparent objectivity of what is to be read in favour of the subjectivity of the reader and the fluidity of the reading process.

The idea of lifting up a word and putting a space around it is congenial to such theories because it is based upon a spatial analogy, specifically upon the way in which people look at modern paintings in which there is much diction but no syntax. I find the idea congenial, too, but for a different reason. I have written a good deal about American literature, especially in my *Connoisseurs of Chaos, The Ordinary Universe, The Sovereign Ghost,* and *Thieves of Fire,* but in each case the context, I now think, was peremptory, it forced the authors I wrote about to obey, or to seem to obey, the terms of discourse I prescribed for them. In *Connoisseurs of Chaos* I wrote about the poetries of Whitman, Tuckerman, Melville, Dickinson, Robinson, Frost, Stevens, J. V. Cunningham, Robert Lowell, Theodore Roethke, and—in the second edition—Elizabeth Bishop. I construed those poets in a severe context. The subtitle of the book was *Ideas of Order in Modern American Poetry.* The relation between order and the anarchy that threatens to subvert it imposed fairly strict limits upon the freedom with which I read the poems. In *The Ordinary Universe* the American writers I discussed—Henry James, William Carlos Williams, Saul Bellow, and Marianne Moore among them—were again curtailed by my concern for the relation between the poetic imagination and the ordinary world it often proposes to transcend. In *Thieves of Fire* Melville appears as an example of a type of imagination I call Promethean, but I was more interested in describing the type, and the overreaching motive it exemplifies, than in doing full justice to the writers—Milton, Blake, Melville, D. H. Lawrence—I used to clarify it. In *The Sovereign Ghost* the chapter on *The Waste Land* is perhaps decently free from the obligation of illustrating a thesis, but not as free as I would now wish.

The present selection from my uncollected essays and reviews on American themes is not, of course, without a context, but the context in each case is as loosely defined as it could well be. In several cases I was writing for a magazine—*The New York Review of Books, The New York Times Book Review, The Times Literary Supplement, The New Statesman*—whose readers were, I trusted, interested in American literature but not at the cost of their other interests. In some cases there was the different pleasure of writing for readers—of *Salmagundi, Nineteenth Century Fiction, The Hudson Review, Sewanee Review, The Southern Review*—whose interests were likely to be literary to begin with and to give a literary tone to their social, political, and moral observances. I hoped that the variety of such readerships would protect me from the danger of being pedantic in questions of theory.

The title of the book is not as outlandish as it may seem. In the Introduction to the revised edition of *Connoisseurs of Chaos* I have described my experience of American literature and the first steps I took to read it, in Dublin, before I ever had occasion to visit the United States. My relation to American literature, like my presence in the United States, is that of a "resident alien": I feel I hold the Green Card in both capacities. The literature is, I assume, an epitome of the society that has provoked it, and may be read on that understanding. I read it by spelling it, a little at a time. Sometimes—as on April 15, 1986, the dreadful day of President Reagan's bombing attack on Benghazi and Tripoli—I'm sure I don't understand anything of America, and can only stare at it in dismay. But when I read Wallace Stevens's "The Course of a Particular," I feel not entirely blank about it.

Reading these essays and reviews again, I appreciate afresh the particular debts I owe to R. P. Blackmur and Kenneth Burke. Blackmur helped me to gain access to the literature where it counted most, in the detail of poems and novels. He was not always right. His essay on *Moby-Dick*—the supreme work of American literature, as I now think—needs to be completed and corrected by thinking of all the things its obliquity prevented Blackmur from saying. But Blackmur's sense of the modern American poets and how they might be read was extraordinarily acute. As for Burke: his relation to American literature is intermittent and opportunistic. Even more than Blackmur, he is an American writer: his novel *Towards a Better Life* is unique, yet typically American in the demented dance of its sentences. His *Counter-Statement* is the first American book of criticism I recall reading, and it still strikes me as fulfilling the glowing possibility that a book of criticism may also be a work of art.

An alternative title for my book would be "With the Help of My Lips." Or "Lipreading as a Second Language."

ESSAYS

AMERICA IN THEORY

I n April 1975 a conference on American Studies was held at the
Schloss Leopoldskron in Salzburg as the first act in a celebration of
the bicentennial of the American Revolution. It was arranged by the
European Association for American Studies, the American Studies
Association, and the Salzburg Seminar in American Studies. Our theme
was "the impact of the U.S.A. and Europe upon each other." Four further
conferences were held within a few months, in Lagos, Tokyo, Tehran,
and San Antonio. The intention in those events was "to provide full
critical analyses of the United States."

The conference at Salzburg did not engage in much analysis, but it
began and ended with incidents worth recalling. In the first, Andrew
Sinclair left the Great Hall of the Schloss in protest against what he called
"the sad and terrible words" delivered by Gordon Wood in his opening
address, which Mr. Sinclair declared "a travesty." The protest seemed to
me dramatic but obscure. Sinclair couldn't have expected Professor Wood
to beg Europe's forgiveness for the crimes of the American government,
or to denounce Richard Nixon according to ethical criteria exemplified
by Che Guevara. Wood's address seemed to me acceptable, especially in
its implication—I recall this just as vividly as Sinclair's protest—that

American administrations must reconsider their involvement in the lives of others.

The second incident was not dramatic, but memorable in its way. Robert Forrey, coordinator for the Bicentennial Committee on International Conferences of Americanists, suggested at a plenary discussion of "The Future of American Studies" that we should examine the relation between American money and the development of American Studies in Europe. It was not clear to me whether he had in mind that those who paid the piper should have the privilege of calling the tune; or that we should examine more generally the relation between tunes and patronage. A Scandinavian scholar welcomed the suggestion, made a few remarks about money and power, and was squashed by one of his senior colleagues who accused him of borrowing more books than anyone else from the American Library, an institution entirely dependent upon American dollars. The question was dropped.

I mention Mr. Forrey's suggestion and Mr. Sinclair's protest only to remark that the academic pursuit of themes in American Studies can't be neutral or disinterested. You think you are talking about an American novel, but before you are well begun you find yourself reflecting on the exercise of power in the world. This doesn't happen when you talk about *Ulysses.* In Europe, we have at least intermittently adverted to the fact that our part in American Studies is implicated in a network of sentiments and purposes partly our own, no doubt, but at least equally the concern of diplomats and officers of the State Department. An entirely reputable academic interest has been furthered—sponsored, indeed—by other motives: American foreign policy, the spasmodic rhetoric of the cold war, the self-consciousness of American society. The relations between these motives are matters for argument and definition: they are not beyond the reach of syntax. It is absurd to suggest that scholars should turn away from their academic interests lest they find themselves corrupted by American hospitality, the embrace of the State Department, the Library of Congress, the American Council of Learned Societies, and the United States Information Service. But the relation between scholarship and money and power is an issue in American Studies, whereas it is not an issue in, say, Irish Studies, a pursuit in which worldly temptations are few.

I shall mention another occasion, and then move beyond these preliminaries.

On October 19, 1957, Lionel Trilling gave a lecture at the University of the South on "English Literature and American Education," in which he complained that American undergraduates were no longer interested in English literature, and had turned their sole attention to themselves and to the history and literature of America. Trilling was dismayed by this inclination—he took it as a sign of provincialism—and by the significance of its having happened so recently. He mentioned that in 1930 Carl Van Doren had given up his Columbia University lectures on American literature since the Civil War, and that it was only in 1944 that the university found it necessary to provide a new course on the subject.

The year 1944 marks pretty accurately, not indeed the beginning of the academic study of American history and literature, but the establishment of American Studies as an officially sponsored activity in Europe and elsewhere. In Germany, immediately after the war, the American government undertook a severe programme of "denazification," but it was soon abandoned in favour of more affable forms of persuasion, including the provision of democratic images and motifs for a people long deprived of them. American Studies in Europe became a significant part of that programme.

I have referred to these episodes as an indication of the context in which many European scholars have come to think of America through its history and literature. But for another reason, too. I recall from Salzburg and other similar occasions that in the European gatherings of Americanists we were especially concerned with two related considerations. The first was the idea that there was something sufficiently identifiable to be called "the American experience," whatever forms its description might take. The historical source of the experience was a matter of endless dispute: it might be attributed, we argued, to the Frontier, or to New England Puritanism and covenant theology, to democracy, Transcendentalism, slavery, the divisions of North and South, utopian sentiment, the Indians, Unitarianism, immigration, the idea of America as Redeemer Nation, or to what Reinhold Niebuhr once called "the ironic incongruity between our illusions and the realities which we experience." America, after all, is one of the few countries in which a sense of a particular destiny was prescribed at its origin: if this is true, the relation between origin and aftermath must be peculiarly tense. We interpret an origin as if it marked a principle. A country characterized by its origin has its proper destiny already inscribed. All it can do in the meantime is live up to that destiny or renounce it. In 1823 Emerson thought that life in America had been spared the corruptions which beset every other country. Surely this sentiment was worth pondering. And so forth: in Europe we discussed these origins, these destinies, as if we had to comprehend them or give up the hope of reading an American novel.

The second consideration arose from the first. We thought that what we needed was a theory of American life, and that we must begin with a theory of American literature. It should be a paradigm, a little story, or a simple formula legal enough to hold the multitudinous detail in place and yet flexible enough to admit further detail. I recall, too, that the working theory most regularly invoked was derived from the famous chapter of Henry James's monograph on Hawthorne in which James reflects upon the alleged thinness of the social and public life available to Hawthorne, and named several of the European institutions missing from the American scene. We were gratified to think that American life, so demonstrably affluent, was chiefly to be understood as marked by a disability, and that we had James's warrant for proceeding on that assumption. The most arduous instances of American literature were responses to penury of relations. We did not inquire how James came to think himself justified in patronizing Hawthorne for the impoverished character of his "contemplative saunterings and reveries." Nor did we pursue the consequence of James's saying, in *Notes of a Son and Brother,* that Hawthorne "proved to what a use American matter could be put by an American hand," and that he showed how "an American could be an artist, one of the finest, without 'going outside' about it . . . ; quite in fact as if Hawthorne had become one just by being American enough." Perhaps it amounted to a major concession on James's part. But it was clear that he didn't think the commitment of an American artist to being American enough would turn him into a great artist—a Balzac, to be specific—or that it would suffice for the largest ambition. There was always a further achievement which would have to be approached in a different way, and presumably by the addition of perceptions necessarily European.

It is my impression that European scholars in American Studies didn't pursue the question beyond the point where James had left it. I don't recall that we stayed with it even long enough to take sides in the argument on the point between James and Howells. James, we knew, had Cooper and indeed Hawthorne himself on his side, but Howells was sufficiently American to insist, in his review of James's monograph, that the catalogue of civic institutions which James listed as deplorably missing from Hawthorne's America still left "the whole of human life remaining, and a social structure presenting the only fresh and novel opportunities left to fiction, opportunities manifold and inexhaustible."

I recall, too, not understanding what T. S. Eliot meant by saying, in one of his essays on James, that "it is the final perfection, the consummation of an American to become, not an Englishman, but a European—something which no born European, no person of any European nationality, can become." I assumed that James came close to making himself a European by making himself an Englishman entirely at ease among the French; and that Eliot was content with the minor achievement of making himself a sort of Englishman, with some critical recourse to the values he deemed to issue from "the mind of Europe."

I don't say that the question of "the American experience" held us back from the daily business of reading American books; but that we read them tentatively and felt the lack of an enabling theory which would make sense of them. A theory might not, indeed, make sense of them, but it would indicate what kind of sense we should look out for. So the scholarly books we especially valued were those which offered to arrange the literature in advance of particular need. All we asked was that we be given an idea of American experience by analogy, perhaps, with the idea of a university we could learn from Newman. The idea would be based upon high examples of the literature, but it would hold out further possibilities and keep us alert to them.

In the event, the scholarly books we resorted to numbered about ten. I recall that at Salzburg we referred with particular respect to Perry Miller's *The New England Mind* (1939) and *Errand into the Wilderness* (1956), F. O. Matthiessen's *American Renaissance* (1941), Alfred Kazin's *On Native Grounds* (1942), Henry Nash Smith's *Virgin Land* (1950), Trilling's *The Liberal Imagination* (1950), Charles Feidelson's *Symbolism and American Literature* (1953), R. W. B. Lewis's *The American Adam* (1955), Richard Chase's *The American Novel and Its Tradition* (1957), Leslie Fiedler's *Love and Death in the American Novel* (1959), Leo Marx's *The Machine in the Garden* (1964), Richard Poirier's *A World Elsewhere* (1966), and Quentin Anderson's *The Imperial Self* (1971). These were the books we took as indicating that American experience was indeed exceptional, and that it was best understood as involving a refusal, upon principle, of the values derived from history and society. The American hero, these books encouraged us to see, enters into fellowship with nature—with a continent barely domesticated, still in its essence a wilderness—to forestall the constraints that in every other respect would be enforced by considerations of politics and economics, money and greed. Acting upon Emerson's distinction between the "biographical ego" and the "grand spiritual ego," the American Adam regards his biographical ego as a mere bundle of circumstances, the victim of crass conditions: his essential self is spiritual, and it finds its true place in the wilderness. Indeed, Richard Poirier's book uses such words as "environment," "place," and "world" as pure tropes: they have nothing to do with places in which one might live, and everything to do with the resources of language, they are figures within the space of a vocabulary. Poirier distinguishes "between works that create through language an essentially imaginative environment for the hero and works that mirror an environment already accredited by history and society." The first are likely to be American, the second European and, mostly, English or French.

The differences among these several works of scholarship are real, and I should allow for them. But their similarities are even more striking. Indeed, the theory they imply has been augmented by more recent work. I am thinking of Quentin Anderson's "Practical and Visionary Americans" (*The American Scholar,* Summer 1976), some recent essays by Nina Baym and Annette Kolodny, and the work Irving Howe has done in the spirit of his "Anarchy and Authority in American Literature," a chapter of his *Decline of the New* (1971), which I'm afraid we neglected at Salzburg. Perhaps I should say a word or two about these to show that they are indeed compatible with a theory I shall then try to name.

Howe maintains that the deepest desire in American literature is to be rid of every authority except that of the individual self, and he asks, in dismay, how and why American readers have made the unprecedented demand upon their writers that they create values "quite apart from either tradition or insurgency." American readers ask to see created a realm of values they wouldn't dream of living in or acting upon; values deliberately conceived at a distance from any world in which those readers might live. Quentin Anderson's essay proposes to explain the demonic element in American literature as responding to an appalling disaffection in American society. The disaffection arises, he believes, "from a projection of the loathing felt by individuals for a part of themselves"—the part that goes along willingly enough with acquisition and greed. According to this interpretation, American literature is called upon to enable readers "to fantasize a guiltless possession of the world" for themselves. Nina Baym's argument in "Melodramas of Beset Manhood" is that the myth of the American experience, as described in the scholarly books I have named, sets the hero free to disengage himself from a society he regards as embodied in women and the responsibilities of domestic life: as a result, he transfers to the open landscape his desire for sexual freedom. Annette Kolodny argues, in *The Lay of the Land* (1975), that the open wilderness to which the hero resorts symbolizes the compliant woman upon whom he exercises his power.

I am not claiming that these essays in the theory of America are "all the same." There are differences and disagreements among them. Poirier's review of *The Imperial Self,* for instance, is extremely severe: he doesn't believe that there can be, in literature, such a self, if only because language doesn't allow it. There are critical differences, too, in the use of such concepts as "property" and "premise." But I recur to the irrefutable compatibility among the several books, and to the episodes in American literature which they regularly call upon for testimony.

One of these is a passage from *The Portrait of a Lady* which Quentin Anderson and other critics have taken as especially significant. The passage comes in Chapter 19 when Madame Merle and Isabel Archer are much in each other's company at Gardencourt and are getting along splendidly. Isabel doesn't yet know anything she wouldn't wish to know about Serena Merle, and she admires virtually every quality she sees in her. If she feels any misgiving, it is that she associates her entirely with the social amenities and appearances. She permits herself to wonder, though not aloud, what commerce Madame Merle "could possibly hold with her own spirit." The question comes up again a few pages later when Isabel disavows every interest in the property of the young men who have sought her affections. That's very crude of you, Madame Merle insists.

> When you've lived as long as I you'll see that every human being has his shell and that you must take the shell into account. By the shell I mean the whole envelope of circumstances. There's no such thing as an isolated man or woman; we're each of us made up of some cluster of appurtenances. What shall we call our "self"? Where does it begin? Where does it end? It overflows into everything that belongs to us—and then it flows back again. I know a large part of myself is

in the clothes I choose to wear. I've a great respect for things! One's self—for other people—is one's expression of one's self; and one's house, one's furniture, one's garments, the books one reads, the company one keeps—these things are all expressive.

Isabel disagrees. "I think just the other way," she says.

I don't know whether I succeed in expressing myself, but I know that nothing else expresses me. Nothing that belongs to me is any measure of me; everything's on the contrary a limit, a barrier, and a perfectly arbitrary one.

It is in some respects a specious argument. The things which Madame Merle chooses as appurtenances are clearly expressions of her; though by expressing herself in these ways she may deceive people and deceive herself. If her attitude didn't have much to recommend it, James couldn't have written *The Spoils of Poynton,* where similar attitudes are the gist of the matter, and are thought worth fighting about. There would be a better argument about the things which are not matters of choice. It is commonly supposed, I think, that Isabel has the better part of the dispute, and that she is speaking up, quite properly, for the self as a spiritual attribute and not at all as a quality to be found in one's wardrobe. The sense in which Isabel is pert and, indeed, spiritually pretentious is normally brushed aside in favour of the sense in which her spiritedness is seen to be characteristically American. It is the moral and rhetorical aim of American literature, after all, to separate essence from existence, and to protect essence—or call it selfhood—from the vulgarity imposed by mere conditions.

The fact that a theory of American experience is even attempted means that such experience is deemed to be distinctive in kind or in degree. If in kind, it amounts to essentialism in the sense described and deplored by Karl Popper in the first volume of *The Open Society and Its Enemies,* where he writes of "methodological essentialism" as "the theory that it is the aim of science to reveal essences and to describe them by means of definitions." Popper disapproves of the theory, and wants to replace it by "methodological nominalism," which doesn't search for essences but "aims at describing how a thing behaves in certain circumstances." The main objection to essentialism is that it depends upon intellectual intuition, which can't serve as a basis of discussion since your intuition is likely to differ from mine.

An essentialist theory of American experience is as implausible as an essentialist theory of any other society. On the other hand, there may indeed be a difference of degree, enforced by conditions far more pressing in one society than in another. The situation of an embattled self finding its freedom in a wilderness is certainly a myth in American literature so frequent and so enduring that it must amount to a difference in the structure of forces and motives to which it refers. What that structure is may be inferred, I think, from Georg Simmel's *The Philosophy of Money* (1900), even though he leaves us free to apply his findings as we wish. I point particularly to passages in which he doesn't refer especially to America but to forces he regards as increasingly pervasive. He maintains, for instance, that the modern division of labour permits the number of dependencies to increase just as it causes personalities to disappear behind their functions. The reason is that only one side of them operates, at the expense of all the other sides which together would make up a personality. These conditions, Simmel argues, make the most favourable situation for bringing about the sentiment of true independence as an entirely private possession. As soon as we rebel against the implication that we are truly identified by our functional presence in the world, and that there is nothing more to us, we establish an interior life and declare it to be our real life. We say with Hamlet that we have that within which passes show and may indeed never be shown. We are, we assert, our own "property," the most private possession.

But don't the conditions which Simmel describes exist in every industrial society: shouldn't they be just as pressing in Glasgow as in Detroit?

Yes, but there is still an American difference: it arises from the incongruity between, on the one hand, a continent given over to commercial expansion and aggrandizement and, on the other, the promise of individualism and selfhood implicit in the once open expanse of virgin land. Thoreau's recourse to Walden Pond acquires its moral point from its relation to the other forms of property and desire it rejects. He lived there for two years to renew a promise or an offer to which the American landscape bore witness. No such offer was ever made in Glasgow. Nothing in English literature encourages a worker in Glasgow to feel that his true life is lived elsewhere. Much in American literature responds to the

Detroit worker's sense—or to his desire to feel—that his true life is indeed a world elsewhere, and that he does not coincide with his conditions.

I am describing the theory of America which is still predominant in American Studies: it supposes an ego psychology which is in turn predicated upon a national typology. Pressed far enough, it would come to a metaphysic, though it is rarely pressed as far as that. But it may be a matter of surprise that I have not included in my list of theoretical books one which long preceded them and gave the interpretation of American literature a metaphysical cast. D. H. Lawrence's *Studies in Classic American Literature* was mentioned at Salzburg. I recall that Malcolm Bradbury made much of it and argued that the contradictions of American fiction and poetry which Lawrence registered so powerfully can't be accommodated in a neat theory. But Bradbury didn't force the issue to the point of challenging the dominant theory.

The reason is that Lawrence's sense of American literature doesn't, in fact, challenge the theory. He was determined to find in America, Mexico, Sardinia, and Etruscan places the dark gods he thought merely suppressed by the bourgeois amenity of England. "The essential American soul," he says in the chapter on Cooper's Leatherstocking novels, "is hard, isolate, stoic, and a killer. It has never yet melted." The true rhythm of America, he says, is in Whitman: "he is the first white aboriginal." But the power of Lawrence's book arises not only from his sympathy with the aboriginal forces running loose in Poe, Whitman, Hawthorne, and Melville, but from his rejection of Franklin and the pedestrian mentality for which Franklin spoke. If we think of Franklinism as the sentiment that willingly fulfils itself in work and business, we come upon the same theory in a truculent form.

Indeed, Lawrence's sense of America sustains the dominant theory by locating itself between a psychology and a metaphysic. So does Charles Olson's, which is achieved by translating the relation between self and nature into one between the soul and space. "I take SPACE to be the central fact to man born in America," Olson says in *Call Me Ishmael;* and in the same book he identifies self as the force of will. But it is a particular direction of force. "To Melville," he says, "it was not the will to be free but the will to overwhelm nature that lies at the bottom of us as individuals and a people." The nature to be overwhelmed was not denoted, for Olson, by the Frontier or the central plains or Nantucket, but by the Pacific Ocean. Melville, too, understood, according to Olson, "that America completes her West only on the coast of Asia."

If you start with two richly implicative terms—in this case, self and space, or self and nature—it requires only a change of mood to throw your energy upon one term or the other. Olson insisted on the second term—space or nature—as testifying to the latitude of possibilities he refused to see constricted by politics or economics; and he let the first term—self—enforce itself as will.

I find much the same rhetorical structure, though a different tone, in Harold Bloom's theory of the American Sublime, especially when he describes it in Emerson's terms. Emerson, according to Bloom, "opens us to more power in ourselves," and prescribes no limit to that power. A sense of unlimited power of will and mind—and the two are one and the same for Bloom—is the American Sublime, and Bloom regards it as the only American religion. If the self is driven or drives itself to overwhelm nature, that is because Bloom means the Gnostic true or antithetical self which is "absolutely alien to the cosmos, to everything natural." The psyche or soul would indeed wish to make a home for itself in the world, but the antithetical self is, upon principle, a creator of the worlds it insists on imagining. No wonder Bloom is sullen in the presence of poems which are content to document life and the given world—Lowell's, Berryman's— and to leave their contents nearly as opaque as they found them.

The theory I have been describing first appeared, so far as I know, in the second (1840) volume of Tocqueville's *Democracy in America:*

> Among a democratic people, poetry will not be fed with legends or the memorials of old traditions. The poet will not attempt to people the universe with supernatural beings, in whom his readers and his own fancy have ceased to believe; nor will he coldly personify virtues and vices, which are better received under their own features. All these resources fail him; but Man remains, and the poet needs no more. The destinies of mankind, man himself taken aloof from his country and his age and standing in the presence of Nature and of God, with his passions, his doubts, his rare prosperities and inconceiveable wretchedness, will become the chief, if not the sole, theme of poetry among these nations.

Since God is not an historical principle, and Nature is historical only according to a slow rhythm of change or growth, man in Tocqueville's paragraph is seen, in effect, under the aspect of eternity, free of history, politics, and society. The presence of God and Nature may or may not constitute a condition: as in Bloom's version of the American Sublime, the *pneuma* is free to invent God and to assert its independence of Nature. Fidelity is entirely optional in either case. The attempt to understand man as such, free of social and historical contingencies, is the axiom upon which the several variants of our theory proceed.

If we add to Tocqueville's paragraph Hawthorne's famous Preface to *The House of the Seven Gables,* and in particular his distinction between the novel—which aims "at a very minute fidelity, not merely to the possible, but to the probable and ordinary course of man's experience"— and the romance—which presents "the truth of the human heart" under circumstances largely of the author's own devising and free of all consideration of probability—we turn the theory in a specifically American direction. The romance is the genre in which the American hero takes to himself immunity from every social condition. He has only one question to ask: what then?

Or rather: now that I am free, what am I free to do? W. H. Auden has added a footnote to Tocqueville and Hawthorne in an essay on James's *The American Scene:* it is in *The Dyer's Hand.* The crucial difference between Europe and America, Auden says, is that America has established its society by rejecting the *romanitas* upon which Europe was founded and which Europe has not ceased trying to preserve. The fundamental presupposition of *romanitas* is that virtue is prior to liberty: "what matters most is that people should think and act rightly." It would be splendid if they did so of their own accord, but if they don't, they must be forced; persuaded by education and tradition, or required by law. The opposite assumption, which Auden ascribes to American society, is that liberty is prior to virtue: liberty is the prerequisite without which virtue and vice are meaningless. Virtue is preferable to vice, but to choose vice is better than having virtue chosen for you or required of you.

If freedom is deemed to be prior to virtue, the question arises: where is one free? The clearest answer, and the answer most compatible with our theory of America, is: in the aesthetic dimension. I use Marcuse's phrase because he, more resolutely than one would expect of him, given his political affiliations, has argued that the aesthetic dimension is valuable because it is preeminently the domain of freedom. He goes further:

there is no reason, he says, why individuals should be shamed out of their subjectivity by having it derided as a bourgeois consolation prize. "With the affirmation of the inwardness of subjectivity," Marcuse maintains, "the individual steps out of the network of exchange relationships and exchange values, withdraws from the reality of bourgeois society, and enters another dimension of existence." This recourse to inwardness, this insistence on a private sphere "may well serve as bulwarks against a society which administers all dimensions of human existence." The aesthetic dimension is a space of freedom, cleared for privacy. Art, by virtue of its aesthetic form, is "largely autonomous vis-à-vis the given social relations." The work of art, in its composition, its presence, and its reception by individual minds, offers a rival space within the much larger domain of public and social life.

There are many difficulties with Marcuse's argument. He regards as opportune what Simmel presents mostly as a predicament: the separation of private and public life. Irving Howe is dismayed to find people evidently gratified by the aesthetic production of values by which they wouldn't even consider living. He is bewildered by such flagrant discontinuity between theory and practice. Marcuse is willing to make a kind of freedom out of conditions amounting otherwise to necessity. Perhaps he believes that the consignment of the arts to the domain of subjectivity and private life is the only way to give them a purpose in the world; since poetry, according to Auden, makes nothing happen. But this is another day's argument.

At Salzburg we received a strange message from Leo Marx, strange because it was not in keeping with the essentialist spirit of *The Machine in the Garden.* I was surprised to find him urging us, as he did in a message Hans Bungert was asked to convey, to regard the uniqueness of American experience as a nationalistic fantasy. We should "expose, once and for all, the dangers inherent in all variations of the idea of American exceptionalism." European scholars, according to Professor Marx, were "well qualified to help correct the record, and to demonstrate the extent to which American society, for good or evil, is chiefly to be understood as a development of Anglo-European history."

I am not sure whether Professor Marx's advice issued from a settled conviction or from a mood. The involvement of America in Vietnam made many American scholars feel that the role of Redeemer Nation must be abandoned. But it has not been shown, in the years since 1975, what form a diminished role in the world might take. I agree with Professor Marx that we should prescind from an essentialist theory of American culture, but I can't see that we gain much by thinking of American history as "a development of Anglo-European history." Such a formula would force us into the predicament of regarding blacks, Chinese, Puerto Ricans, and Mexicans in the U.S.A. as marginal to an official narrative.

It would of course be possible to put the question of theory aside for a while. James, reviewing Theodore Roosevelt's *American Ideals and Other Essays Social and Political* in April 1898, said that Roosevelt was proposing "to tighten the screws of the national consciousness as they have never been tightened before." And this at a time when, James thought, people all over the world were showing "a tendency to relinquish the mere theory of patriotism in favour of—as on the whole more convenient— the mere practice." It is not the practice, but the theory, that is violent, he said. Roosevelt urged Americans to live and breathe "purely as Americans," but he didn't indicate what that regimen would entail. James maintained that, in any case, an American's thought could only be recognized as such after the fact; it couldn't be predicted.

> To say that a man thinks as an American is to say that he expresses his thought, in whatever field, as one. That may be vividly—it may be superbly—to describe him after the fact; but to describe the way an American thought *shall* be expressed is surely a formidable feat, one that at any rate requires resources not brought by Mr. Roosevelt to the question. His American subject has only to happen to be encumbered with a mind to put him out altogether.

After this vivacity, James rebukes Roosevelt for making free with the "American name":

> . . . it is after all not a symbol revealed once for all in some book of Mormon dug up under a tree. Just as it is not criticism that makes critics, but critics who make criticism, so the national type is the result, not of what we take from it, but of what we give to it, not of our impoverishment, but of our enrichment of it. We are all making it, in truth, as hard as we can, and few of us will subscribe to any

invitation to forgo the privilege—in the exercise of which stupidity is really the great danger to avoid.

In short, Roosevelt should leave the doctrine alone.

I have quoted James's rebuke—apart from the intrinsic satisfaction of its comedy—to point to an aspect of theory which makes it a problem. We felt at Salzburg that we needed a theory to gain access to the literature. But we didn't appreciate that the theory, once we received it, would dictate to us how we should read the major works. Works which are a scandal to the theory can hardly be read at all: or, at best, they are read in a brittle relation to the theory they affront. I have no doubt that the dominant theory of American literature has often enforced a severe judgement upon a particular work of fiction or poetry, for no better reason than that it fails or refuses to fulfil the theory. I'm thinking, for the moment, of several works in the literature of the South, which are often regarded as marginal, too European to be quite acceptably American. Indeed, any American writer who asserts the authenticating force of history is bound to feel that he is working against the American grain. Allen Tate, as a case in point: his early poems seem querulous until we bear in mind that he regards the modern world, and especially the North, as humiliating the historical analogies and continuities in which he finds high moral value. In "Aeneas at Washington" and "Retroduction to American History," Tate ascribes the terrible "serenity of equal fates" to the lack of a genuine historical sense: the inevitable consequence of this refusal of history is narcissism. Antiquity "breached mortality with myths," but modern America makes do with mimicry of the ancients, even in the South, where an imitated Parthenon is found in Tennessee stucco. Instead of the individual will acting upon conditions taken seriously enough to provide a human context, decision is handed over to heredity:

> *Intellect*
> *Connives with heredity, creates fate as Euclid geometry*
> *By definition.*

But Tate's poems, and his novel *The Fathers,* are generally regarded as extraneous to American literature, morally a rearguard action, linguistically archaic. In a society less doctrinal, they would be appreciated far more warmly.

I feel sure, too, that the particular judgements enforced in Parrington's *Main Currents in American Thought* issued not from a disinterested sense of the works in question but from Parrington's certainty that he knew what the main currents were and wanted to see the particular works as constituting the force of the flow. Trilling was entirely justified, indeed, in arguing against Parrington that the culture of a nation "is not truly figured in the image of the current." A culture, he maintained, is not a flow or even a confluence: the form of its existence is struggle. It is a significant circumstance of American culture, he remarked, that an unusually large proportion of its notable writers of the nineteenth century contained "both the yes and the no of their culture, and by that token they were prophetic of the future." I don't think Trilling always acted upon this consideration: his theory of American literature didn't regard the faculty of containing the yes and the no as a sufficient merit. But his emphasis upon conflict and contradiction had the effect of mitigating the ferocious lucidity of a theory, and of qualifying its insistence.

Finally, I recall that at Salzburg we tried to evade or postpone a question I'm sure we didn't want to articulate: to what extent does our professional interest in American literature, and our participation in State Department cultural enterprises, commit us to general sympathy with the aims of an American administration? Andrew Sinclair had no problem here: he made his position dramatically evident. But the rest of us preferred to ensure that the question would not arise.

It would have to arise if we were to assemble at Salzburg now: April 12, 1986. We would have to find some courteous method of indicating that while we remained professionally concerned with American literature, and therefore with the society it expresses, we do not feel bound to approve this official policy or that. It is clear that President Reagan's foreign policy, in its bearing upon Nicaragua, El Salvador, Libya, and other countries, arises with appalling directness from a vision of America's destiny in the world. It is impossible to distinguish a vision from a theory in this context. The President's private war with the duly elected government of Nicaragua is his version, righteous and unquestioning, of the theory of America as Redeemer Nation. It is not even necessary for him to say that he regards America's destiny as one of saving the world from Communism: it is a matter of course. His more immediate problem is to convince millions of Americans that their security is threatened by the existence of one form of government rather than another in Nicaragua.

The easiest way, for a student of American literature, is to keep literature separate from a President's missionary zeal. I have no gift to set this statesman right. Perhaps it is enough to keep the political consequences of an inherited vision in mind, and to let it darken one's lucidity from time to time.

EMERSON AT FIRST

I have Emerson's licence for beginning before the beginning, as his *Nature* (1836) started with two items before coming to Chapter 1. The first was an epigraph from Plotinus, the second a body of two or three hundred words which might well enough have been called Chapter 1. My own preliminary matter goes into several paragraphs, and consists of observations which have no other aim than to indicate my general sense of Emerson: they haven't at all the merit of supplying the qualifications they would need if they aspired to be precise. I give them in a stark sequence, numbering them to mark their limitations.

One: I assume that Emerson's essays propose to assert "the sufficiency of the private man," a phrase he uses in "New England Reformers" a page or two before his more elaborate version of it, "the private, self-supporting powers of the individual." It follows that "an institution is the lengthened shadow of one man," as Emerson maintained in "Self-Reliance," a phrase T. S. Eliot recalled inaccurately in "Sweeney Erect"—

> *(The lengthened shadow of a man*
> *Is history, said Emerson*

Who had not seen the silhouette
　　Of Sweeney straddled in the sun.)

—but accurately enough, since Emerson went on to say that "all history resolves itself very easily into the biography of a few stout and earnest persons."

Two: I interpret the sufficiency of the private man as Emerson's gloss on what in *Nature* he calls the soul. I assume, too, that the soul is not synonymous with the mind or the will, but with their conjoint power. I haven't found any passage in which Emerson refers to the mind as separable from the will.

Three: Emerson works on the conviction that the soul is adequate to whatever obstacles it encounters and lifts every burden. He acknowledges necessity under the name of Ananke, but it is only a condition or circumstance; it doesn't defeat the soul or bring its activity to an end. The soul acts by giving its objects a certain form of attention. As Santayana says in "The Optimism of Ralph Waldo Emerson," "he passes easily from all points of view to that of the intellect."

Four: The adequacy of the mind isn't entirely dependent upon its power of abstraction. Nothing in Emerson contradicts the assumption, in Valéry and Stevens, that the mind fabricates by abstraction, unless they mean solely by abstraction. Emerson's sense of the mind's adequacy is closer to Coleridge's, especially in *On the Constitution of the Church and State,* where Coleridge describes an idea as "that conception of a thing, which is not abstracted from any particular state, form, or mode, in which the thing may happen to exist at this or at that time; nor yet generalized from any number or succession of such forms or modes; but which is given by the knowledge of *its ultimate aim.*" In Emerson, the particular form of attention the mind gives to an object is such as to respect not its immediate attributes but its ultimate aim. The act of the mind is concerned not with the object as it is or as it appears to be but with its destiny. Only the mind can say what that destiny is.

Five: In the gap between the object and its destiny we come upon a problem Robert Martin Adams has considered, without reference to Emerson, in his *Nil,* where he resorts to a vocabulary of void and nothingness. His theme is not the rift between experience and consciousness, so far as that might be considered a wretched predicament; it is the rift insisted on and gloried in, as if only a vulgar satisfaction could accom-

pany the coincidence of mind and experience. "From Julien Sorel to des
Esseintes, from Keats to Mallarmé, from Novalis to Ibsen, they all testify
that anticipation, imagination, and memory (any relation as long as it is
distant) are richer experiences than experience itself." In Emerson, the
mind holds its power by keeping its distance, and by enforcing the
distance between an object and its destiny. It is the mind's power to do
this which ensures that no account of life is necessarily predicated upon a
crisis or a rupture. Two forms of satisfaction are entailed. The mind is not
intimidated by what it deals with, and a sense of history can proceed on
the assumption not of ruptures and dissociations but of a continuous
sufficiency of soul to the world it lives in.

Six: The characteristic defect of thought is prematurity: the mind
settles upon familiar forms of itself, and loses the force of a contingent
relation to its occasions. To counteract this tendency, Emerson trusts to
the whim he praises in "Self-Reliance," and takes as his motto a sentence
from "Circles": "our moods do not believe in each other." He repudiates
consistency and rest. Again in "Self-Reliance" he says that "power ceases
in the instant of repose; it resides in the moment of transition from a past
to a new state, in the shooting of the gulf, in the darting to an aim." It is
true that in "Art" he says that "the virtue of art lies in detachment, in
sequestering one object from the embarrassing variety," and praises artists
and orators for giving "an all-excluding fullness to the object, the thought,
the word, they alight upon." Emerson's own affection for the character of
an essay speaks to the same sentiment: a genre that takes contradictions
lightly because it doesn't claim to be comprehensive. But what Emerson
takes pleasure in is his assurance that the mind, having committed itself to
"the tyrant of the hour," then passes to some other object, "which rounds
itself into a whole, as did the first." The same rhetorical process could be
applied to a few objects, seeing them from the vantage of different
moods, thus introducing mobility where there seemed to be nothing but
fixity. As Santayana wrote of Emerson in *Interpretations of Poetry and
Religion:* "He differed from the plodding many, not in knowing things
better, but in having more ways of knowing them."

Seven: Emerson's persuasiveness is based on the renewed claim that
all men are equal—a charming claim, especially at a time when social and
economic arrangements, notably industrialization and capitalism, were
conspiring to make people unequal and to emphasize their inequality by
giving them unequal wages and conditions of employment. Emerson told

his readers and audiences that people who are treated unequally in social and economic life can find their dignity in themselves, by seeing society in the light of nature and diminishing its force in that light. When people feel that they are dominated by systems and institutions, Emerson offers to disconnect these structures of power, on condition that each person will take up the slack upon his own responsibility.

Eight: The offer Emerson's essays make goes somewhat like this: "Wouldn't our lives be much as I describe them, if we took seriously the sufficiency of the private man, exerted mind and will together as power, and regarded the whole world as having been given to us for our instruction and use?" It is not surprising, then, that Emerson was just as readily available to Pragmatism as to Transcendentalism: the vocabulary of property, commodity, use, exchange, instrumentality, and value made him available to William James, Peirce, Dewey, and any other sages who wanted to make the best of the given world.

So much for preliminaries and prejudices.

Emerson begins *Nature* by dissociating himself from belatedness and the acceptance of it: insisting on the new as providing "an original relation to the universe." Paul's First Epistle to the Corinthians (Chapter 13) prophesied the supersession of prophecy and knowledge: the time will come when we shall see God face to face, without mediation. Emerson reverses Paul's vision. Our forefathers, he says, "beheld God and nature face to face": why must we see them only through their eyes?

So the oppositions begin: originality, against retrospection; insight, against tradition; revelation, not history; the living generation, against sundry masquerades; "floods of life" against the "dry bones of the past," this last being another reversal, since Ezekiel 37 has always been interpreted by Christian readers as a sign of resurrection. Emerson says that the universe is composed of Nature and the Soul; otherwise put, the Me and the Not-Me. Man is like and unlike Nature in the sense that action in him precedes knowledge and presumably can persist without knowledge. But man has the faculty of apprehending as truth what he has acted as life. Nature hasn't. Nature can only do, ignorantly and slavishly, what Wisdom ordains it to do, so the possibility of discovering what Wisdom is by divining its plan for Nature can only devolve upon man. This discovery would amount to a new relation to the universe: it would be indistinguishable from firstness. Hence the aim of Science is to propound a theory of Nature, sufficiently abstract to explain everything that needs to be explained. Man's destiny is in knowing; but since knowing and willing are never found apart, the terminology of action still applies.

Chapter I: Nature

Appropriately, the "attitude" that prefigures the "act" of science is that of walking out into the fields and looking at the stars; astronomy being the privileged science to a sage who would set his thinking astir by reflecting upon the soul and nature. Not so appropriately, the stars are humanized by a flick of the sentence, the paragraph ending with reference to "their admonishing smile." The reason for the personification is clear enough, but hardly justifies grandiloquence.

The chapter begins with sensory events—the stars and their rays as a man sees them—but soon rises to concepts of understanding, invoking the faculty of recognizing unity among a multiplicity of sensory events: "the integrity of impression made by manifold natural objects." So the mind sees as a tree the bits of timber Nature supplies; distinguishes a landscape from the several farms which provoke this understanding; sees distant objects and calls the impression they make the horizon. What gratifies the mind is not the natural objects but the unity they unknowingly make. "There is a property in the horizon which no man has but he whose eye can integrate all the parts, that is, the poet." A few sentences later this property becomes "virtue"; in either case, a capacity of the mind is fulfilled. The allusions are mostly to Wordsworth, and to childhood as he praised it. But in the most famous passage, ideas of reason are transposed into modes of "the sublime" by way of Wordsworth and Schiller: "Crossing a bare common, in snow puddles, at twilight, under a clouded sky, without having in my thought any occurrence of special good fortune, I have enjoyed a perfect exhilaration. I am glad to the brink of fear. . . . Standing on the bare ground—my head bathed by the blithe air, and uplifted into infinite space,—all mean egotism vanishes. I become a transparent eyeball; I am nothing; I see all; the currents of the Universal Being circulate through me; I am part or particle of God." "Mean" shows that the egotism Emerson mentions is an attribute of the understanding when it refuses to allow a man to rise above it or otherwise disengage himself from its claims. In "New England Reformers," anticipating Stevens's "major man," Emerson says that "the man who shall be born, whose advent men and events prepare and foreshow, is one who shall enjoy his connection with a higher life, with the man within the man." Here, in *Nature,* Emerson is such a man, transparent rather than opaque—a juxtaposition that comes readily to Emerson when the despotism of sense and understanding is set against the higher fact of Reason.

"I am glad to the brink of fear." Emerson's version of "the sublime" involves, like many other versions, the presence of two contradictory perceptions. Schiller says, in his essay on the sublime, that such a combination irrefutably demonstrates our moral independence: "For since it is absolutely impossible for the very same object to be related to us in two different ways, it therefore follows that we ourselves are related to the object in two different ways; furthermore, two opposed natures must be united in us . . . By means of the feeling for the sublime, therefore, we discover that the state of our minds is not necessarily determined by the state of our sensations, that the laws of nature are not necessarily our own, and that we possess a principle proper to ourselves that is independent of all sensuous affects." Reason is Emerson's word, as it was Coleridge's, for the principle proper to ourselves: the exercise of it is further proof that, as Schiller goes on to say, "man's will is in his own hands."

Chapter 2: Commodity

Virtually a commentary on George Herbert's poem "Man," two lines of which Emerson quotes here, postponing till Chapter 8 a more ample selection of stanzas. But the two lines—"More servants wait on Man, / Than he'll take notice of"—are enough to establish the affiliation between "service" in Herbert and "commodity" in Emerson. "Under the general name of Commodity, I rank all those advantages which our senses owe to nature": the O.E.D. quotes this sentence to document "commodity" as "advantage, benefit, profit, interest: often in the sense of private or selfish interest." Not that it has that latter sense in Emerson: on the contrary, in him it means the availability of natural objects for entirely proper use, "Nature, in its ministry to man." Indeed, the chapter is a somewhat secularized version of Herbert's notion of "service" as the human form of mediation between Nature and God: "That, as the world serves us, we may serve thee, / And both thy servants be." If for "God" or "thee" we read Reason, we can still retain Herbert's domestic analogies and Emerson's vocabulary of use, profit, and service—with a fine equivocation on "ministry."

Chapter 3: Beauty

The love of beauty is a human attribute, but Emerson has to take care not to present Beauty as an intrinsic good: it must be seen as useful, of instrumental value. He concedes, in the first of his three numbered paragraphs, that "the simple perception of natural forms is a delight," but the delight is quickly made to consist of the exercise of certain human powers, notably the power of seeing a horizon, and of having eye and light cooperate to enforce a perspective upon natural forms. Perspective is an integrating act. There is also the admitted desire to find natural forms somehow significant: this paragraph asks "what was it that nature would say?" and "was there no meaning in the live repose of the valley behind the mill?" "What are the wild waves saying?" was an incorrigible question, not only in *Dombey and Son*. But Emerson's version of it can't allow the natural forms to say or intend anything, since that would make Nature share some of Man's power of knowledge. So he must hold Nature at the point of trying to say something, but failing: he gives it an air of meaning, short of meaning. The word he uses for that condition is "expression," which is responsive to the human desire for communication but not committed to saying anything in particular. The word is especially convenient because it can lean toward meaning or be held in reserve, as in a later reference to "the face of the world."

At the end of this first numbered paragraph Emerson warns that the beauty of Nature should not be sought. Why not? Because it should be ancillary to the human acts it accompanies. But also because, if it is sought, enjoyed, or intrinsically cultivated, it prevents us from going further. So, in the second numbered paragraph, Emerson has these revealing sentences: "The presence of a higher, namely, of the spiritual element is essential to its perfection. The high and divine beauty which can be loved without effeminacy is that which is found in combination with the human will." Without effeminacy? There is no point in fudging the issue. Emerson thinks of the face of the world as a woman's face, and of that as expressive without expressing anything in particular. Nature is a woman.

Mind is a man. Effeminacy is what a man falls into, or indulges himself in, when he is less than himself: Samson yielding to Delilah. Here, Emerson is warning us against cultivating the beauty of Nature, and the sentiment of being present to it: such a thing would mean luxuriating in matter, and suspending the will. In the fifth chapter of *Nature* he refers to "the analogy that marries Matter and Mind," and it is clear how the analogy goes. In the fourth chapter the assertion couldn't be clearer: "That which, intellectually considered, we call Reason, considered in relation to nature, we call Spirit. Spirit is the Creator. Spirit hath life in itself. And man in all ages and countries embodies it in his language as the FATHER." If a doubt remains, consider this passage, again from the fourth chapter: "All the facts in natural history taken by themselves have no value, but are barren like a single sex. But marry it to human history, and it is full of life." It follows that the beauty that can be loved without effeminacy is that of the human will; a manly act, acknowledged for the heroic character it has by the feminine expressiveness that accompanies it. So the second numbered paragraph gives several instances of human virtue, all of them in a man's world.

In the third numbered paragraph the beauty of the world is linked to a still higher consideration; not delight or even virtue but thought: beauty "as it becomes an object of the intellect." This is work for scientist and artist. The scientist—Emerson refers to "the intellect" but it is clearly the work of science—"searches out the absolute order of things as they stand in the mind of God, and without the colors of affection"; without, that is, effeminacy. He seeks a theory of nature. Meanwhile the artist creates his work of art as "an abstract or epitome of the world": "it is the result or expression of nature, in miniature." As an aesthetic, Emerson's argument is unsatisfactory: it doesn't allow for an artist's creativity, his work is confined to an epitome of what is already there. In fact, the artist's faculty, according to Emerson's description here, is merely an extreme instance of the general human power of composing "the integrity of impression made by manifold objects." The artist's subject, like the orator's, is for the time being the sequestered object on which he lavishes attention: integrity of impression, provoked by the object but transcending it, is in turn an epitome of the integrity of the world.

At the end of the chapter, Emerson reverts to the vocabulary of use, Nature's ministry to man. "The world thus exists to the soul to satisfy the desire of beauty": truth, goodness, and beauty "are but different faces of the same All." Goodness is clearly a moral virtue, truth a moral discovery: lest beauty appear to be an attribute of the natural object rather than of the mind that perceives it, Emerson makes it, in any event, entirely instrumental: "But beauty in nature is not ultimate. It is the herald of inward and internal beauty, and is not alone a solid and satisfactory good." The 1870 edition has "eternal," not "internal" beauty, presumably because inward and internal are nearly synonymous and the herald may be allowed to proclaim his master's message in the grandest terms. The relation between herald and master—between the message and its authoritative source—is a problem Emerson leaves for the next chapter.

Chapter 4: Language

Three numbered assertions set this chapter in motion. One: Words are signs of natural facts. Two: Particular natural facts are symbols of particular spiritual facts. Three: Nature is the symbol of Spirit. But Emerson doesn't distinguish between sign and symbol; we are free to think them synonymous. The scheme of things would work out somewhat like this. Start by positing Reason or Spirit or Universal Soul. Then allow that Spirit—choosing one of the synonyms for easy reference—necessarily manifests itself in material forms, the ensemble of which is called Nature. Finally, link words to Nature as "signs of natural facts." I concede that Emerson prefers to take the opposite direction: he likes to start with sensory events, and move with decent speed to a higher perspective, and thence to the perspective-beyond-other-perspectives which he calls Reason or Spirit or Universal Soul.

While the doctrine of this chapter is Swedenborgian, the details are organized in such a Wordsworthian manner as to make the chapter a devout allusion to the Preface to the second edition of *Lyrical Ballads*. But the arguments, if put together in a more prosaic sequence than Emerson's, would culminate in yet another defence of Science.

Such a sequence would begin with the assertion that the Original Cause has ordained the world on the principle of "the centrality of man in nature, and the connection that subsists throughout all things"—phrases I have taken from the chapter on Swedenborg in *Representative Men*. The laws of Nature include relations and correspondences, and a privileged relation between mind and matter. Man's access to these mysteries is by way of analogy: nature is a text he tries to read in the light of radical consanguinities. The linguistic forms of kinship are figures, notably metaphor: the conceptual forms are types, emblems, and allegories.

Man's knowledge of the laws of nature is merely partial. Some people have no sense of the relation between mind and matter, but even those who are alive to it have only partial apprehension. "By degrees," Emerson says, "we may come to know the primitive sense of the permanent objects of nature, so that the world shall be to us an open book, and every form significant of its hidden life and final cause." There are far more symbols in nature than we can interpret; our dictionary is incomplete, and therefore so are we. "Did it need such noble races of creatures, this profusion of forms, this host of orbs in heaven, to furnish man with the dictionary and grammar of his municipal speech?" At this point Emerson glances at a question alien to him, whether the natural forms—mountains, waves, and skies—are significant of themselves, or "have no significance but what we consciously give them, when we employ them as emblems of our thoughts." Strictly speaking, Plotinus should have settled the question, but Emerson is struck by what seems to be the disproportion between the profusion of natural forms and the penury of our meanings. If "the whole of nature is a metaphor for the human mind," we don't seem to have learned much. It is a difficult moment in the chapter. Emerson turns away from it and finds consolation again in Coleridge. "Every object rightly seen unlocks a new faculty of the soul," Coleridge said in a passage Emerson quotes now from *Aids to Reflection.*

Chapter 5: Discipline

The most scandalous chapter, this one is largely responsible for the assumption, audible as clearly in the elder Henry James as in W. B. Yeats, that Emerson was totally devoid of a sense of evil. I don't know whether or not it would improve Emerson's reputation in this respect to explain that when he appears a monster—as again in parts of "Self-Reliance"—it is because he has committed himself to the dominion of the act of consciousness over any conditions it meets. If those conditions include objective facts of evil, suffering, and pain, so much the more resolutely is the particular act of consciousness urged to transcend them. It could be argued, then, that the lack of a sense of evil and suffering in Emerson is a consequence of his logic rather than a defect of sympathy: but this doesn't help much, since it invites the retort that it is monstrous to take one's logic more strictly than the suffering of others. The mind can transcend the conditions it meets only by keeping them at a distance or by rising above the level on which they are met.

The second of these devices is favored by Schiller, who thought that the mind should exercise itself upon artificial or imagined misfortunes and assert its independence in that practice. "The more frequently the mind repeats this act of independence, the more skilled it becomes, the greater the advance won over the sensuous impulse, so that finally, should an imaginary and artificial misfortune turn into a real one, the mind is able to treat it as an artificial one and transform actual suffering into sublime emotion." For most people, Schiller's argument is nonsense: imagined pain is not the same as actual pain, and can't be mistaken for the real thing, unless the mind in the case is deranged. But I have to concede that Schiller's point has many ancient traditions behind it, and not merely Epicureanism: as a method of dealing with one's alienation, it has had its adherents.

Emerson's life had more than its share of sorrows, he saw those he loved in pain and misery. It is true that he brought his notion of compensation to bear upon these occasions: also that in his distinction between Understanding and Reason he insisted on regarding the inexplicable opacity of evil as a matter for the first, and every uplifting consideration as issuing from the second. Quentin Anderson has argued in *The Imperial Self* that Emerson "played with the idea that every evil was in the end compensated for, not because he deeply believed in it, but because it offered a defense against the notion that the self could not embrace the world if the world was indeed fatally plural, intractable, and evil." This is well said, but I don't think it disposes of the question. We would then have to ask why Emerson so desperately needed what Anderson calls "his fantasy of the primacy of the self"—needed it so badly that he couldn't allow it to be threatened by appalling evidence.

The passage of most extreme scandal in this respect turns up in the present chapter, where Emerson argues that Nature is a discipline, and that every property of matter is a school for the Understanding. His general point is that the lessons the Understanding learns from the disposition of the natural world are the exercise of the will and the experience of power. Reason then "transfers all these lessons into its own world of thought," where they are translated into moral terms. Even the tedious details of daily life are valid, seen as instruction: "The same good office is performed by Property and its filial systems of debt and credit. Debt, grinding debt, whose iron face the widow, the orphan and the sons of genius fear and hate; debt, which consumes so much time, which so cripples and disheartens a great spirit with cares that seem so base, is a preceptor whose lessons cannot be foregone, and is needed most by those who suffer from it most." There is no point in saying that this is heartless: it is clear from the cadences ("Debt, grinding debt . . . ") that the experiences it generalizes are as familiar to Emerson as to anyone else. It is the lack of a dramatic context, sufficient to question the generalizations and bring them to the test of particular suffering, that distinguishes it from passages of fiction that might be produced from *Hard Times* or *The Mayor of Casterbridge.* What the sentences mostly evince is not hard-heartedness but pedantry, which pursues the logic beyond any reasonable degree of need. If the passage had stopped before its last phrase, the pedantry would not have to be insisted on; but that phrase ("and is needed most by those who suffer from it most") offers the poorest people an educational program when what they need at once is bread and money.

The first device I mentioned, by which the mind keeps its distance from whatever conditions it has to meet, is a technique of generalization and survey: in Emerson, it depends upon his privileging the sense of sight, and the light in which that sense acts. One of the consequences of this privilege is that when we see an object in the light of its idea, what we mostly see is the idea, not the object. But even if this is not necessarily the case, the privileging of sight has other consequences. Hans Jonas has pointed out, in *The Phenomenon of Life,* that "seeing requires no perceptible activity either on the part of the object or on that of the subject": "Neither invades the sphere of the other: they let each other be what they are and as they are, and thus emerge the self-contained object and the self-contained subject. . . . Thus vision secures that standing back from the aggressiveness of the world which frees for observation and opens a horizon for elective attention. But it does so at the price of offering a becalmed abstract of reality denuded of its raw power." Denuded, too, of its power to hurt.

It is idle to ask which came first in Emerson, his privileging of the sense of sight rather than, say, the sense of touch and the conviction of reality which a sense of touch insists on; or his "fantasy of the primacy of the imperial self" in a world that threatened to undo it.

Chapter 6: Idealism

Emerson doesn't indicate, in this chapter, what form or degree of Idealism he favours, but it is clear enough that it is Critical or Transcendental Idealism: "a system of thought in which the object of external perception, together with the whole contents of our experience, is held to consist, as known to us, but not necessarily in itself, of ideas." In "The Transcendentalist" he sufficiently describes the position. The Idealist "affirms facts (which are) not affected by the illusions of sense, facts which are of the same nature as the faculty that reports them, and not liable to doubt." These are facts "which it only needs a retirement from the senses to discern." The Idealist manner of looking at things "transfers every object in nature from an independent and anomalous position without there, into the consciousness."

It is enough for Emerson to make these assumptions. One: Nature is a phenomenon, not a substance; but there is no need to deride it for that or any other reason. Two: "to the senses and the unrenewed understanding belongs a sort of instinctive belief in the absolute existence of nature." But the presence of Reason "mars this faith." "The first effort of thought tends to relax this despotism of the senses, which binds us to nature as if we were a part of it, and shows us nature aloof, and as it were, afloat." (Emerson's position here coincides with Coleridge's, especially when Coleridge attacks "the delusive notion that what is not *imageable* is likewise not *conceivable.*" The idea that the eye is "the most despotic of our senses" is also found in Wordsworth.) Three: Imagination, which Emerson describes as "the use which the Reason makes of the material world," perceives "real affinities between events (that is to say, ideal affinities, for only those are real)" and thus enables the poet — Shakespeare is Emerson's example — "to make free with the most imposing forms and phenomena of the world, and so assert the predominance of the soul." Four: Idealism has this advantage over the popular faith, "that it presents the world in precisely that view which is the most desirable to the mind."

I assume that this phrasing alludes to Bacon's description of poetry, that "it doth raise and erect the mind, by submitting the shows of things to the desires of the mind; whereas reason doth buckle and bow the mind unto the nature of things." Bacon's vocabulary in the latter part of the sentence wouldn't suit Emerson, who has a quite different idea of Reason and wouldn't attach such weight to "the nature of things." No wonder he misquoted Bacon, as René Wellek has noted, and turned him into an out-and-out Platonist. Poetry, Emerson has Bacon saying, "seeks to accommodate the shows of things to the desires of the mind, and to create an ideal world better than the world of experience." Not that it much matters: the only point is that what Bacon attributes to poetry, Emerson attributes to Reason as such. It is then from Emerson that Stevens begins, brooding upon poetry, fictiveness, and the desires appeased by the fictive capacity of mind.

Chapter 7: Spirit

The title is misleading, so it is not a surprise that the chapter has little to say about Spirit and much about more tangible things. Emerson's concern with Spirit was nearly exhausted by the act of positing it. He was far more interested in the consequences of the act than in the act itself or its meaning. He remarks in his journal for April 22, 1837: "I say to Lidian that in composition the *What* is of no importance compared with the *How.* The most tedious of all discourses are on the subject of the Supreme Being." If someone were to ask him what he meant by Spirit, Emerson would have to answer: by Spirit I mean the Supreme Being or the Creator or the Universal Soul. But he wouldn't have wished the interrogation to go much further. Whereof one may not speak, thereof one might as well be silent.

So here we have him referring to "Spirit, that is the Supreme Being," and to God, the Creator, and "the divine mind." The elder Henry James once complained that Emerson "found certain transcendentalist and platonic phrases named beautifully that side of the universe which for his soul . . . was all-important." The problem was and is: can the reader do anything more with these phrases than take them as lyric cries, sites of desire?

Emerson posits Spirit, and then derives from it two further terms, Man and Nature. "The world proceeds from the same spirit as the body of man. It is a remoter and inferior incarnation of God, a projection of God in the unconscious." The world differs from the human body in one respect: it exhibits a serene order, independent of the human will. For that reason, the world is to us "the present expositor of the divine mind." There is another difference, which Emerson doesn't specify here.

The world is ignorant of itself, but Man—as a projection of God in consciousness—"has access to the entire mind of the Creator, is himself the creator in the finite."

But Emerson is moody with these terms. Sometimes he represents Nature as an unconscious drudge, a donkey; sometimes as the Christ who sat on one. These discrepancies wouldn't matter, indeed, if they were merely signs of compensatory moods within a genial acknowledgement of man and nature. If a Wordsworthian sense of man and nature were to obtain, as "a wooing both ways"—Blackmur's phrase in another connection—one's mood of the moment could safely tip the balance now in favour of one, now of another. But in this chapter Emerson deduces from the inviolable order of nature and the supposed disorder of man that "we are as much strangers in nature, as we are aliens from God." But the only proof he offers is that we're not on easy terms with bears and tigers; we don't know much about birdsong. The chapter ends with a very strange notion: "Is not the landscape, every glimpse of which hath a grandeur, a face of him? Yet this may show us what discord is between man and nature, for you cannot freely admire a noble landscape, if laborers are digging in the field hard by. The poet finds something ridiculous in his delight, until he is out of the sight of men." Why so? A Marxist would say that a middle-class poet should indeed be embarrassed, indulging himself in intimations of the grandeur of a landscape at a time when labourers are digging in the next field. But the embarrassment wouldn't have anything to do with discord between man and nature; it would testify to discord between man and man, and invite a strictly historical explanation. If Emerson finds something ridiculous in his delight, it can only be because he is in a position to turn fields into a landscape by raising his mind above the stubble, while the labourers aren't.

Chapter 8: Prospects

The crucial word in this chapter is "idea." Each fact is to be seen "under the light of an idea." The question is not: what is an idea? But rather: how is the correlation established between a particular fact and a particular idea? If we look again at Coleridge's definition of an idea, it now appears more questionable—that conception of a thing "which is given by the knowledge of its ultimate aim." On the next page Coleridge associates it with Law, his reiterated point being that an idea in mind is to a law in nature as the power of seeing is to light. Specifically: "That which, contemplated objectively (i.e., as existing externally to the mind), we call a LAW, the same contemplated subjectively (i.e., as existing in a subject or mind) is an idea." But it's not clear whether an idea, or a law, in Coleridge's sense, is deemed to be already known or still to be known. Is "its ultimate aim" already known to the mind, so that at most it only needs to be fulfilled; or is it already fulfilled?

The question is crucial for our sense of Emerson, because he is hostile to fixity; an idea would have to be sufficiently mobile to have a further life. Mobility could be gained if we said that while the laws of Nature are in force, we don't yet know them. Science knows some of them, but not all. A total theory of Nature is Emerson's project for Science, so the activities of Understanding and Reason should continue indefinitely. The power of an idea would consist in the power of the mind lavished upon achieving a more and more complete knowledge of it; it would not be already in place, fixed and retrospective.

This distinction is well established: it is possible to distinguish between two meanings of the word "idea." Erwin Panofsky's book *Idea* recalls Michelangelo's use of the words *concetto* and *immagine*. "Both of these words might reasonably be translated as 'idea,' " Panofsky says, "but with a crucial difference." In its proper and literal sense, already formulated by Augustine and Thomas Aquinas, "*immagine* means that notion which *ex alio procedit,* that is, which reproduces an already existing object." *Concetto,* on the other hand, "when it does not simply stand for 'thought,' 'concept,' or 'plan,' means the free creative notion that constitutes its own object, so that it in turn can become the model for external shaping: as the Scholastics put it, the *forma agens,* not the *forma acta.*" The distinction turns on a matter of grammatical tense. *Immagine* is the code of past feelings, invoked even at the risk of replacing them with a code. *Concetto* is a project, a gesture—Newman's idea of a university, Eliot's idea of a Christian society— toward a future in which the project may or may not be fulfilled. If we brought this meaning—*concetto*—to bear upon "idea," then a fact seen in the light of an idea would mean "in the light of the further possibilities of the fact, its possible development by correlation with the further phases of the mind that attends to it." Awkwardly phrased, I know, but the important point is that the fact would have a future commensurate with the most developed activities of the mind.

Coleridge's way of gaining mobility for his Idea was by compromising its ultimacy and "perfection": not that that was his intention. In
"Constancy to an Ideal Object," he invokes the ideal object as an absolute,
"the only constant in a world of change"; then thinks of another absolute,
his love for Sara, a passion just as constant. Emerson's writings—his essays
and poems—are not as immediately personal as Coleridge's poem; so in
theory he could be content to regard an idea as an archetype, which
doesn't depend upon its embodiment in a substance. But he, too, like
Coleridge, disturbs the archetype to the point at which it becomes a
concetto rather than an *immagine;* but for a different reason. He hasn't any
particular need to concentrate his mind on the merging of an absolute
with a human embodiment; or on the hyperbole to which Coleridge's
feeling drives him. But he has an interest, just as keen, in giving his mind
the latitude of experience and the indefinitely extensive scope which I
have been describing as mobility. Mobility is the quality of Emerson's
desire, too, though the object of the desire is the "supreme fiction" of his
mind: the "ultimate aim" which characterizes an idea must be such as to
give the mind that aspires to it—or yearns for it—an historical development as large as Emerson's ambition.

Postscript

Granted that Emerson is not a philosopher; it is enough that he is a poet
and a sage. He is not in competition with Hegel or Schelling. But the site
of his poetry and his sageness is the history of voluntarism. The more we
read *Nature,* the more clearly it appears that the whole essay is predicated
upon the capacity of Will. Not knowledge but power is its aim; not truth
but command. Human will is deemed to participate in the vitality of
natural forms. Mind is a chosen direction of Will. In "The Poet" Emerson
writes: "This insight, which expresses itself by what is called Imagination,
is a very high order of seeing, which does not come by study, but by the
intellect being where and what it sees, by sharing the path or circuit of
things through forms, and so making them translucent to others. The
path of things is silent. Will they suffer a speaker to go with them?" The
vitality of natural forms is the circuit of things through forms; the aim of the
poet and sage is to present the circuit as if it were subject to his command.
Mind, as a chosen direction the will takes, is charted in *Nature* through

the phases of sensibility, understanding, and reason. An extreme "moment" in the progress is self-command, which corresponds to Heidegger's notion, in *Being and Time,* of choosing to "let be." So if we go back to the transparent eyeball passage and read it as a voluntarist act rather than an instance of the Sublime, we find that the eyeball becomes transparent because a light higher than its own sensory light is made to shine through it. "The currents of the Universal Being circulate through me"; that is, I will that no sensory obstacle—and therefore no opacity—shall impede the progress of the power that is in me.

Voluntarism is an accurate name for this commitment, provided we do not think of it as issuing in an ego psychology. Harold Bloom well distinguishes, in his *Agon,* between *psyche* and the Emersonian spark or *pneuma* — "this Gnostic true or antithetical self, as opposed to *psyche* or soul." The difference can only be that *psyche,* as asserted by ego psychology, is known by the particular structure of the attributes which embody it: *pneuma* has only this sole attribute, that it is one's wilful possession of the energy at large in a living world. *Pneuma* is a spark of life, of the force of life as such, before any further attributes are located or recognized. Not a psychology but a pneumatology explicates Emerson's work: we have access to it only by recourse to the vocabulary of Will and to its social form, a pragmatics of the future.

Reference to such a pragmatics is enough to remind us that Emerson is not merely a poet and a sage: he is the founding father of nearly everything we think of as American in the modern world. To the extent to which the sentiments of power, self-reliance, subjectivity, and independence attract to themselves a distinctly American nuance, its source is Emerson. Harold Bloom has named as Emersonian the only form of religion he is willing to recognize as American. So it is clear that American scholars and artists have invested much of their energy in the values we associate with Emerson.

That there are "answers" to Emerson is well understood, but we hear little of them nowadays. Twenty or thirty years ago a critic writing on Emerson would have felt obliged to face Yvor Winters's argument, in *Maule's Curse,* that Emerson presented the commonplaces of the Romantic movement in the language of a Calvinistic pulpit: "He could speak of matter as if it were God; of the flesh as if it were spirit; of emotion as if it were Divine Grace; of impulse as if it were conscience; and of automatism as if it were the mystical experience." It follows, according to Winters's argument, that Emerson and those who listened to his lectures and read his essays "were moral parasites upon a Christian doctrine they were endeavoring to destroy." At this point the argument merges with another, which we find in the Southern critics and especially in Allen Tate and Robert Penn Warren, that Emerson made available a genteel form of secularism which was particularly attractive to people who wanted to escape from the responsibilities of crime and punishment, sin and expiation.

Eliot's poem "Cousin Nancy" extends these arguments: its implication is that Emerson and Arnold, by encouraging Nancy to think of herself as the privileged centre of culture and experience, merely released her to fall for every fashion that came along, mistaking futile rebelliousness for self-determination:

> *Upon the glazen shelves kept watch*
> *Matthew and Waldo, guardians of the faith,*
> *The army of unalterable law.*

The irony of "guardians" reaches conclusion in the mockery of "law." The total effect of Arnold's philosophy, Eliot maintained in his essay on Arnold and Pater, "is to set up Culture in the place of Religion, and to leave Religion to be laid waste by the anarchy of feeling." So Arnold was responsible for the easiest forms of Humanism, and for Pater and Wilde. What Emerson was responsible for, Eliot doesn't explicitly say. But the strongest indication of Eliot's condescending estimate of Emerson is the fact that he excluded him from the American tradition he took most seriously. In "The Hawthorne Aspect" he said of Emerson, Thoreau, and Lowell that "none of these men . . . is individually very important; they can all, and perhaps ought to be made to look very foolish; but there is a 'something' there, a dignity, about Emerson for example, which persists after we have perceived the taint of commonness about some English contemporary, as for instance the more intelligent, better educated, more alert Matthew Arnold." But in describing the kinship of Hawthorne and James, which he presented without wishing to diminish James's relation to Balzac and Turgenev, Eliot pointed to what he regarded as the best the New England mind had to give, a best by comparison with which nothing in Emerson, Lowell, Thoreau, Longfellow, or Margaret Fuller was quite good enough. What Hawthorne and James had, a possession requiring full consideration in any account of their genius, was "a very acute historical sense," a sense even more acute in Hawthorne than in James. By the criteria this sense enforced, Emerson didn't come into the reckoning.

It is not my intention to document "the case against Emerson." Indeed, I wouldn't have mentioned it but for the fact that such a case appears to have been quite forgotten. In the past several years, Emerson has been called upon to sponsor many different programmes: he can be quoted to nearly any purpose. There is no question of adjudicating between Emerson's adherents and his opponents: one would have to start with a consideration of Original Sin. The critical question might be met, far more briefly and delicately, by yet again reading *Nature:* if our first reading concentrated upon the privilege according to Mind, and the second upon the primacy of Will, a third would register not chiefly Will, but the misgivings that should attend the claims Emerson makes for it as nothing less than a moral principle.

From Stephen Donadio, Stephen Railton, and Ormond Seavey (eds.), *Emerson and His Legacy: Essays in Honor of Quentin Anderson* (Carbondale and Edwardsville: Southern Illinois University Press, 1986).

THOREAU

I

few weeks after Thoreau's death on May 6, 1862, Emerson
wrote in his *Journal:*

Henry T. remains erect, calm, self-subsistent, before me, and I
read him not only truly in his Journal, but he is not long out of mind
when I walk, and, as today, row upon the pond. He chose wisely no
doubt for himself to be the bachelor of thought & nature that he
was—how near to the old monks in their ascetic religion! He had no
talent for wealth, & knew how to be poor without the least hint of
squalor or inelegance.

   Perhaps he fell, all of us do, into his way of living, without
forecasting it much, but approved & confirmed it with later wisdom.[1]

"For himself": nothing of the kind would have suited Emerson, who
found the idea of hermitage tiresome, even though he could not have
regarded himself as gregarious. Tiresome, but seductive:

Henry Thoreau is like the woodgod who solicits the wandering poet & draws him into antres vast & desarts idle, & bereaves him of his memory, & leaves him naked, plaiting vines & with twigs in his hand. Very seductive are the first steps from the town to the woods, but the End is want & madness.[2]

The last phrase echoes Wordsworth's "Resolution and Independence": "We Poets in our youth begin in gladness; / But thereof comes in the end despondency and madness." I interpret Emerson's attitude as rueful acknowledgement that Thoreau's Walden may well be a place for poets, but that in every social consideration it is intolerable. Again, on May 10, 1858, when Thoreau at Walden Pond described a life even more retiring than his own, Emerson confided to his *Journal:*

I hear the account of the man who lives in the wilderness of Maine with respect, but with despair. . . . Henry's hermit, 45 miles from the nearest house, is not important, until we know what he is now, what he thinks of it on his return, & after a year. Perhaps he has found it foolish & wasteful to spend a tenth or a twentieth of his active life with a muskrat & fried fishes.

My dear Henry,
    A frog was made to live in a swamp, but a man was not made to live in a swamp. Yours ever,
        R.[3]

II

The biographical facts are not dramatic. David Henry Thoreau, to give him the name he was christened—as a young man he reversed the first names for the sake of euphony—was born on July 12, 1817, at Concord, Massachusetts, where his father had a small but quite successful factory for making lead pencils. David Henry went to school at Concord Academy, and in 1833 entered Harvard College to read classics and Eastern languages. He was a difficult, edgy student, but he managed to graduate in 1837. In 1838, with his brother John, he set up a private school, and moved toward a literary life of lectures, essays, and poems. In 1841 he lived with the Emersons, and worked for them as handyman. In March 1845 he decided to build a shack beside Walden Pond and try the experiment of living according to Emersonian principles of individualism, simplicity, and self-reliance. He stayed there for two years, growing beans, keeping a journal, and recording the daily life of pond and shore. In the summer of 1847, refusing to pay his poll tax and thereby expressing his disapproval of slavery and the Mexican War, he was arrested and spent one night in jail, till his aunt Maria paid the tax and gained his release. The experience provoked him to give a lecture, eighteen months later, in justification of "civil disobedience," specifying the conditions which made it necessary, in his view, to reject allegiance to the state. In 1847, too, he went back to the Emersons; later, to his father's house, making occasional excursions, once to Canada, four times to Cape Cod, three times to Maine. In 1861, suffering from tuberculosis, he went to Minnesota for a change of air but returned to Concord again, where he died.

It is generally agreed that Thoreau was in some degree in love with a local girl, Ellen Sewall: she turned him down. It is widely if not generally agreed that a few years later he fastened his affections upon Lidian, Emerson's wife, and maintained a spiritual attachment to her till his relation to Emerson himself cooled and illness dispensed Lidian from the trouble of caring. It is now commonly but not universally assumed that Thoreau's sexual inclination was homoerotic; a conclusion scholars found easy to reach once they had set out in its direction. Still, there is some evidence for it.

It is beyond dispute that Thoreau was a difficult, truculent character. Emerson had cause to complain that Thoreau always found it easier to say no than yes, an attribute "a little chilling to the social affections." Not that Emerson's own social affections were at all warm: in his domestic character he was a cool if not a cold fish. He assumed that people would keep their distance, and he helped them to keep it. But he expected them to be conversationally amenable, and Thoreau regularly disappointed him in that regard:

> If I knew only Thoreau, I should think cooperation of good men impossible. Must we always talk for victory, & never once for truth, for comfort, & joy? Centrality he has, & penetration, strong understanding, & the higher gifts—the insight of the real or from the real, & the moral rectitude that belongs to it; but all this & all his resources of wit & invention are lost to me in every experiment,

year after year, that I make, to hold intercourse with his mind. Always some weary captious paradox to fight you with, & the time & temper wasted.[4]

Besides, Emerson regarded Thoreau—when he was annoyed by his truculence—as an unambitious fellow, self-indulgent and vain. Thoreau, in turn, and with particular force after 1850, found Emerson disappointing, and his patronage an irritant. He wrote in his *Journal:*

Talked, or tried to talk with R.W.E. Lost my time—nay, almost my identity. He, assuming a false opposition when there was no difference of opinion, talked to the wind—told me what I knew—and I lost my time trying to imagine myself somebody else to oppose him.[5]

But the main difficulty between them was that Thoreau resented having a master, and Emerson wanted disciples to be genial.

III

Only two of Thoreau's books were published in his lifetime. The first was *A Week on the Concord and Merrimack Rivers* (1849), an account of a trip he took with his brother—two weeks, in fact, from August 31 to September 13, 1839—a trip sufficiently meandering to allow for sundry ruminations on mythology, fish, the status of the New Testament, the nature of history, Homer, music, the village of Nashua, and anything else that came into his head or could be conveniently removed from his *Journal.* The second was *Walden: or, Life in the Woods* (1854), a description of Thoreau's life at Walden Pond from July 4, 1845, the Independence Day on which he moved into his shack, to September 6, 1847, the day on which he took up the next of what he regarded as his several lives. Commercially, both books were failures. In 1853, the publisher of *A Week* sent Thoreau the remaining 706 copies of the book. "I have now," Thoreau wrote in his Journal, "a library of nearly nine hundred volumes, over seven hundred of which I wrote myself."

After Thoreau's death, Emerson and others started gathering for publication the best of his essays, sketches, and letters, a process that produced a new book every year: *Excursions* (1863), *The Maine Woods* (1864), *Cape Cod* (1865), *Letters to Various Persons* (1865), *A Yankee in Canada, with Anti-Slavery and Reform Papers* (1866). Unfortunately, these books established Thoreau's reputation as that of a naturalist, a botanist, a travel writer, to be compared with Gilbert White or William Gilpin. The passages Emerson selected made Thoreau sound like Emerson, continuously sententious and quotable. When H. G. O. Blake made a first selection from the *Journal,* he set it out as a calendar of notes and reflections to accompany the seasons: *Early Spring in Massachusetts* (1881), *Summer* (1884), *Winter* (1888), and *Autumn* (1892). The *Journal* was published in 1906 as fourteen of the twenty volumes which make up the Walden edition of Thoreau's *Writings:* the fourteen were reprinted as two by Dover in 1962. But selections continue to be published which emphasize Thoreau's relation to a few seasonal themes.

IV

Thoreau's reputation, while he lived, was a local matter: he was regarded as one of Emerson's several meek philosophers, hardly distinguishable from the younger William Ellery Channing or Bronson Alcott. In 1853 he thought of himself as "a mystic, a transcendentalist, and a natural philosopher to boot," but only the last of these would have differentiated him from the general run of Emersonians. Emerson, too, saw him as, in a limiting sense, his ephebe. In September 1841 he reported what must have been a painful conversation:

> I told H.T. that his freedom is in the form, but he does not disclose new matter. I am very familiar with all his thoughts—they are my own quite originally drest. But if the question be, what new ideas has he thrown into circulation, he has not yet told what that is which he was created to say.[6]

Only after Thoreau's death did Emerson find a virtue to redeem the limitation:

> In reading Henry Thoreau's Journal, I am very sensible of the vigor of his constitution. That oaken strength which I noted whenever he walked or worked or surveyed wood lots, the same unhesitating

hand with which a field-laborer accosts a piece of work which I should shun as a waste of strength, Henry shows in his literary task. He has muscle, & ventures on & performs feats which I am forced to decline. In reading him, I find the same thought, the same spirit that is in me, but he takes a step beyond, & illustrates by excellent images that which I should have conveyed in a sleepy generality. 'Tis as if I went into a gymnasium, & saw youths leap, climb, & swing with a force unapproachable—though their feats are only continuations of my initial grapplings & jumps.[7]

But even in this posthumous tribute Thoreau is still the young disciple.

Henry James, too, saw Thoreau in that diminishing light. In an essay of 1887 on the correspondence of Carlyle and Emerson, he included Thoreau in those "Concord-haunting figures which are not so much interesting in themselves as interesting because for a season Emerson thought them so."[8] More damagingly still, James thought first of Thoreau when he wanted to illustrate how Emerson allowed it to be assumed that he found his associates interesting, letting his courtesy "pass for adhesion." Emerson's fidelity "as an interpreter of the so-called transcendental spirit" consisted—or was made to consist—with "his freedom from all wish for any personal share in the effect of his ideas." Thoreau, according to James, remained with Emerson's ideas to the bizarre point of turning them into practice. It was Thoreau "who took upon himself to be, in the concrete, the sort of person that Emerson's 'scholar' was in the abstract, and who paid for it by having a shorter life than that fine adumbration."

> The application, with Thoreau, was violent and limited (it became a matter of prosaic detail, the non-payment of taxes, the non-wearing of a necktie, the preparation of one's food one's self, the practice of a rude sincerity—all things not of the essence), so that, though he wrote some beautiful pages, which read like a translation of Emerson into the sounds of the field and forest and which no one who has ever loved nature in New England, or indeed anywhere, can fail to love, he suffers something of the *amoindrissement* of eccentricity. His master escapes that reduction altogether.[9]

Not that James had much regard for nature writing as a thing separate from the social transactions which might be imagined as taking place in an emphatic setting: the New England of *The Europeans,* for instance. In July 1865 he thought of reviewing Thoreau's *Letters to Various Persons,* but lost interest after taking a trip to the White Mountains: "His nature is very good in town: but it will not stand juxtaposition with nature's own," he told Charles Eliot Norton in September.[10]

Some years later, in his monograph on Hawthorne (1879), James recurred to the question of Thoreau as if he had still not got him quite right:

> Whatever question there may be of his talent, there can be none, I think, of his genius. It was a slim and crooked one; but it was eminently personal. He was imperfect, unfinished, inartistic; he was worse than provincial—he was parochial; it is only at his best that he is readable. But at his best he has an extreme natural charm, and he must always be mentioned after those Americans—Emerson, Hawthorne, Longfellow, Lowell, Motley—who have written originally. He was Emerson's independent moral man made flesh—living for the ages, and not for Saturday and Sunday; for the Universe, and not for Concord.[11]

But it was James Russell Lowell who said nearly everything that could be said against Thoreau. In *A Fable for Critics* he ridiculed Thoreau as a little man trotting after Emerson. In an essay of 1865 he derided Transcendentalism as "the maid of all work for those who could not think," and went on to refer to Thoreau's writings as strawberries from Emerson's garden. Thoreau's imagination, Lowell said, was receptive rather than active: he had powers of appreciation, but his critical power, "from want of continuity of mind," was inadequate. What Lowell mainly deplored was Thoreau's high conceit of himself: it was such "that he accepted without questioning, and insisted on our accepting, his defects and weaknesses of character as virtues and powers peculiar to himself." He valued everything "in proportion as he fancied it to be exclusively his own." He "seems to have prized a lofty way of thinking (often we should be inclined to call it a remote one) not so much because it was good in itself as because he wished few to share it with him." Morbid, egotistical, Thoreau sought "a seclusion which keeps him in the public eye." As for his relation to the wilderness: it was a gross example of "the modern sentimentality about Nature," a sign of disease, and entirely compatible with a cynical revulsion against humanity:

> While he studied with respectful attention the minks and woodchucks, his neighbors, he looked with utter contempt on the august drama of destiny of which his country was the scene, and on which the curtain had already risen.

Thoreau's experiment at Walden Pond "presupposed all that complicated civilization which it theoretically abjured."

> He squatted on another man's land; he borrows an axe; his boards, his nails, his bricks, his mortar, his books, his lamp, his fish-hooks, his plough, his hoe, all turn state's evidence against him as an accomplice in the sin of that artificial civilization which rendered it possible that such a person as Henry D. Thoreau should exist at all.[12]

After that indictment, it hardly matters that Lowell found in Thoreau's style, at its best, a quality he associated with Donne, Sir Thomas Browne, and Novalis.

V

It is clear that the publication of Thoreau's *Journal* in 1906 made it possible for scholars to make a far higher claim for Thoreau than any put forward by his contemporaries. But it is still true that his popular reputation is based entirely on "Civil Disobedience" and *Walden*. The first, largely because it caught Gandhi's attention and he wrote to Tolstoy about it, became a textbook of nonviolent dissent, and was established in that capacity by Martin Luther King, Jr. The second is still read as an American pastoral, just as fundamental as *Huckleberry Finn* in offering, against the conventions of acquisition and advancement, a self-ordained life in harmony with the seasons. *The Maine Woods* and *Cape Cod* can hardly be popular; even if Thoreau's account, in *Cape Cod,* of the wreck of the Irish emigrant ship *St. John* in October 1849 is indelible, and several phrases from it have taken on new life in the first stanza of Robert

Lowell's "The Quaker Graveyard in Nantucket," the description of the drowned sailor: "Light / Flashed from his matted head and marble feet." The common reader is unlikely to read the *Journal*.

But a good deal has changed. Thoreau is no longer regarded as merely a lesser Emerson. He has emerged from that shadow. But his independence is still a tendentious matter. There are those who maintain, in the line of argument which Philip Rahv traced in "The Cult of Experience in American Writing," that Thoreau, just as much as Emerson, construed experience in merely theoretical terms. These readers do not see Thoreau, as James did, carrying Emerson's theories into gullible practice. They think of the issue in the terms James made available in his book on Hawthorne, where he said that "the doctrine of the supremacy of the individual to himself, of his originality and, as regards his own character, unique quality, must have had a great charm for people living in a society in which introspection, thanks to the want of other entertainment, played almost the part of a social resource."13

Rahv's version of that sentiment is:

> On a purely theoretical plane, in ways curiously inverted and idealistic, the cult of experience is patently prefigured in Emerson's doctrine of the uniqueness and infinitude, as well as in Thoreau's equally steep estimate, of the private man. American culture was then unprepared for anything more drastic than an affirmation of experience in theory alone, and even the theory was modulated in a semiclerical fashion so as not to set it in too open an opposition to the dogmatic faith that, despite the decay of its theology, still prevailed in the ethical sphere.14

One result, according to Rahv, was that Transcendentalism declared itself most clearly in the form of the essay, "a form in which one can preach without practicing." It declared itself even more clearly, I think, in the lecture and, for private brooding, the journal.

But the distinction here between theory and practice, or between preaching and practicing, is misleading. Strictly assigned, everything in literature, everything in writing, should fall into the category of theory. If a reader of Thoreau gives up his job and retires to a shack in the mountains, that is another matter. Thoreau hasn't required such logic of him. It is enough that a reader of Thoreau—or of any other writer—is impelled to imagine a life different from his own: the merit consists in the vividness and latitude of the imagining.

We need a vocabulary which doesn't, in advance, split experience into theory and practice. Perry Miller's *Consciousness in Concord* (1958), a book much hated by Thoreau's devoted critics because of Miller's harsh sense of Thoreau's character, provides a more useful way of indicating a discrepancy, a fissure, the refusal of Thoreau's mind to coincide with its contents.

VI

Miller's argument, like James Russell Lowell's, is that Thoreau was a man of outlandish egotism; such that, after the failure of *A Week* and *Walden,* he sought failure as the only condition adequate to his self-conceit. Not only in his writings but in his friendships: every relation was required to show its inadequacy. What was apparently good had to be shown to be bad, by applying to it an absolute criterion in the light of which nothing could stand. From the *Journal* of July 30, 1840:

> Defeat is heaven's success. He cannot be said to succeed to whom the world shows any favor. In fact it is the hero's *point d'appui,* which by offering resistance to his action enables him to act at all. At each step he spurns the world. He vaults the higher in proportion as he employs the greater resistance of the earth. . . . When we rise to the step above, we tread hardest on the step below.[15]

Miller doesn't remark that this passage brings together three otherwise separable sentiments: those of the Transcendentalist, the tragic hero, and the Promethean, as I have described—in my *Thieves of Fire* —an over-reaching type of imagination which scorns amenity. Emerson, Nietzsche, and Melville may be taken as indicating each sentiment, separately considered. The passage also indicates the tone in which Thoreau was always ready, whether he knew it or not, to go beyond Emerson and perhaps to disavow him. Where the Transcendentalism is found by itself, its mark is indeed the one which Miller finds decisive in Thoreau, that his characteristic stance is always one of anticipation. Anticipation in the worldly sense: instead of a heavy, uncomprehending readership, he will one day be received by an ideally qualified reader named Posterity. Anticipation in the naturalist's sense: as a mind responsive to the rhythm of the seasons anticipates the spring, and brings his *Walden* to a triumphant recognition of its first intimations. Anticipation in the spiritual sense: as the mind desires to reach through and beyond the senses and come to the unity felt as constituting a soul. From the *Journal* of September 28, 1840:

> The world thinks it knows only what it comes in contact with, and whose repelling points give it a configuration to the senses—a hard crust aids its distinct knowledge. But what we truly know has no points of repulsion, and consequently no objective form—being surveyed from within. We are acquainted with the soul and its phenomena, as a bird with the air in which it floats. Distinctness is superficial and formal merely.
>
> We touch objects—as the air we stand on—but the soul—as the air we breathe. We know the world superficially—the soul centrally. In the one case our surfaces meet, in the other our centres coincide.[16]

I don't claim that the passage is philosophically novel: it shares a common version of Idealism with Kant, Coleridge, Carlyle, Emerson, and many other writers who thought they must refute Locke or capitulate to materialism. I quote it as illustrating a form of anticipation which Miller didn't mention. If I live my life, for the most part, according to my senses; but if I know, as a good Transcendentalist, that the senses are merely transitional as my will aspires to the condition of soul; then I live in anticipation of that state, and refuse to coincide with objects of sense.

It was this aspect of Transcendentalism that gave it, to many people, a foolish name, and sometimes a sinister one. The view taken of it in State Street, according to Emerson in his *Journal* (October 1841), is that "it threatens to invalidate contracts." As indeed it might: if you took a sufficiently lofty view of reality, paying your debts wouldn't interest you much. As a good naturalist, Thoreau studied the plants and animals he saw at Walden and elsewhere; especially the things in nature which could be studied on the ground. But he studied these things not in themselves or for their own sake but as provisional events, moments in the process of moving toward soul, the highest form of cognition. He valued contingency only so far as it enabled him to anticipate the revelation of truth as myth.

But this had the effect of making his relation to the natural world equivocal. He paid attention to what he saw and heard: that is easily granted. He was far more observant than Emerson or Alcott. But it is not clear whether the attention he paid to an object was such as to enable his mind to coincide with it for the gratification of losing himself in its detail; or to participate in the life common to the object and the mind that perceived it; or—a more seductive possibility—to establish himself apart from it.

It is still common to praise Thoreau for being willing to look at things—an American Hopkins, on the evidence of journal entries in each case. But it is misleading to make much of his relation to Louis Agassiz, or the influence of Audubon, or to see Thoreau as prefiguring D'Arcy Thompson. These names denote different ways and degrees of paying attention. The fact that Thoreau conversed with Agassiz, to Emerson's embarrassment, about the mating habits of turtles, and that he sent Agassiz dozens of contributions to the never-finished *Natural History of the United States,* doesn't prove that their minds worked similarly even in the matter of turtles.

At this point recourse to the *Journal* is necessary. To the connoisseur, as Walter Harding has remarked, "it is the best of Thoreau."[17] But the relation between the *Journal* and the two books Thoreau prepared for publication is still disputed. Many readers think of the *Journal* as omnivorous writing from which Thoreau took the most publishable bits. But there are scholars who regard it as an autonomous work having complicated bearing upon the published books, which are by definition secondary. Guy Davenport has argued that "Thoreau's finest thought remained in the privacy of his rich notebooks because of the dullness of the public interest, which he treated to inspired insults and ironic exhortations, daring to risk his meditations on its blank surface."[18] If this is the case, a reader would expect to find Thoreau's published work evasive or, in some fundamental way, unforthcoming, and to find the truth of his subversive mind chiefly in the *Journal.*

This is substantially the argument of Sharon Cameron's *Writing Nature: Henry Thoreau's Journal.*[19]

VII

Thoreau started keeping a journal in the autumn of 1837 and continued till November 2, 1861, when he became too ill to persist. Sharon Cameron claims that the *Journal* is "the great nineteenth century American meditation on nature."

The busiest years of the *Journal* were between 1851 and 1861. Professor Cameron concentrates on the years 1850–52 because "it is during this time that Thoreau began to regard—and to speak of—the *Journal* as an autonomous composition," indeed as his central literary enterprise.

It is an essential part of Cameron's argument that the *Journal* must be separated from Thoreau's published writing, and especially from *Walden*. Indeed, she proposes to show that the relation between mind and the natural world which we find in the *Journal* differs in nearly every respect from the relation as it obtains in *Walden*. Most students of Thoreau have tried to reconcile his apparently conflicting allegiances to the natural and the social worlds, and have rebuked him for any residual incompatibility. Cameron hopes to resolve the matter by regarding *A Week* and *Walden* as merely partial and socially prudent expressions; the complete truth is in the *Journal*. Thoreau's motive in the *Journal* was "a passion for nature divorced from social meaning." In the *Journal*, "contemplation of nature bereaves the mind of natural counterparts"; that is, I assume, bereaves it of analogies between natural law and moral law. In *A Week* and *Walden*, Thoreau gratified his readers by giving them images of the mutuality of nature and man. *Walden*, according to Cameron, presents "not nature but the seductive rapprochement of the natural and the social to which, put in the harshest terms, nature is sacrificed." In the *Journal*, Thoreau released the natural world from the obligation of providing congenial analogies.

On April 11, 1852, Thoreau wrote in the *Journal*:

> It appears to be a law that you cannot have a deep sympathy with both man & nature.

A Week, "Ktaadn," and *Walden* pretend that you can be equally and continuously sympathetic to both. To produce "an account of nature visible for others," and to ingratiate himself with his readers, Thoreau diverted himself from his best subject, his "unmediated relation to nature."

The privacy of the *Journal* enabled him to tell the truth, that—as in the *Journal* of January 5, 1850—"there is no interpreter between us and our consciousness."

Cameron describes three technical procedures by which Thoreau, in the *Journal,* tries to express an unmediated relation to nature. The first is to unsettle perspectives "by raising the question of how part of a phenomenon is related to the whole of that phenomenon or to another phenomenon." This is a version of "perspective by incongruity," in Kenneth Burke's phrase, a technique for achieving new orientations by arranging wilful incongruities, impious juxtapositions which dislodge old pieties.

Thoreau's second procedure, according to Cameron, is to write human beings "virtually out of the picture," and to insist on "nature's infinite self-referentiality." It entails the rejection of Wordsworth's genial sense, in the Preface to *The Excursion,* of the mutual fittingness of mind and the external world.

The third procedure involves—though Cameron doesn't quite say this—Thoreau's making an exception in his own favour. Wordsworth has deluded himself. Nature is alien to man. But Thoreau can "impersonate the alienness," can "voice nature or be nature's voice," according to his formula: Not I, but nature in me. To do this, he projects as speaker of the *Journal* a "second person," a recording consciousness whose sole function is "to reflect natural occurrence." Thus, according to Cameron:

> If the *Journal*'s second person is the speaker, is the access to the *Journal*'s subject, the "I" is the observer, is its audience.

So Thoreau must ventriloquize a discourse such that "as far as possible it is its own first and second person." Presumably the "I" who listens corresponds to an ideally responsive Posterity. The "I" who speaks is a projected self capable of internalizing natural events which to other people remain opaque.

The first problem with this argument is that it depends upon seeing the *Journal* and *Walden* as distinct and incompatible works. But J. Lyndon Shanley has shown, in *The Making of Walden* (1957) and his edition of *Walden* (1971), that Thoreau started writing the book, sometime after February 1846, by gathering "the material which lay everywhere in his journals," reverting to journal entries he had written at various times between 1840 and 1845. For the successive versions of *Walden* he took further material from the journals, and "in some cases he assembled notes on a topic by tearing pages out of his journals." After the publication of *A Week* in May 1849, he worked intermittently on revisions of the first three versions of *Walden,* but he didn't write much more of it till January or February 1852. The decision to make the *Journal* an autonomous work was taken, according to Cameron, in 1850, but Professor Shanley has shown that on January 17, 1852, Thoreau wrote two items in the *Journal* which he clearly intended using in the book. More material for *Walden* "appears frequently in the journals of succeeding weeks and months." Shanley reports:

> He wrote version IV at various times during 1852. He drew much of the new material for it from his journals for 1850, 1851, and the first half of 1852; there are also a few items from September, October, and November 1852.[20]

The final version of *Walden* was sent to the printer in late February or early March 1854.

In any ordinary sense, therefore, there is a close, not to say continuous, relation between the *Journal* and *Walden.* Cameron is well aware of this, but she seems to think it doesn't matter to any of the considerations she cares about. It is conceivable that a journal written over a period of twenty-four years would feature an epistemology (or several epistemologies) different from the one implied in *Walden,* a work of about eight years. It would not be surprising if, after the failure of *Walden* in 1854, Thoreau turned inward and confided to his *Journal* every changing mood, every dark speculation; especially those which excluded other people. Such a turning could, I think, be shown. But Professor Cameron has a far more daring argument in view. She finds *Walden* deeply evasive about mind and nature, and the *Journal* more honest because it disposes the question of mind and nature in "multiple theatricalizations of attitudes." It would demean her argument if I were to take it as merely claiming that Thoreau told the truth when he talked to himself and, when he wrote for the general public, gave the dullards what they wanted to hear. But to substantiate her argument Professor Cameron would have to show that even when Thoreau used notes from the *Journal* for his revisions of *Walden* he changed the text and made it amenable to conventionally Wordsworthian expectations.

She has tried to do this, but it has required desperate pleading. For instance, she compares a passage in the "Brute Neighbors" chapter of *Walden* ("Why do precisely these objects which we behold make a world?") with the corresponding passage in the *Journal* for April 18, 1852 ("Why should just these sights & sounds accompany our life?"). The question in *Walden,* she says, "suggests an equative relationship between the objects beheld and the world they compose." The question in the *Journal* "suggests juxtapositions."

> In addition, because the question in the *Journal* is not a self-sufficient sentence in its own paragraph, it requires expansion. The passage from the *Journal* entry is itself the termination of a lengthy meditation in which one impression verges on another. The questions in the *Journal* and in "Brute Neighbors" do not differ from each other only in their respective wordings, but also because one precedes a list of observations (and preempts a meditation) and the other follows a list of observations opening into a meditation from which it is inseparable.

But the question from "Brute Neighbors" isn't a self-sufficient sentence in its own paragraph: it is immediately explicated by the next sentence in the same paragraph: "Why has man just these species of animals for his neighbors; as if nothing but a mouse could have filled this crevice?" The relation between "precisely these objects" and "make a world" isn't equative: they make a world only by our beholding them, so "which we behold" isn't an equals sign. The two questions make up a whimsical improvisation, a coy introduction to the long paragraph about Thoreau's intimacy with a particular variety of mouse, the *Mus leucopus.* It is bizarre to take them as seriously annotating an epistemology. As for the question from the *Journal* — "Why should just these sights & sounds accompany our life?" — I can't see the juxtapositions as at all pointed. It comes after a bland paragraph which, if Cameron's sense of *Walden* were accurate, should have been comfortably placed in that book rather than in the *Journal:* "I am serene & satisfied when the birds fly & the fishes swim as in fable, for the moral is not far off." The moral, no less. Every incident in nature, Thoreau goes on to say, "is a parable of the great teacher." Then comes the quoted sentence, and "accompany" is well enough explained not by its enactment of a juxtaposition but by the fact that not seen objects alone but those objects and heard sounds together accompany our lives as in music. Specifically: the chattering of blackbirds and the smell of skunks. "I would fain explore the mysterious relation between myself & these things," Thoreau immediately says, and we are left wondering how Professor Cameron can maintain that, according to the *Journal,* there is no mystery because there is no such relation.

Some of Professor Cameron's commentaries on particular passages from the *Journal* are quite brilliant: these passages have never before been read with such precision. The commentaries which strike me as perverse are those which are offered to illustrate, with notable insistence, an argument already enforced in more general terms. My own sense of the *Journal* is that you can find in it nearly anything you look for, and you can quote it to any purpose. It provides texts for virtually any epistemology you care to describe. Much of it seems to me philosophically naïve; as in Thoreau's complaint (October 6, 1857) that *Modern Painters* isn't "a more out-of-door book," and that Ruskin "does not describe Nature as Nature, but as Turner painted her."

How much is written about Nature as somebody has portrayed her, how little about Nature as she is, and chiefly concerns us, i.e. how much prose, how little poetry!

But I agree that it is in the *Journal,* more than in the published books, that we find an un-Emersonian Thoreau.

We find him in his style, rather than in any novelty of theme or motif. Thoreau is a moody writer, often insecure in tone as if he couldn't decide whether the theme in hand was really adequate to his sensibility or not. Or whether he was addressing a person or a void. It is probably as vain to turn Thoreau into a philosopher as to turn Wallace Stevens into one. They are both misleading when we take them seriously on their own terms. The range of their moods, too, is about equal, and might be charted accurately enough by saying that in one mood Thoreau, like Stevens, tended to say, "Soldier, there is a war between the mind / And sky," and in a more specifying mood that

> *we live in a place*
> *That is not our own and, much more, not ourselves*
> *And hard it is in spite of blazoned days . . .*

and nevertheless—a third mood—that

> *Ecstatic identities*
> *Between one's self and the weather and the things*
> *Of the weather are the belief in one's element ...*

Thoreau, like Stevens, seems to me a poet of one's self and the weather and the things of the weather, best read as an expert in pleasure rather than in knowledge. It is edifying to find him ready to pay attention, nearly always, to outer and inner weather. But I can't see him as an epistemologist. The claims he makes upon an unmediated relation to nature are vain, if for no other reason than the fact that language has already vetoed the possibility. Relatedness is a linguistic category. Only angels, according to Scholastic philosophy, have unmediated access to objects of knowledge. Nineteenth-century writers liked to think of children as little angels for that reason. William Empson studied the sentiment in *Some Versions of Pastoral,* and commented on the notion "that no way of building up character, no intellectual system, can bring out all that is inherent in the human spirit, and therefore that there is more in the child than any man has been able to keep."[21] In one mood, Thoreau seems to have felt that the mind could become like a little child by taking the right decision: it accounts for a certain weightlessness he seems to seek as an attribute of his way of being in the world. He was observant, committed to details, but he seems in a curious way to have distrusted the objects he attended to, and thought they would intrude upon his numinous sense of a greater life they merely punctuated. This may be what Cameron has in view when she says that in the *Journal* Thoreau has to an especial degree "an interest in relations which seem devoid of content, or whose content could be specified as man's pleasure in his ability to negotiate the continuously reiterated terms of likeness and change." When I first read that sentence, I thought it made Thoreau sound too much like Stevens, who often sets his mind, that necessary angel, astir upon a play of resemblance and difference between events which hardly survive the play. But I see now that what mainly bothered me was that if we make Thoreau sound like Stevens, it becomes harder to keep him close to Frost, which is where my first prejudice wanted to have him.

The same problem arises with any artist whose thinking has a

pronounced tendency to aspire. If we describe it at an arbitrary point in
its trajectory, we interrupt the process and give a misleading account of
its character. But the problem is compounded in Thoreau by the fact that
his desire always seems to be located aside from what he's talking about.
His official theme is always secondary, by comparison with some primary
relation which is characterized, of necessity, by its absence. Take a simple
example from the *Journal,* December 22, 1851:

> If I am thus seemingly cold compared with my companion's warm,
> who knows but mine is a less transient glow, a steadier and more
> equable heat, like that of the earth in spring, in which the flowers
> spring and expand? It is not words that I wish to hear or to utter, but
> relations that I seek to stand in; and it oftener happens, methinks,
> that I go away unmet, unrecognized, ungreeted in my offered
> relation, than that you are disappointed of words.

On one level, this is only the familiar complaint that I can't express
myself; with the corresponding claim that my feelings are such, and so
exalted, that I shouldn't be expected to be able to find words for them.
The relations I seek to stand in are evidently the constituents of an
element so fine that words are bound to degrade it. But this wordless
communion is then transformed into a totality to which, as the negations
show—"unmet, unrecognized, ungreeted"—only a recognition at once
bodily and spiritual could fully correspond. Nothing becomes All, according to a trope familiar in Transcendentalism. But before anything can
become All, it has to be reduced to Nothing from whatever it has
been.

A more complicated version turns up in the *Journal* for January 17,
1852, when Thoreau is pondering the status of his thoughts. It pleases him
to regard them as objects he has discovered in the natural world, and to
give them, but only to begin with, the same God-ordained status as any
other objects found there. But in that mood, each object already in the
natural world becomes a symbol of some capacity in himself; and each
thought-object becomes a symbol of something in himself deeper than
thought:

> In proportion as I have celestial thoughts, is the necessity for me to
> be out and behold the western sky before sunset these winter days.

That is the symbol of the unclouded mind that knows neither winter nor summer. What is your thought like? That is the hue, that the purity, and transparency, and distance from earthly taint of my inmost mind, for whatever we see without is a symbol of something within, and that which is farthest off is the symbol of what is deepest within.

The unclouded or inmost mind is the capacity of passing through sensory distinctions to a conviction of unity. The equation of distance and depth is easily made, and made with particular force by a natural scientist who takes another kind of pleasure in noting the veins in a leaf. Hopkins says, somewhere in his journal: "what you look hard at seems to look hard at you." In one mood, Thoreau was willing to encounter that hard look. But in another he wanted to soften it to the point at which it would seem to fade from view and there is nothing left but the mind communing with itself. It is that mood to which one of Cameron's sentences most richly applies: "Thoreau wants to be the externality on which he reflects, to be away from the self, to be out of the mind." In the end he is his own desired object of attention, and has dislodged every rival.

But now we have made Thoreau sound like Valéry's Monsieur Teste, and we have to put up with it. It is only in language, and not in nature, that Thoreau could find conditions at all responsive to his desire; to his desire, that is, for unmediated access not to any object of his attention but to its essence. Indeed, only in language can we find the desire tolerable: elsewhere it is repellent, since it amounts to an insistence that the mind's life must be absolutely free of conditions. In language, we can tolerate the majesty of the claim, and take it equably enough as a justified indication of the quality of Thoreau's desire. In life, it is obnoxious.

Emerson recognized Thoreau's majesty, and described it well. Reading the *Journal* in the summer of 1862, he wrote:

Thoreau's page reminds me of Farley, who went early into the wilderness in Illinois, lived alone, & hewed down trees, & tilled the land, but retired again into newer country when the population came up with him. Yet, on being asked, what he was doing? said, he pleased himself that he was preparing the land for civilization.

If there is a little strut in the style, it is only from a vigor in excess of the size of his body. His determination on natural history is organic: he sometimes felt like a hound or a panther &, if born among Indians, would have been a fell hunter: restrained, modified by his Massachusetts culture he played out the game in this mild form of botany & ichthyology.

I see many generals without a command, like Henry.[22]

VIII

The strut in Thoreau's style marks his way of being in language: experimental, quirky, cutting a dash. In *A World Elsewhere,* Richard Poirier makes the important point that Thoreau, rather than Emerson, is concerned "to make the rational, physical, mundane side of a given experience inseparable from its visionary aspects."[23] It is his capacity to move swiftly between the two worlds, the virtuosity he knows he commands, which issues in the strut.

Normally, this power in Thoreau is associated with his recourse to English seventeenth-century writers, especially Browne, Donne, and Herbert: the metaphysical conceit was far more congenial to him than to Emerson, and he practised it with evident pleasure. Sometimes it became a trick, his darting between the literal and the figurative character of the words as if to assure himself (and, for the moment, his putative reader) of a correspondence between nature, language, and mind. He couldn't examine a leaf without thinking of turning over a new one. Sharon Cameron argues that both the literal and the figurative are produced, in the *Journal,* under the sign of despair. "While figurative language may command an ample repertoire to 'identify' what is seen," she says, "in the *Journal* such language seems ultimately at the same loss as the literal language to whose rescue it has come." But the examples she chooses— "grass like a sea of mowing," for one—seem to me to be free of the particular disability she describes. But while the manners of Browne and Donne especially gratified Thoreau—and mainly in their play of figures— he also caught a particular gleam of his own time, flashing as if between Carlyle and Byron. Some readers of Thoreau are dismayed by the flash— "he writes with the taunt of the virtuoso," Irving Howe complains in *The American Newness*—and there is indeed a question of vulgar display. But Thoreau's poorest writing is done not when he shows off but when he hesitates before deciding how wildly to show off; when he thinks of

Concord before dashing off to Walden. A touch of Massachusetts gentility keeps coming in to spoil what we have good reason to call the effect.

I think this conventionally good taste is what Margaret Fuller sensed in an essay Thoreau submitted to *The Dial* in the summer of 1840. Turning it down, she told him:

> Last night's second reading only confirms my impression from the first. The essay is rich in thoughts, and I should be pained not to meet it again. But then, the thoughts seem to me so out of their natural order, that I cannot read it through without pain. I never once felt myself in a stream of thought, but seem to hear the grating tools on the mosaic. It is true, as Mr. Emerson says, that essays not to be compared with this have found their way into *The Dial*. But then, these are more unassuming in their tone, and have an air of quiet good-breeding, which induces us to permit their presence. Yours is so rugged that it ought to be commanding.[24]

I take the move from "pained" to "pain" as an irony: this is the sort of thing Thoreau was in the habit—because it became a habit, and didn't become him then—of doing. A stream of thought was Mr. Emerson's way of doing things, and it accounts for some of his fame as lecturer, essayist, and sage: to feel oneself in such a stream was the sensation his devotees evidently wanted. Thoreau's method of commuting between his *Journal* and the writings he offered for publication was indeed mosaic work: he may have had a scruple against stream work, preferring striking juxtapositions to an element in which surprises came rarely and a sense of being suffused was the richest gratification.

IX

Two passages from *Walden* will enable us to see something of its range. I take the first from the first chapter, deliberately entitled "Economy" because, even more daringly than Emerson when he used such words as "commodity" and "compensation," Thoreau laid claim to the entire latitude of its meanings:

Finding that my fellow-citizens were not likely to offer me any room in the court house, or any curacy or living anywhere else, but I must shift for myself, I turned my face more exclusively than ever to the woods, where I was better known. I determined to go into business at once, and not wait to acquire the usual capital, using such slender means as I had already got. My purpose in going to Walden Pond was not to live cheaply nor to live dearly there, but to transact some private business with the fewest obstacles; to be hindered from accomplishing which for want of a little common sense, a little enterprise and business talent, appeared not so sad as foolish.

I have always endeavored to acquire strict business habits; they are indispensable to every man. If your trade is with the Celestial Empire, then some small counting house on the coast, in some Salem harbor, will be fixture enough.[25]

Quentin Anderson has remarked that Thoreau, trying to establish a visionary world in a society given over to commerce, repudiates commercial values by stealing their language for visionary use.[26] He appropriates for his own high-minded purpose the low vocabulary of trade. But there is further piquancy in the theft. Thoreau is not merely saying that his values are so high that they can withstand the strain of an alien vocabulary. He is saying that as a poet he has just as strong a claim to those words as any entrepreneur. The passage I've quoted isn't merely a parody of Franklinism. Thoreau had to outflank the businessmen, but he had also to show, by taking over their vocabulary, that he knew the way of life he was choosing to renounce. They couldn't write him off as a fool. Part of the irony is that Thoreau is about to describe a modern experiment, but in a vocabulary drawn largely from the English tradition of common sense, its chief exemplar Daniel Defoe. Thoreau's gospel of self-reliance takes on a sturdier manner—"I must shift for myself"—than Emerson gave it, its inward conviction entirely answerable to the range of demands in such words as "business," "capital," "transact," and (after repeated business with "business"), "enterprise" and "trade." "Curacy or living": the pun is stirred into life by the Latin of "curacy," which is at once *curatus,* meaning having a cure or charge, and *cura* meaning care, hence a spiritual benefice. Translated into ecclesiastical English, the irony of "living" sends it beyond itself into every kind of livelihood. My fellow citizens don't care whether I live or die.

The second passage comes near the end of *Walden,* the chapter called "Spring": it corresponds to a passage in the *Journal* for December 31, 1851. At one point Thoreau describes how the thawing sand and clay flow down the side of a cut in the railroad. The forms the thawing stuff takes suggest to Thoreau other forms in vegetable and animal life:

> Thus it seemed that this one hillside illustrated the principle of all the operations of Nature. The Maker of this earth but patterned a leaf. What Champollion will decipher this hieroglyphic for us, that we may turn over a new leaf at last? This phenomenon is more exhilarating to me than the luxuriance and fertility of vineyards. True, it is somewhat excrementitious in its character, and there is no end to the heaps of liver, lights, and bowels, as if the globe were turned wrong side outward; but this suggests at least that Nature has some bowels, and there again is mother of humanity. This is the frost coming out of the ground; this is Spring. It precedes the green and flowery spring, as mythology precedes regular poetry. I know of nothing more purgative of winter fumes and indigestions. It convinces me that Earth is still in her swaddling-clothes, and stretches forth baby fingers on every side. These foliaceous heaps lie along the bank like the slag of a furnace, showing that Nature is "in full blast" within. The earth is not a mere fragment of dead history, stratum upon stratum like the leaves of a book, to be studied by geologists and antiquaries chiefly, but living poetry like the leaves of a tree, which precede flowers and fruit,—not a fossil earth, but a living earth; compared with whose great central life all animal and vegetable life is merely parasitic. Its throes will heave our exuviae from their graves . . . [27]

And so forth.

Let us read the passage with a particular consideration in mind. In *Permanence and Change,* Kenneth Burke proposes, instead of a metaphysics, a metabiology:

> Essentially, it involves the selection of a purposive or teleological metaphor (the metaphor of human action or poetry) as distinct from a mechanistic metaphor (the *vis a tergo* causality of machinery) for the shaping of our attitude toward the universe and history. And it bases this choice upon the most undeniable point of reference we

could possibly have: the biological. It aims less at a metaphysic than at a metabiology. And a point of view biologically rooted seems to be as near to "rock bottom" as human thought could take us.[28]

Have we not in Thoreau's passage an applied metabiology, beginning not at rock bottom but at sand-and-clay bottom, and featuring in the image of thawing—at once solid and liquid—the rudimentary and irresistible force of life, the "great central life" which he celebrates? (A few sentences later, beginning a sentence with a reference to Thaw, Thoreau puns his way to Thor, as if his own surname were but a further development of the kinship.) The entire passage proposes a comparison between thawing sand and "the world's body." Appropriately, it deploys not only the most fundamental vocabulary we have, that derived from the experience of our own bodies, but a vocabulary that recognizes the lowliest parts of the body. The big dictionaries give three meanings of excrementitious: having to do with (a) dregs, lees, refuse, leftovers from the process of refinement, (b) superfluous matter cast out of any animal body, and (c) an outgrowth of an animal body, such as hair, nails, and feathers. They are all active in Thoreau's passage. It is typical of him, too, that he moves swiftly from liver, lights, and bowels—figurative, here, and heaped together to display Nature's grand excess—to "bowels" in an even more figurative sense. The O.E.D. gives as one of the meanings of bowels, by transference: "Considered as the seat of the tender and sympathetic emotions, hence pity, compassion, feeling, heart." Two of the citations are Lytton (1832): "I am a man that can feel for my neighbors. I have bowels—yes I have bowels"; and Carlyle (1865): "Had idle readers any bowels for him; which they had not." So in Thoreau: "but this suggests at least that Nature has some bowels, and there again is mother of humanity." Humanity in two senses, the human race which Nature anticipates, and compassion, the sentiment we learn from our mothers.

A few more details.

1. " . . . the principle of all the operations of Nature." Thoreau assumes that there is only one principle, and that it subsumes every form of geological, vegetable, and animal life. In this chapter its emphasized form—the moment toward which *Walden* itself strives—is the coming of Spring, the endless manifestation of creativity. And we should put beside that phrase a passage in Emerson's *Journal,* January 1858:

I found Henry T. in my woods. . . . We talked of the willows. He says, 'tis impossible to tell when they push the bud (which so marks the arrival of spring) out of its dark scales. It is done & doing all winter. It is begun in the previous autumn. It seems one steady push from autumn to spring. I say, How divine these studies! Here there is no taint of mortality.

2. "The Maker of this earth": an artist, genius of one work, epitomized in the design of a leaf. Guarantor, therefore, of every true artist, each a God in little.

3. " . . . will decipher this hieroglyph": so that interpretation becomes the means to a new life, punningly a new leaf turned over. The Spring "precedes the green and flowery spring, as mythology precedes regular poetry": precedes, Miller's motif of anticipation again.

4. " . . . that Earth is still in her swaddling-clothes": a rejection of the commoner sentiment that the world is coming to an end.

5. Thoreau's strut is evident again in his appropriation of the language of mechanism: having said that there is nothing inorganic, he proves it by saying that the "foliaceous heaps lie along the bank like the slag of a furnace, showing that Nature is 'in full blast' within." Everything that man has invented, Nature has already conceived.

6. And just as the Earth in Spring is a child, so a few sentences later Thoreau puns or "joyces" the withered vegetation into widows' weeds, "decent weeds, at least, which widowed Nature wears." So the principle governing all the operations of Nature accommodates death, too, as widows wince and die.

Where is Thoreau in this passage? He takes part in the festival, dances attendance upon the Spring, but with a certain reserve. I think it significant that in the first chapter he speaks of himself as having become, after the experience of Walden Pond, "a sojourner in civilized life again"; and in the second says that "the very simplicity and nakedness of man's life in the primitive ages imply this advantage, at least, that they left him still but a sojourner in nature." Think of Cameron's argument again, and translate it into vulgar terms, at whatever cost. Perhaps we can accept it in a vulgar more readily than in a subtle form. Let us say that Thoreau regarded people as nuisances in his recourse to the natural world; and that, at least in some moods, he regarded Nature as a nuisance in his desire to transform Nothing into All. Existence in any form is a nuisance if nothing less than Essence will satisfy you. If you have to be in the world, then be there with reserve; be a sojourner. The Bible (I Chronicles 29:15) has this: "For we are strangers before thee, and sojourners, as were all our fathers: our days on the earth are as a shadow, and there is none abiding."

It is only in language, and not even in Nature, that Thoreau is content to reside. His verve in playing words for all their various lives are worth—puns, literal and figurative meanings, allusions, the tension between Anglo-Saxon and Latin affiliations—shows that only among sentences was he willing to be at home.

NOTES

1. Joel Porte (ed.), *Emerson in His Journals* (Cambridge, Mass.: Harvard University Press, 1982), p. 502.
2. *Ibid.,* p. 391.
3. *Ibid.,* pp. 481–82.
4. *Ibid.,* p. 465.
5. Thoreau, *Journal,* eds. Francis H. Allen and Bradford Torrey (Boston: Houghton Mifflin, 1906), V, 188.
6. *Emerson in His Journals,* p. 264.
7. *Ibid.,* p. 511.
8. Henry James, *Essays on Literature: American Writers, English Writers* (New York: Library of America, 1984), p. 264.
9. *Ibid.,* p. 265.
10. Henry James, *Letters,* Vol. I: 1843–1875, ed. Leon Edel (London: Macmillan, 1974), p. 62.
11. Henry James, *Hawthorne* (London: Macmillan, 1902 reprint), pp. 96–97.
12. James Russell Lowell, *Literary Essays* (Boston, 1890), pp. 361–81.
13. Henry James, *Essays on Literature,* p. 383.
14. Philip Rahv, *Image and Idea* (New York: New Directions, 1957), p. 18.
15. Perry Miller, *Consciousness in Concord: The Text of Thoreau's Hitherto Lost Journal, 1840–1841* (Boston: Houghton Mifflin, 1958), p. 162.
16. *Ibid.,* p. 163.
17. Walter Harding, *The Days of Henry Thoreau* (rev. ed.; Princeton: Princeton University Press, 1982), p. 71.
18. Guy Davenport, *The Geography of the Imagination* (San Francisco: North Point Press, 1981), p. 231.
19. Sharon Cameron, *Writing Nature: Henry Thoreau's Journal* (New York: Oxford University Press, 1985).
20. J. Lyndon Shanley, *The Making of Walden* (Chicago: University of Chicago Press, 1957), pp. 18–33.
21. William Empson, *Some Versions of Pastoral* (London: Chatto & Windus, 1950 ed.), pp. 260–61.
22. *Emerson in His Journals,* p. 502.

23. Richard Poirier, *A World Elsewhere* (New York: Oxford University Press, 1966), p. 89.
24. Quoted in Miller, *Consciousness in Concord,* p. 137.
25. Thoreau, *A Week, Walden, The Maine Woods, Cape Cod* (New York: Library of America, 1985), p. 338.
26. Quentin Anderson, "Practical and Visionary Americans," *The American Scholar,* XLV, No. 3 (Summer 1976), 414.
27. Thoreau, *A Week...,* p. 568.
28. Kenneth Burke, *Permanence and Change* (Los Altos, Calif.: Hermes Publications, 1954 ed.), pp. 260–61.

From (in part) *The Times Literary Supplement,* April 25, 1986.

WHITMAN

It is proper to declare that we are concerned with Whitman the poet; allowing, with whatever degree of irony, that it is permissible to reflect upon Whitman the prophet, the laureate of Democracy, the good grey messenger of revolution, the American, Lincoln's elegist, champion of freedom, and so forth. But it is easier to avow this scruple than to act upon it. Whitman lives in his poems, we say, or he does not live at all. True, in one sense; but the poems do not reach us in such purity. It is disingenuous to maintain that the words "Walt Whitman" mean the collected works of a certain poet as the words "T. S. Eliot" mean the collected works of a certain poet. Walt Whitman is a myth, as Eliot is not: that is, whatever Eliot means is to be found, definitively secreted, in the poems themselves, but the meaning of Whitman sprawls far beyond his lines. We see this in the first stanza of Wallace Stevens's poem "Like Decorations in a Nigger Cemetery":

> In the far South the sun of autumn is passing
> Like Walt Whitman walking along a ruddy shore.
> He is singing and chanting the things that are part of him,
> The worlds that were and will be, death and day.

Nothing is final, he chants. No man shall see the end.
His beard is of fire and his staff is a leaping flame.

It would be absurd, or a merry quip, to compare the sun, in the first two
lines, with any other figure in American literature: try inserting, for
instance, the names of Emily Dickinson, Henry James, T. S. Eliot, or
Robert Frost. Melville is the only other writer who might survive the
comparison. This does not mean that, to Stevens or to us, Whitman is
obviously the greatest American writer; but rather that, in a peculiar
degree, he occupies a special place in the landscape of American feeling.
He is an emblem, a moral force, a personage: the poetry, in certain
respects, does not matter. This is why Whitman has a particular profile in
the iconography of American literature; his status is heroic, whether the
poems are good or bad. He lodges in the mind as a certain gesture, a
stance; the last line of Stevens's invocation makes it clear. That line is not
offered as description or notation: it testifies, rather, to Whitman's epic
character, as if he were a certain feeling, personified. If feelings had
proper names, one of them would be Whitman. He is, in Emerson's sense,
a Representative Man. So if we say of the words on the page that they alone
matter, we can hardly say it until, late in the evening, we have disengaged
ourselves from considerations which, in other respects, matter more.

Whitman was born on May 31, 1819, at West Hills, Long Island,
New York: "well-begotten," as he writes in "Starting from Paumanok,"
"and rais'd by a perfect mother." His father, less than perfect, meant little
to the boy. In 1823 the family moved to Brooklyn, where the father tried
his luck as a builder. Walt's education was vague and random. At the age
of seventeen, he attached himself to a printer in New York, and thereafter,
for many years, he lived in close touch with printing rooms, newspapers,
editorial desks. In 1848 he spent some months in New Orleans, working
on a newspaper, the *Crescent*. In 1862 he went to Washington and
attended upon Civil War soldiers as a "wound dresser": as he wrote in
"Song of Myself":

> *I am he bringing help for the sick as they pant on their backs,*
> *And for strong upright men I bring yet more needed help.*

To support himself, he took a job as a clerk in the Army Paymaster's
Office, but in 1864 his health failed and he went back to his mother's

house in Brooklyn. Later, he worked again, as a clerk in the Indian Bureau of the Interior Department, where he spent nine years, but after 1873 he was never to recover his health. He left Washington and went to live with his brother George in Camden, New Jersey. In 1884 he moved to his own house in Mickle Street. In the last seven or eight years of his life he lived as a sage, visited and admired by a succession of literary men: he was now famous. He had published the first edition of *Leaves of Grass* in 1855; thereafter, several larger books appeared under that title until the famous "deathbed" edition of 1892. He had also published *Drum-Taps* (1865), *Democratic Vistas* (1871), and *Specimen Days* (1882). He died on March 26, 1892.

The life was not, indeed, as diverse as the poems claim: many of the ostensibly autobiographical moments in the poems are the work of fancy and desire. The rhetoric of the poetry required a sustaining experience multitudinous and free: confinement to the facts would have impeded the flow. It may be argued that Whitman found, in the way of experience, whatever he needed for the good of the poems; but at the same time the poems often give an impression of cultural emaciation, as if desire and fancy were not enough. Some passages are written, apparently, on the assumption that to say a few things well it is necessary to say everything anyhow: if there is enough of it, some of it is bound to be good. Whitman's culture may have given him what he needed, so that the poems became what they are; but there is the other possibility, that the culture did not give him what he needed to make the poems greater than they are. It is often necessary to say of Whitman what R. P. Blackmur said of Hart Crane, that he represents "every ignorance possible to talent when it has genius, every wilfulness tolerable because of expressive intention." Certainly, Whitman's culture gave him material enough for his grandest purposes, but it did not force him to survey those purposes, to criticize his high intention: his individual talent was not, in any profound sense, curbed or rebuked by a critical tradition.

But these are premature questions. We must allow to Whitman's "expressive intention" at least this: that we take him at his word and on his terms before we insinuate other words, other terms. Reading poets like Whitman and Crane, who pursue the American Sublime, we have to take the will and the deed as making a continuum; or at least we have to give these poets the benefit of every doubt, until the doubts are resolved or transcended. Eliot's intention does not offer itself as interesting apart from the deed, but to engage with Whitman and Crane at all, we have to strike a liberal bargain with them: a word is to be justified by the line, the line by the stanza, the stanza by the poem, the poem by the whole work, *Leaves of Grass;* and even then we are not released, there is still the larger *oeuvre,* the life.

"Of all mankind," Whitman writes in the Introduction to the first edition of *Leaves of Grass,* "the great poet is the equable man." He may have been encouraged in this sentiment by Emerson, who said, in the essay "The Poet," that the poet is representative: "He stands among partial men for the complete man, and apprises us not of his wealth, but of the commonwealth." To Whitman, the poet is seer, arbiter, standard, and key; the self, so far as the self is complete and expressive. In "Song of Myself," he speaks of "the Me myself," saying it is not "contain'd between my hat and boots": it is not even the sum of its experiences, but rather that sum, apprehended:

> *Apart from the pulling and hauling stands what I am,*
> *Stands amused, complacent, compassionating, idle, unitary,*
> *Looks down, is erect, or bends an arm on an impalpable certain*
> *   rest,*
> *Looking with side-curved head curious what will come next,*
> *Both in and out of the game and watching and wondering at it.*

The pulling and hauling: that is, the events of life, one thing after another, the matter of relevant things. But the self is not identified with its casual contents; the contents are transfigured by the imagination. Poems are "psalms of self" if in thinking of song we mark the singer. The poet's theme is "my own diversity," the range and amplitude of those experiences which the self has apprehended. Ultimately, the self is identified with "the soul," and that with God. "To be this incredible God I am!" Whitman exults in "Song at Sunset." In the "Song of Myself": "Divine am I inside and out, and I make holy whatever I touch or am touched from." Man is God in the measure of his senses and his imagination: it makes little difference whether we think of divine attributes and then ascribe them to man, or think of certain human powers and equate them, transfigured, with God. All roads lead to that romantic Rome. The idiom is philosophically idealist, to begin with; as

Coleridge thought of the human imagination as the finite counterpart of God's creative power, the infinite I AM. But Coleridge did not press the analogy to the pitch of identifying God and man; Whitman's pitch, in fact. Whitman speaks of God as of man in his most extreme reach of imagination.

The pattern is clear in "Passage to India" and other poems. Whitman cannot think of God and the universe as separate from himself; such a thought would leave him wrecked, dissociated. So he refutes the thought by thinking of himself, "the soul," and endowing that phrase with divinely creative attributes: at that stage there is no longer any need to use an idiom of divine things or divine powers; the soul is God:

> *Swiftly I shrivel at the thought of God,*
> *At Nature and its wonders, Time and Space and Death,*
> *But that I, turning, call to thee O soul, thou actual Me,*
> *And lo, thou gently masterest the orbs,*
> *Thou matest Time, smilest content at Death,*
> *And fillest, swellest full the vastnesses of Space.*

It is a characteristic curve of feeling: the poet redeems himself, constantly renews himself, until he fills all the world. This partly explains why, to Whitman, poetry consists in the entire life of feeling. Feeling is the divine spirit, the great poem is the great life, and the mere words on the page are only one form of this activity. The ultimate poem is life itself; the poems are merely one part, consistent with other parts. Ideally, poems intervene between one great silence and another. What is crucial is the process, the continuity and diversity of feeling; process rather than product. Look after the process and the product will look after itself. The enemy is "stagnation." The poet never stagnates: "if he breathes into any thing that was before thought small it dilates with the grandeur and life of the universe"; like God.

So the poet is, in Emerson's phrase, the secretary. "I find a provision, in the constitution of the world," Emerson writes in *Representative Men*, "for the writer or secretary, who is to report the doings of the miraculous spirit of life that everywhere throbs and works." Add to this the further assumption that the miraculous spirit is most clearly found in "the Me myself," and we have the gist of Whitman's rhetoric. It is given, implicitly, in the last paragraph of Emerson's book:

The secret of genius is to suffer no fiction to exist for us; to realize all that we know; in the high refinement of modern life, in arts, in sciences, in books, in men, to exact good faith, reality, and a purpose; and first, last, midst, and without end, to honour every truth by use.

There is enough here for Whitman's purposes. The idealist slant of his aesthetic need not be extreme, there is no need of solipsism. It is possible to assimilate the Romantic imagination to intimations of divine purpose and power, but it is also possible to act as secretary, writing the miraculous truths of nature and self. There is no contradiction, especially if the post of secretary is not restricted to mere transcription. The secretary reports what he sees, hears, touches, tastes, and smells, but these impressions are related and, indeed, transfigured by the imagination: what the secretary writes is the imaginative record, not a blunt paraphrase. The secretary has his own diversity.

To use a standard philosophical idiom: the object is qualified by the subject's reception of it. The point, in relation to Whitman, must be enforced. There is a sense in which he is nonchalant about the self: as if the self were the sum of its experiences and could safely, beyond that, be taken for granted. "I become as much more as I like," he says in "Song of Myself," reciting several experiences to display his possessions. "A shroud I see—and I am the shroud," he says in "The Sleepers." Whitman's sense of self may often be defined as a sense of its possessions. But a complete merging of subject and object is rare in his poetry: there are dangerous moments in certain meditations upon death and the sea. Nearly always, subject and object are held in poise, each is itself. "Clear and sweet is my soul . . . and clear and sweet is all that is not my soul." The characteristic act of the self is to attract appearances and impressions, the chosen objects of experience:

> *And I know I am solid and sound,*
> *To me the converging objects of the universe perpetually flow.*

The fuller the flow, of course, the better: the self lives well, never short of converging impressions. What happens to these impressions when they converge is the history of Whitman's imagination.

The language is idealist in the sense that the primary act is deemed to be the act of feeling: normally, there is no quarrel between subject and object, but if a quarrel should break out, subject must be asserted. "All architecture is what you do to it when you look upon it," Whitman says in "A Song for Occupations." Everywhere the governing idiom is personal, subjective: what is objective is acknowledged, but Whitman emphasizes the subjective force of attraction and perception, the force of convergence toward a centre. Poetry is great because it is personal, it comes from the person, the self, the soul:

> *My words are words of a questioning, and to indicate reality;*
> *This printed and bound book . . . but the printer and the*
> *   printing-office boy?*
> *The marriage estate and settlement . . . but the body and mind*
> *   of the bridegroom, also those of the bride?*

In "Song of the Answerer," "Every existence has its idiom . . . every thing has an idiom and tongue." In "To a Historian," Whitman distinguishes between historian and poet, the historian celebrates "bygones," the poet, "Chanter of Personality," projects "the history of the future." If we ask the secretary whether his text contains more subject than object, he is likely to reply that objects are, indeed, acknowledged but, finally, they minister to the subject. As in "Out of the Cradle Endlessly Rocking," "the sea whisper'd me."

If the poet is God, poetry is everything, it encompasses everything, religion, science, fact, life, everything. Poetry is Being: so the idiom of Being is superior to all other idioms, as the poet is superior to all other persons, complete where they are partial. It is typical of Whitman to use one idiom to refute another, as the single category of Being refutes all other categories. The distinction between good and evil vanishes, at least in this stringent theory, when both terms are dissolved in the higher language of Being. Hence Whitman's ethic is his aesthetic: his sense of the world is an aesthetic sense, in which good and evil are featured as neutral terms. William Carlos Williams wrote, in the essay "Against the Weather," that "the blessed and the damned are treated by Dante, the *artist*, with scrupulous impartiality. . . . Pan is the artist's patron." This is in Whitman's spirit. It was William James, I think, who brought into critical currency the notion that, in practice, Whitman lacked a sense of evil. In a lecture of 1895 he spoke of "our dear old Walt Whitman's works" as the handbook of that "temperamental optimism" which is "incapable of believing that anything seriously evil can exist." What James started, Yeats continued, in a famous passage in *A Vision*. But it will not do. Some of the most haunting passages in "Song of Myself" are apprehensions of sickness and pain, "the silent old-faced infants and the lifted sick." The fact is that Whitman was determined to erect one terminology and place it above all: in that terminology, such words as "feeling," "poetry," and "being" would be strong enough to put any rival terminology down. The conventional distinction between good and evil, respectable and illicit, would be dissolved, on the superior ground that anything which exists and is felt is good. Any object which exists and converges upon the subject is good. This is why Whitman says, in "Starting from Paumanok":

> *Omnes! omnes! let others ignore what they may,*
> *I make the poem of evil also, I commemorate that part also,*
> *I am myself just as much evil as good, and my nation is—*
> > *and I say there is in fact no evil.*
> *(Or if there is I say it is just as important to you, to the*
> > *land or to me, as any thing else.)*

In a battle, success and defeat are good: all things which exist are equal in their perfection, each is miraculously itself. Whitman recognizes every thing for what it is, good or bad, but he is not daunted by its nature. *Etiam peccata.* The reasoning in these passages is not severe, and it entirely depends upon the governing rhetoric in which existence is the only and greatest good. If that rhetoric is deemed to fail, the case is lost, and Whitman the loser is humiliated as a fool.

Taking precautions against this fate, Whitman tries to make the language of Being so compelling that resistance is discouraged: only an extraordinarily wilful reader is likely to resist. "The flush of the known universe" is his theme, if we allow that, equally, the divine powers of the "knower" are engaged. "He brings everything to the test of himself": who does not? To ease the strain of belief, Whitman sometimes translates the ostensible terms of good and evil into the language of the Hero, so that the rivals may each appear as heroic. The account of the frigate fight in "Song of Myself" is a case in point; another is the levelling ethic of "A Song for Occupations." Or again, as in "To Think of Time," Whitman posits a perspective so lofty that the distinction between good and bad, from that height, is invisible:

> *The vulgar and the refined . . . what you call sin and what you*
> *call goodness . . . to think how wide a difference;*
> *To think the difference will still continue to others, yet*
> *we lie beyond the difference.*

Later:

> *What is called good is perfect, and what is called sin is*
> *just as perfect.*

Another procedure is to assimilate the language of poetry and Being to that of irrefutable things—stones, trees, animals—in which the distinction between good and bad hardly arises. In the Introduction to *Leaves of Grass,* Whitman says that "to speak in literature with the perfect rectitude and insouciance of the movements of animals and the unimpeachableness of the sentiment of trees in the woods and grass by the roadside is the flawless triumph of art." "I will have purposes," he continues, "as health or heat or snow has." The rhetorical trick here—to speak of it in these sullen terms—is to take advantage of the several meanings of "perfection"; the state of being complete in its own kind, and—a separate meaning— the state of moral excellence. The first meaning is neutral, according to the dictionaries; the second is of course eulogy. Whitman's strategy is to use the word as a term of praise, to prevent the second meaning from assuming any airs. Anything may be perfect, in its kind: so pious folk may not preen themselves. But meanwhile animals know how to live; they toil not, neither do they spin, sweat, whine, worry, weep, kneel, or discuss. In "Me Imperturbe," Whitman says:

> *Me imperturbe, standing at ease in Nature,*
> *Master of all or mistress of all, aplomb in the midst of*
> *irrational things,*
> *. . . O to be self-balanced for contingencies,*
> *To confront night, storms, hunger, ridicule, accidents,*
> *rebuffs, as the trees and animals do.*

Like Thoreau in this respect, Whitman counsels: "Simplify." We are to live as little children: between children and natural forms there is a "wooing both ways." In this version of pastoral the liaison of subject and object is continuous; objects converge upon the subject, and in reply the subject directs his feeling toward the objects:

> *There was a child went forth every day,*
> *And the first object he looked upon and received with wonder*
>   *or pity or love or dread, that object he became,*
> *And that object became part of him for the day or a certain*
>   *part of the day . . . or for many years or stretching cycles*
>   *of years.*

Finally, everything ministers to the subject, the child: objects willingly celebrate the child, incorporating themselves in him. But the supreme analogy for poetry is the human body itself, simple, uncompounded, stark, but capable of everything. "I sing the body electric." "And your very flesh shall be a great poem," Whitman promises the reader, "and have the richest fluency not only in its words but in the silent lines of its lips and face and between the lashes of your eyes and in every motion and joint of your body." "If life and the soul are sacred the human body is sacred." In turn, the canonical terms in Whitman's vocabulary are those which are drawn immediately from a bodily source: many are phrenological terms. A short list includes: adhere, inhale, respiration, adhesiveness, meeting, inspiration, acceptation, realization, give, receive, press, swallow. The poet distrusts abstract terms not because of a fussy cult of "the concrete," but because the best words are continuous with the intimate life of the body.

Naturally, the great moment, then, is the moment at which subject and object meet; in bodily terms, the moment of contact. "I am mad for it to be in contact with me," he says in "Song of Myself," and the object might be anything. Of the great poet, he writes in the Introduction to *Leaves of Grass:* "What balks or breaks others is fuel for his burning progress to contact and amorous joy." Sight is good, but not as good as touch: touch is immediate, indisputable, perhaps erotic. "The press of my foot to the earth springs a hundred affections." "Is this then a touch?" he asks later, "quivering me to a new identity." In "A Song for Occupations," he writes: "I pass so poorly with paper and types. . . . I must pass with the contact of bodies and souls." So he tries to use papers and types as if they, too, were modes of contact. Sight is good, but it holds the object of sight at a distance. This is scandalous to Whitman, who resents distance: things are certified by touch. In the passage about the "common farmer" in "I Sing the Body Electric," the proof of intimacy is touch, "that you and he might touch each other."

As there is no conflict, ideally, between one body and another, so there is none, ideally, between body and soul. "I am the poet of the body," Whitman says, "and I am the poet of the soul." Yeats speaks of body being bruised to pleasure soul, and he often thinks of these terms in incorrigible rivalry. True, there are moments in which he, too, thinks that the body in splendid animation might certify a great "unity of being." But more frequently the poor soul is "fastened to a dying animal." Whitman starts with the body and makes the soul at home there: if all else fails, he is prepared to make the body the chief term, but he sponsors amity. "Behold, the body includes and is the meaning, the main concern, and includes and is the soul." If a more elaborate definition of soul is demanded, he is ready to say:

> Was somebody asking to see the soul?
> See, your own shape and countenance, persons, substances,
>   beasts, the trees, the running rivers, the rocks and sands.

So there should be no quarrel: let the soul be the shine upon the face of nature, the animation of the human body.

The optimism is part of Whitman's time, since he chose to take it from his time. In "Great Are the Myths" and other poems the leading terms are evolutionary, excelsior terms, promissory notes: the earth's progress is unlimited. A two-line poem, "Roaming in Thought," was written in Hegel's light:

> Roaming in thought over the Universe, I saw the little that
>   is Good steadily hastening towards immortality.
> And the vast all that is call'd Evil I saw hastening to merge
>   itself and become lost and dead.

After talking to a German spiritualist, Whitman wrote "Continuities," celebrating the myth of the eternal return, promising that "nothing is ever really lost." Even life and death may be reconciled:

> Great is life . . . and real and mystical . . . wherever and whoever,
> Great is death. . . . Sure as life holds all parts together, death
>   holds all parts together;

Sure as the stars return again after they merge in the light,
death is great as life.

[from "Great Are the Myths"]

In "Out of the Cradle Endlessly Rocking," the sea whispers to Whitman "the low and delicious word death." But this is not the Romantic swoon of death: Whitman sets up, in full lucidity and daylight, those great opposites which he then proceeds to reconcile; the opposites are invoked for the sake of the reconciliation. The imagination must be declared, exhibited: its characteristic act is to accept whatever experience offers, but to make the acceptance a strikingly personal act. The personal gesture redeems the content of experience, reconciles all dichotomies. The process is Hegelian.

The political equivalent is democracy, the American version. "The United States themselves are essentially the great poem," Whitman claims, because the American democratic style is the greatest style, the most liberal, the most capacious. It may be maintained that Whitman's cult of "the common people" is, in the limiting sense, a "literary" gesture. It is certainly true that he derived his politics from his aesthetic, as he derived his ethic from the same source. He did not start with democracy or even with "these States": his sense of these matters was, in the first instance, an aesthetic sense, governed by the primacy of Being. "The Americans . . . have probably the fullest poetical nature"; not on the demonstrable strength of American poems already written, but on the promising strength of a society in tune with an aesthetic feeling, a certain way of life, a style. At this stage, that is, before the Civil War, Whitman did not look very closely at the practical versions of democracy, local politics, the detailed organization of wards, cities, and states. He sponsored the idea of democracy, regardless of its local manifestations. After the war, he became disenchanted, as the sharp prose of *Democratic Vistas* indicates: his critique of practical democracy is as vigorous as, say, Henry Adams's image of the Age of Grant in his novel *Democracy*. But that was far ahead. In the first editions of *Leaves of Grass*, America was presented as God's new Eden, where every diversity is received, every contradiction reconciled, "her athletic Democracy" a wonderful invention. The terms of praise are poetic terms, in the sense that they may be applied, with equal conviction, to poetry and to America; the metaphors are the same. The possibility of poetry is the possibility of America: the great poet is the American Adam, the secretary. So at this stage, there was no need to ask hard questions, as

Adams would ask them in one way, Henry James in another. Whitman's concern was the metaphorical congruity of American democracy and a correspondingly liberal poetry. So he celebrates this largesse, and it is hardly surprising that, in this mood, he blurred the difference between the actual and the possible, promiscuous in his attendance upon the future tense.

But we must not exaggerate. Every self-conscious country needs an apostle: if he serves that purpose, it is irrelevant if he serves any other. For many years, Whitman offered himself as the American bard, chanter of democratic personality: at first the offer was spurned, but gradually it was accepted. America agreed to take him at his proffered word; he was received as the spirit of unity, force, diversity, cohesion. So it has taken readers a long time to realize that this image of Whitman is partial. We are still encouraged to think of him as representing a simple, honest unity; with the further implication that this is a better thing than its rival, a Jamesian image of irony, critique, and sophistication. That is, we are invited to read the poetry as if it were politics, all the better for a vulgar touch, proof of honesty and unity. It must be conceded that Whitman lends himself to these purposes: if a politician needs a slogan, he is bound to find what he needs in Whitman, perhaps on the first page. But the truth is more complex. Whitman was never entirely the unified man of popular legend, liberal, androgynous, available; he was not completely liberated from the common anxieties and divisions of his time. Even when his poems end in reconciliation, they begin, many of them, in division: "wandering and confused . . . lost to myself . . . ill-assorted . . . contradictory." Often the division can be healed only by pointing to a happier future implicit in Whitman's terminology. "Do you suppose I could be content with all if I thought them their own finale?" he asks in "Faces": one face is "a dog's snout sniffing for garbage," but it is a human face; Whitman rages against it, but he contents himself by thinking of a future in which that man, too, will be a true man. In such a future, all things are possible. But meanwhile there are poems like "As I Ebb'd with the Ocean of Life," in which Whitman is just as confused and dispirited as any of his contemporaries:

> *O baffled, balk'd, bent to the very earth,*
> *Oppress'd with myself that I have dared to open my mouth,*

Aware now that amid all that blab whose echoes recoil upon
    me I have not once had the least idea who or what I am,
But that before all my arrogant poems the real Me stands yet
    untouch'd, untold, altogether unreach'd,
Withdrawn far, mocking me with mock-congratulatory signs and
    bows.

The poem does not end there: Whitman never leaves such feelings as his last word, he tries again until, by force of will, the reconciling motives begin to assert themselves. But the evidence is indisputable: Whitman lives, at least on certain days, in the world of Arnold's "The Buried Life," Hopkins's "terrible sonnets," Clough's *Amours de Voyage.* If they are divided, so is he. In Whitman, theory is one thing, practice another. Sometimes he is the chanter of fellowship, but again he seems dissociated, alien, "withdrawn far." Sometimes he is open, expansive, a comrade; at other times, secretive, furtive. Now clear, now ambiguous; now healthy, now morbid; singing "the song of companionship," proclaiming his exile. Even in *Calamus,* where the leading figures are moved in Whitman's direction, there are moments in which the entire structure of his world seems doomed:

Of the terrible doubt of appearances,
Of the uncertainty after all, that we may be deluded,
That may-be reliance and hope are but speculations after all,
That may-be identity beyond the grave is a beautiful fable only,
May-be the things I perceive, the animals, plants, men, hills,
    shining and flowing waters,
The skies of day and night, colors, densities, forms may-be
    these are (as doubtless they are) only apparitions, and
    the real something has yet to be k own,
(How often they dart out of themselves as if to confound me
    and mock me!
How often I think neither I know, nor any man knows, aught of
    them!)
May-be seeming to me what they are (as doubtless they indeed
    but seem) as from my present point of view, and might
    prove (as of course they would) nought of what they appear,
    or nought anyhow, from entirely changed points of view;

To me these and the like of these are curiously answer'd by
    my lovers, my dear friends . . .

It is a characteristic movement: the slide from "appearances" to "apparitions," and then, the beginning of the return to solid ground, the "real something" conceived now not in terms of philosophical thought but of "contact." The effort to disengage himself from one terminology and to grasp another is mimed in the poem itself: a crucial moment is "yet," "and the real something has yet to be known." The word is seized as if with physical strain, and the return begins. Now the only truth is physical, human in that sense, erotic:

> *When he whom I love travels with me or sits a long while*
>   *holding me by the hand,*
> *When the subtle air, the impalpable, the sense that words and*
>   *reason hold not, surround us and pervade us,*
> *Then I am charged with untold and untellable wisdom, I am*
>   *silent, I require nothing further,*
> *I cannot answer the question of appearances or that of identity*
>   *beyond the grave,*
> *But I walk or sit indifferent, I am satisfied,*
> *He ahold of my hand has completely satisfied me.*

This may appear simple, merely an abdication of judgement, the terrible doubt resolved by turning away from it; but in fact the resolution at the end is not achieved, in the poetry, without strain. In life, such a resolution may be easy or hard, but in poetry it is achieved only by exerting great pressure upon certain crucial terms. Notice, for instance, what is done with the sequence, holding/hold/ahold: the lovers, holding hands, surround the middle word, "the sense that words and reason hold not," with the force of their rhetoric. In the presence of physical certainty, the uncertainty of words and reason seems more extreme than ever. These poor things are bound to break. In the physical context, now, even the impalpable is redeemed: "Then I am charged with untold and untellable wisdom," the body electric again, driving its hero beyond all doubt. He is now indifferent, "I am satisfied"; a word rescued from a context in which he suffered, intellectually, always dissatisfied. Now "satisfied" means answered as well as fulfilled; but the answer has reached Whitman, as always, from an alteration of terminologies.

The decisive moment in these matters is the moment at which one terminology shifts toward another: often the change is begun with an important word, used now in a slightly odd sense, pointing to the new area of feeling. It is like the change from the present to the future tense. The exemplary occasion in Whitman is the moment when the present event is seized, fully acknowledged, and all the relevant energies are directed toward the future. "The direct trial of him who would be the greatest poet is today," Whitman writes: such a poet must "flood himself with the immediate age," must "attract his own land body and soul to himself." In "Song of Myself," everything converges upon the present:

> *There was never any more inception than there is now,*
> *Nor any more youth or age than there is now;*
> *And will never be any more perfection than there is now,*
> *Nor any more heaven or hell than there is now.*

Or in "A Song for Occupations":

> *Happiness not in another place, but this place . . . not for another*
> *hour, but this hour.*

But the conclusion is not merely: seize the day. Whitman is bringing everything to bear upon this moment, "now," because this is the turning point, the start of a new age. If new terminologies must be enforced, a start must be made now.

Inevitably, the past is ambiguously treated. Emerson said that "man is explicable by nothing less than all his history," but his account of history is self-centred, history as a gathering of man's affinities. The past is reduced to the history of consciousness. Emerson does not value gone times for the critical force they exert upon man, or the instances of objective existence they provide. The modern self is the centre of every circle. Indeed, a sense of the past as different from ourselves and compelling for that reason is rarely found in American literature. Hawthorne's relation to the past was fruitful so long as he could personify the past as a family immured in sin and guilt. James, to whom Eliot ascribed not a sense of the past but a sense of the sense, dealt with gone events successfully—that is, warmly and vividly—only when they were already halfway toward becoming a composition, a picture. Nothing was really understood, he seemed to say—nothing really appreciated, until it was framed for vision and contemplation. He was pleased with the bustle of things, but only as relevant actions and materials; the human process was incomplete until the bustle was stilled, the relationships composed in the picture. Whitman is utterly different: he is so devoted to process, to bustle and miscellany, that pictures seem to him monstrous, dead things, beyond human contact. The eye, at that extreme, is doing the devil's work. Rather than take such a risk, Whitman is prepared to disengage himself altogether from the past: by definition, in any event, the past is beyond redemption, so let it go. Out of the past, objects converge upon the present, and that is good: better still, the movement of feeling toward the future may now begin.

Whitman has often been rebuked for this. Santayana's rebuke is famous, especially the versions which he included in *Interpretations of Poetry and Religion* and *The Last Puritan.* The complaint has many aspects, but they bear upon one, finally, Whitman's scanting the past. In the *Interpretations,* Santayana says that Whitman reduces experience to a succession of moods: in this the poet is a barbarian, one "who regards his passions as their own excuse for being"; the passions are not to be understood or controlled, they are merely to be entertained. This is Whitman's primitivism: he has gone back "to the innocent style of Adam, when the animals filed before him one by one and he called each of them by its name." He has tried "the imaginary experiment of beginning the world over again": no past is acknowledged as in any degree a restraint. Whitman ignores "the fatal antiquity of human nature," thereby indulging himself in a manner fostered by liberalism and American Transcendentalism. To him, the past was an alien place, and, comparing his own world, he declared the latter a fresh creation. The first result was that he confirmed himself in his chief interest, his own sensations: nothing else was really alive. The world is all surface, no depth: impressions pass before Whitman's senses and he yields himself to each. He sees common life "not in contrast with an ideal, but as the expression of forces more indeterminate and elementary than itself." So the vulgar appears to him sublime. In the discussion of American literature which Santayana inserts in Chapter 13 of *The Last Puritan,* Jim insists that Whitman is "the great, the best, the only American poet"; and, to make a grand claim, he hands Oliver a copy of *Leaves of Grass.* The book opens of itself at a passage heavily scored in the margin, from "Song of Myself":

> *I think I could turn and live awhile with the animals . . . they*
> *   are so placid and self-contained,*
> *I stand and look at them sometimes half the day long.*
> *They do not sweat and whine about their condition,*
> *They do not lie awake in the dark and weep for their sins,*
> *They do not make me sick discussing their duty to God.*

Oliver's reaction is immediate:

> *Dope,* thought Oliver, himself a little somnolent in the noonday heat and the soft air, *dope* in another form. A lazy refusal to look backward, or to look ahead. A hatred of reason, a hatred of sacrifice. The lilies of the field. Work wasn't worth while.

He reads the passage aloud, then asks his father, "Don't you like that?" "I like the first three words: *I could turn,*" his father answers:

> I should have liked it well enough if he had said he could turn and *no longer* live with the animals, they are so restless and merciless and ferocious, possessed with a mania for munching grass and gnawing bones and nosing one another, when they don't make me sick saying they are God's chosen people, doing God's work.

It is sharp: Oliver's father ridiculing the Franciscan Walt Whitman:

> He doesn't see that human conventions are products of nature, that morality and religion and science express or protect animal passions: and that he couldn't possibly be more like an animal than by living like other men. His rebellion is no conversion, no deliverance. He pretends to turn—for it is largely affectation— only from the more refined devices of mankind to a ruder and more stupid existence. He is like Marie Antoinette playing the shepherdess.

The critique then moves into other terms, but it is clear that Whitman's indifference to the past is, in Santayana's eyes, his mortal sin. To Santayana, the past is available as critique, as ideal, as sacrifice: bluntly, the past provides the standard by which present and future acts may be judged. Santayana accepts history as he accepts the difference, once for all, between animals and men. "I could turn"; but he wants the turning to be a real conversion. He wants Whitman to accept the sacrificial record of the past, accept it as critique and, if proper, as rebuke. As a European, Santayana bitterly resents the American facility which sets the past aside, "making it new" with a vengeance directed upon the old.

Perhaps it would not matter, or at least it would not be disastrous, if Whitman were prepared to put any other critical power in place of the past. What Santayana means to force upon Whitman is an acknowledgement that the world was not made today for his sole benefit and pleasure. The trouble is that in freeing himself from the burden of the past Whitman plans to free himself from every other burden: he will not be rebuked, he will be his own free man. In this respect he is far more extreme than Emerson; even the Emerson of "Circles" who wrote:

> Do not set the least value on what I do, or the least discredit on what I do not, as if I pretended to settle anything as true or false. I unsettle all things. No facts are to me sacred; none are profane; I simply experiment, an endless seeker, with no Past at my back.

In "Starting from Paumanok," Whitman claims:

> *I conn'd old times,*
> *I sat studying at the feet of the great masters.*

But he made no commitment to the past; and for that, Santayana berated him.

But we have to ask what Whitman's freedom gave him, besides ease. In one sense he was, indeed, free; he put down burdens which other men sustained. But it may be argued that in another sense he was bound, because he was ignorant of what he disowned. There is no evidence that he conn'd old times sufficiently to know them as sturdy and different from himself: certainly, he did not propose a relation to the past based upon that knowledge. So it is necessary to say that he freed himself from human history without taking the precaution, in the first instance, of thoroughly understanding it. Whatever worth we ascribe to his freedom, it must allow for that limitation, that its facility was not profoundly earned. That is why his message, so far as it may be described as such, is dispensable. He was, by his own assertion, a prophet and a sage, but his prophecy was somewhat meretricious, his wisdom untested. What matters, after all, is the poetry.

To get the beauty of Whitman's poetry hot, one must read it in long, rolling stretches. No poet is less revealed in the single phrase, the image, or even the line. The unit of the verse is indeed the phrase, a loose-limbed structure of several words easily held together and moving along because the cadence goes with the speaker's breath. This is what William Carlos Williams learned from Whitman, the natural cadence, the flow of breath as a structure good enough for most purposes and better for humanity than the counting of syllables. For both poets the ideal is what Williams called "a redeeming language," a language to bridge the gap between subject and object, thereby certifying both and praising bridges. Again in both poets the function of language is to verify an intricate network of affinities and relationships, contacts, between person and person, person and place, person and thing. In Whitman, the number of completely realized poems is small: many poems contain wonderful passages, but are flawed, often by a breach of taste, a provincialism. Where the poem fails, it fails because Whitman thought too well of his excess to curb it; the words converge upon the poem, and he will not turn them aside. Some of his greatest writing is in "Song of Myself," but on the other hand that poem, too, is often provincial, awkward. The best of Whitman, surely one of his greatest achievements, is a shorter poem, "Crossing Brooklyn Ferry." William Carlos Williams once praised a poem by Marianne Moore as an anthology of transit, presumably because the words secured a noiseless progression from one moment to another: they did not sit down to admire themselves. Whitman's favourite subject is movement, process, becoming: no wonder he loved bridges and ferries, which kept things moving while defining relationships, one thing with another.

The first stanza of the poem, in its final version, is a direct invocation to the water, the clouds, the crowds of people crossing on the ferry. But the first requirement in this stanza is to recite these things in personal terms: water and clouds must be translated into personal terms, sharing in that feeling. The translation is effected by the sensory verbs: any object, however resistant, is amenable to the poet's senses, and, once sensed, is rendered personal. Hence: "Flood-tide below me! I see you face to face!"; face to face, marking the personal meeting, equal with equal. The last line of the stanza points the feeling toward a future ("And you that shall cross") and establishes kinship which the subsequent stanzas will enrich. The second stanza defines the exemplary moment as the confluence of present and future; it is Whitman's version of Blake's sentence, that Eternity is in love with the productions of Time. Here, for Whitman, the present moment is certified by its continuity with the future. The specific occasion of this stanza is the poet's sense of "the scheme of things," the unity among instances of diversity. In the light of the scheme, every single object seems "disintegrated," but, a second later, is seen as part of the scheme and therefore redeemed; without the scheme, everything would be mere flotsam. The personal version is the poet's kinship with those "others" who, ages hence, will see and feel the same things. In the third stanza the standpoint is moved directly to the future; from which, now, the present is seen as a shared past, the shared history of feeling: "Just as you feel . . . so I felt." The result is that the present moment is enchanted by being part of an enchanted past, magically sensed and recalled. The work is done, for the main part, by the verbs "watched," "saw," "looked," and so forth. It is typical of Whitman that the only "past" he is willing to acknowledge is the "present," seen from the standpoint of the "future." He does not, in general, acknowledge a past now, in some sense, distinct from his present feeling: there is no stanza in this poem, for instance, which links the "present" speaker to the "past." It is as if Whitman resented any gone time in which he did not participate. He is quite willing to see the present recede, since he has played his part in it, and to be incorporated in a future which he has done something to entertain. But the past is intolerably alien, from the standpoint of a man who has not lived it. In the fourth stanza Whitman is still in a projected future, the language caressing its objects in repeated phrases. The fifth stanza is an anthology of sharing: "I too lived . . . ," the experiences proved by reference to the body: "I too had receiv'd identity by my body." The sixth stanza is a change, a dark place of confession. Whitman looks at himself, his own work, his thoughts, and finds them "blank." He confesses to evil and ambiguity:

> *I am he who knew what it was to be evil,*
> *I too knitted the old knot of contrariety,*

Blabb'd, blush'd, resented, lied, stole, grudg'd,
Had guile, anger, lust, hot wishes I dared not speak.

At the same time Whitman strains toward the idiom of acceptance, the secular equivalent of forgiveness after confession. The movement is effected by the line—"Was one with the rest, the days and haps of the rest"— coming immediately after the lines of confession. Individual guilt is incorporated in universal guilt, and the movement toward forgiveness and unity begins. By the end of the stanza, the poet has been received into amity. But it may be argued that, in fact, the forgiveness was implicit even in the lines of confession.

Whitman does not simply confess, "I was evil," with an implication, "I repent"; what he says is: "I am he who knew what it was to be evil," and in this version the fact of evil is balanced by the fact of knowledge. Evil is bad, let us say, but knowledge of evil is good, especially if the evil is one's own. Whitman is looking at himself as if he were a separate person; a procedure highly respectable in the Emersonian tradition of American literature. In the chapter on Goethe in *Representative Men,* Emerson says:

> An intellectual man can see himself as a third person; therefore his faults and delusions interest him equally with his successes. Though he wishes to prosper in affairs he wishes more to know the history and destiny of man; whilst the clouds of egotists drifting about him are only interested in a low success.

Whitman is speaking of himself as a third person, but he assimilates everything he says to the language of knowledge; according to this rhetoric, every sin committed and acknowledged adds to the sum of personal knowledge. Every acknowledged fall is fortunate. There is a certain complicity, therefore, in Whitman's rhetoric here: the stanza as a whole allows him to find his way out, but the way out is already implicit in the dark detail. The result is that the catalogue of sins, bad as ethics, comes to appear good as experience. In the next stanza, forgiveness takes the form of communion, a conspiracy of feeling: "Closer yet I approach you . . . " In the eighth stanza the same mood is given in terms of tying, fusing, and pouring, self and self. The poem ends with the long stanza of exaltation, beginning: "Flow on, river! flow with the flood-tide . . . " The stanza is a sequence of imperatives, until a change near the end, but the imperatives are designed not to change the direction of their object but to endorse each object in its natural direction: "Live old life!" "Sound out, voices of young men!" "Fly on, sea-birds!" This is the form in which world harmony is heard, the natural action, continuous, flowing, unquestionable. The function of Whitman's lines is not to describe each action, but to encourage it, giving it an endorsing hand. The poet's energy is to answer the energy of the world: this is the form his Sublime takes. Near the end, the mood changes, beautifully, into the indicative: I quote the last two imperative lines and the change:

> *Expand, being than which none else is perhaps more spiritual,*
> *Keep your places, objects than which none else is more lasting.*
> *You have waited, you always wait, you dumb, beautiful ministers,*
> *We receive you with free sense at last, and are insatiate*
>   *hence forward,*
> *Not you any more shall be able to foil us, or withhold*
>   *yourselves from us,*
> *We use you, and do not cast you aside—we plant you permanently*
>   *within us,*
> *We fathom you not—we love you—there is perfection in*
>   *you also,*
> *You furnish your parts toward eternity,*
> *Great or small, you furnish your parts toward the soul.*

This is Whitman at his best. The clue is in the line: "We fathom you not—we love you . . . " It is Whitman's delicacy, his sense of limits, his fine decorum, which prevents him from fathoming the world, moving in upon it to steal its secret. There is always something in an object which Whitman prefers at last to leave untouched: he is content to sense its presence, but he does not grasp it. When this delicacy is present, the proof is in the style. In "Crossing Brooklyn Ferry," Whitman and his style are one, there is no gap when we think of the words on the page and then, by an effort, think of his presence behind the words. He is identical with his style. This happens only when the poetic concern is eminently congenial to his talent, to a sense of the world, and his sense of a corresponding language. It is time to remark that, in these best moments, he has a remarkable feeling for life, for the world as it reaches him through the senses: the world, given to him in appearances, impressions, images, sounds, the press of things. But it is necessary to make a distinction. There are poets who excel in description, in giving a particularly vivid impression of the surfaces of life. Whitman is not one of these; though his descriptive power, when he chooses to use it, is at least good enough for the local purpose. In his greatest poems the world is not given to us, minutely, as *sensibilia,* one apprehended thing and then another: rather, Whitman receives the contents of his experiences as certain great gestures, great cadences of feeling. He touches the world in time, and the experience is enacted as a cadence. The detail is not lost or buried: it is incorporated in the rhythm, contained there like juice in an apple. That is: the detail is not given to the reader as a separable event, but as one phase in the movement of feeling. It is an error, therefore, to speak of his catalogues as if they were lists of undifferentiated things, each one ticked off. The things which are listed are there for the wave of feeling which, in that exact form, they sustain: different things would mean a different wave, a different feeling, or a different direction. Wallace Stevens wrote to Joseph Bennett, February 8, 1955, of Whitman's catalogues:

> I can well believe that he remains highly vital for many people. The poems in which he collects large numbers of concrete things, particularly things each of which is poetic in itself or as part of the collection, have a validity which, for many people, must be enough and must seem to them all opulence and élan. For others, I imagine that what was once opulent begins to look a little threadbare and the collections seem substitutes for opulence even though they remain gatherings-together of precious Americana, certain to remain precious but not certain to remain poetry. The typical élan survives in many things. It seems to me, then, that Whitman is disintegrating as the world, of which he made himself a part, disintegrates.

But this is to read the lines as lists of things, *sensibilia,* and to find poetic value in those things. If they have grown threadbare, the reason is that we have become weary of them, we know them too well, they cannot change. This is, indeed, the fate of objects, congealed. But the way to read Whitman's catalogues is to attend to the rhythm, their flow and ebb, the cadences of feeling which they embody. Poetic value does not depend, then, upon the self-renewing power of feeling. Theodore Roethke's sense of Whitman is, I think, more accurate than Stevens's for this reason. In "The Abyss," Roethke invokes Whitman after a stanza in which he speaks of himself as "neither in nor out of this life":

> Be with me, Whitman, maker of catalogues:
> For the world invades me again,
> And once more the tongues begin babbling.
> And the terrible hunger for objects quails me:
> The sill trembles.
> And there on the blind
> A furred caterpillar crawls down a string.
> My symbol!

Clearly, Roethke does not need Whitman as maker of catalogues: it is impossible to think of Roethke as having much to do with catalogues. Whitman is needed because the poet feels himself "invaded" by the world, those objects which overwhelm him in their demand: answering in himself the "terrible hunger for objects." Whitman the maker of catalogues is also the Whitman who genially disposes the objects listed; genially, so that they are not too demanding and, in turn, his hunger is not too demanding. To Roethke, Whitman's catalogues testify to an agreeable sense of the world, but that sense reaches him, it is clear, through the feeling beneath and between the objects. The phrase we need is in "Crossing Brooklyn Ferry": "We receive you with free sense at last"; free sense, not demand or hunger. In "The Abyss," Roethke's third stanza begins:

> Too much reality can be a dazzle, a surfeit;
> Too close immediacy an exhaustion.

Whitman would answer: only if you insist on possessing every piece of reality your senses deliver; only if immediacy brings out the hunger in you. What Roethke prayed for, calling upon Whitman's intercession, was tact, a certain last propriety. Of Whitman's catalogues he seems to have felt that they, in an obvious sense so material, were in a deeper sense so spiritual, so undemanding. What matters is the feeling. Someone says in The Last Puritan that there is no poetry in identifying things that look alike, "but the most opposite things may become miraculously equivalent, if they arouse the same invisible quality of emotion." In "Crossing Brooklyn Ferry," "Song of the Broad-Axe," "Song of the Exposition," and other poems, particular things are invoked in a particular order for the feeling they define; not for the miscellany; not for the objects as possessions. Whitman does not claim to possess those objects; what he possesses is a flowing sense of them, of their interest, their value, their amazing existence.

The proof is in the delicacy. Almost as random in the "Song of Myself" we read:

> *A child said* What is the grass? *fetching it to me with full hands,*
> *How could I answer the child? I do not know what it is any more than he.*

It is beautiful; mainly because of the transparent language. Whitman lives up to the feeling by giving it in undemanding words, he puts the words in that order to reflect the figure of the feeling, the shape it makes. Neither too much nor too little; not even an excess of moderation: the words do not claim to be interesting, in their own right, but to serve their master, the feeling itself. Again, in "Out of the Cradle Endlessly Rocking":

> *Yes my brother I know,*
> *The rest might not, but I have treasur'd every note,*
> *For more than once simply down to the beach gliding,*
> *Silent, avoiding the moonbeams, blending myself with the shadows,*
> *Recalling now the obscure shapes, the echoes, the sounds and sights after their sorts,*
> *The white arms out in the breakers tirelessly tossing,*
> *I, with bare feet, a child, the wind wafting my hair,*
> *Listened long and long.*

Even here, we are not encouraged to sink to rest upon a word or a phrase: we are to go with the feeling in the long sentence. The meaning is the history of the sentence, the qualifying phrases slowing the movement but not impeding it, since the structure is never in danger. In the last line the feeling is fulfilled, the repeated "long" not an indulgence but a celebration.

It is not fanciful to find, in this delicacy, Whitman's chief value, since delicacy is only the short name for many qualities which run together. The delicacy may be felt to require his doubt as well as his certainty, his trouble as well as his peace, his fear and his assertions: it is all there in the achieved lines and poems.

What the work does not give, however, is proof of development. I suppose our ideal *Collected Works* would feature the wonderfully complete fulfilment of possibilities dimly discerned in the early poems. The career of such poets as Eliot and Yeats is a great consolation in this respect. It is easy to see that in *Prufrock and Other Observations* Eliot laid down, barely knowing what he did and certainly not knowing its implications, seeds of growth and development which would flower, eventually, in the great middle and last poems. *Four Quartets* is continuous with *Prufrock* and *The Waste Land:* every poem seemed to be accomplished in itself and yet to require a further poem for complete lucidity. With the entire work at hand, in poems, plays, and criticism, we think of Eliot's achievement as a major development of the early hints and guesses. With Yeats we feel that somewhere along the line of his work he discovered, perhaps in theatrical metaphors, possibilities which the collected poems and plays fulfil; notably possibilities of drama, one voice answering another, a continuous action. With Whitman, we feel that the first edition of *Leaves of Grass* is, in fact, the whole story. Thereafter, the editions were enlarged, but new possibilities were not discovered; later editions, larger, were not in any important sense different. It is as if Whitman found for himself a settled poetic stance, and discovered that it might be held: there was no reason why it should be questioned. He did not question the basis of his faith. It is possible to argue that the third edition (1860) has special importance, but the categories disposed in that book are not really different from those of the first edition. After the war, a difference is clear, but it arises from the failure of Whitman's faith, its practical misfortune. There is no evidence of possibilities being worked out, challenged, questioned, from one book to another. The reason is that Whitman defined himself, at an early stage, in relation to the world, and the definition was so resolute that it did not call for revision. The later editions present more material, but not different senses of its value. This partly explains how Whitman came to represent, perhaps all too easily, a definable relation to America and to the world: that relation was powerful, engaging, indeed inescapable, but its chief mark was its resistance to change. It did not contain within itself the reason why, under different circumstances, it might be otherwise: more experience merely served to confirm it or to trouble it, not to change it. In a famous moment Yeats distinguished between poetry and rhetoric: rhetoric is made from the quarrel with others, poetry from the quarrel with ourselves. Whitman's aesthetic does not allow for a quarrel with himself: a quarrel with himself would bring his poetry to an end. The poetry contains its own basis, its own strength, but it is the mark of that poetry to make an alternative basis impossible. Whitman may choose, but the choice is limited: either to write that kind of poetry or to remain silent. We often feel that the poet of the first edition of *Leaves of Grass* secured the great advantages of that poetry too easily: he did not have to labour in its cause. He laboured, indeed, with the detail of the lines, but not with the incorrigible burdens attendant upon poets: the problematic relation of the poet to his past, to the life and history of his world. A man must labour to possess a tradition, as Eliot warned. But Whitman secured his first necessity once for all. It has often been maintained that the crucial Whitman is the poet of the first edition of *Leaves of Grass;* everything thereafter being a decay. The argument is not conclusive. But it has at least this merit, that the first effect of reading Whitman is an effect especially akin to that of a poet, this poet, writing his first book. Thereafter, the effect may be greater or less, but there is a sense in which the gist of the case has already been presented. This does not lend support to the common view that Whitman is a naïf, producing one book and spending his life trying to repeat its success. Indeed, Whitman is, if anything, more a decadent than a naïf. But his real problem is to justify to himself the composition of poems which are, in their real nature, merely further expositions of what has already been declared. There are a few remarkable moments in the later editions: sometimes a certain wry wit is audible, the irony directed upon himself. There are transitions which mark Whitman as a comic poet of great merit. But these are local charms. The essential Whitman is already defined, set in his landscape.

Finally, we acknowledge the myth, and the values it declares. To some poets, Whitman is the American inventor of free verse, destroyer of the iambic pentameter. William Carlos Williams thought of him in this context, praised him for helping American poets to free themselves from Europe, rebuked him for not going further. To other poets, Whitman is the spokesman of America as Promises, a doubtful hero in the twentieth century, a sentimentalist smelling of duplicity. But perhaps the permanent strength of Whitman is what Hart Crane saw, especially in that part of *The Bridge* called "Cape Hatteras," virtually an ode to Whitman:

> ... *O, something green,*
> *Beyond all sesames of science was thy choice*
> *Wherewith to bind us throbbing with one voice,*
> *New integers of Roman, Viking, Celt—*
> *Thou, Vedic Caesar, to the greensward knelt!*

From Marcus Cunliffe (ed.), *American Literature to* 1900 (London: Sphere Books, 1973).

EMILY DICKINSON

I

It has long been assumed that the most pertinent question about Emily Dickinson's life is why she was willing to have so little of it. She did not marry. Apart from a trip to Boston and another to Philadelphia and Washington, she restricted her travels to Amherst, and even in that little scene she was selective. Relentless in writing verses, she never stirred herself to have them published. Renunciation was her most practised virtue, pursued so far beyond necessity as to amount to a conviction and, in weariness, to a habit.

When she was about thirty-five, she appeared one midsummer night to Joseph Lyman, her sister Lavinia's temporary suitor, thus:

A library dimly lighted, three mignonettes on a little stand. Enter a spirit clad in white, figure so draped as to be misty, face moist, translucent alabaster, forehead firmer as of statuary marble. Eyes once bright hazel now melted & fused so as to be two dreamy, wondering wells of expression, eyes that see no forms but glance swiftly to the core of all things—hands small, firm, deft but utterly emancipated from all claspings of perishable things, very firm strong little hands absolutely under control of the brain, types of quite rugged health, mouth made for nothing and used for nothing but uttering choice speech, rare thoughts, glittering, starry, misty figures, winged words.

Upon such legendary entrances—the most picturesque her first meeting with a bewildered T. W. Higginson—the common notion of Emily Dickinson as the white nun of Amherst depends. Richard B. Sewall is weary of the legend, and proposes to show that her life was continuous with other lives and remarkable only for pitch and intensity.

Sewall's *The Life of Emily Dickinson* begins with an account of the biographer's problems. Nearly 90 percent of the letters Dickinson wrote have disappeared: of those she received, it is estimated that not one in a thousand has survived. The gaps are filled with rumour, speculation, the stuff of surmise which presents her as the victim of a disastrous passion, vetoed by her father in his role as Mr. Barrett of Wimpole Street. After her death, many clues contained in her poems were suppressed, some by Martha Dickinson Bianchi in an attempt to claim that the friendship which had once obtained between Emily Dickinson and Susan Gilbert stayed sweet during the years of Susan's marriage to Emily's brother Austin. Many of Dickinson's poems and letters can be interpreted as annotations on events or, with an equal show of cause, as fantasies, suppositions, conceits. "When I state myself," she told Higginson, "as the Representative of the Verse—it does not mean—me—but a supposed person." Richard Sewall has pondered the assertion, but he trusts his instinct to tell him when a particular poem means not a supposed person but the historical Emily Dickinson.

This is the biographer's most acute problem. He knows that Dickinson's imagination was to a remarkable degree histrionic, taking pleasure and finding release in projections and suppositions. If many of the poems are indeed clues to the experiences which provoked them, many more indicate nothing but the nature of Dickinson's imagination. But the matter is complex. There are some poems which we can easily read as poems of pure imagination, and with these we are not tempted to confound the work and the life. Other poems make it impossible for us to separate the man or woman who suffered from the mind that created. Reading Frost's poems, we resort to imagined speakers, personae, and so forth, but after a certain point we also know that it is Frost who has imagined them, and this takes us back to him. If someone retorts that the Frost who imagined and the Frost who lived his daily life in certain ways are not one and the same, we can only agree. But still we don't mistake Frost's personae for Stevens's.

R. P. Blackmur complicated the question further by arguing that in Emily Dickinson direct experience, whether invented or originally contingent, was always for the sake of "something else which would replace the habit and the destructive gusto (but not the need) of experience in the world, and become an experience of its own on its own warrant." Attempting a discrimination among Dickinson, Herrick, and Rilke—nuptial poets all three—Blackmur said that "Herrick marries the created world, Dickinson marries herself, Rilke creates within himself something to marry which will—which does—marry and thereby rival the real world." What it means for Dickinson to marry herself is that she makes up for "deprived sensation on the quick" by projecting a personal form of immortality in which alone she truly lives. This was the best, according to Blackmur, that could be done "with the puerile marriage of the self with the self: a sensorium for the most part without the senses, it is sometimes the vision of sense itself."

It would be pleasant to find that the "something else" is the poem, and that the achievement of it coincides with the fulfilment of every desire however inordinate. In that case we could happily say that the mere world was well lost for the poem's sake: readers become the music while the music lasts. But in Dickinson each poem is merely proximate and transitional to a state that has every quality except existence, every heuristic form except embodiment. If many of her poems are at once short and imperfect, the reason is not—or not merely—that she dashed them off in letters and let them have only the status of the letters surrounding them, but that the poetry exists only or chiefly to enable the further excruciations of feeling that ache or rage, otherwise unexpressed, beyond it. Richard Wilbur has written of Emily Dickinson's "sumptuous destitution" as a law with two clauses: one, that when an object has been magnified by desire, it cannot be wholly possessed by appetite; and two, "that food, or victory, or any other good thing is best comprehended by the eye of desire from the vantage of privation." But privation is not enough, since it is merely relative. Emily Dickinson evidently needed to feel that beyond every circle of given or invented experience there were further circles inscribed by nothing but the need of them; unheard melodies, absolute states of feeling. Every particular feeling, however extreme, was only a trial run or an epitome of some ultimacy which could be divined but never expressed. That is why her imagination, to a biographer's despair, would not let her coincide with herself. In the Preface to *The Oxford Book of Modern Verse,* Yeats referred to "that cult of sincerity, that refusal to multiply personality which is characteristic of our time." Emily Dickinson's poetry lives upon multiple personalities, but each of them is merely a half-measure, a device, in the service of consummations measureless as if upon principle.

Dickinson's recourse to multiple personalities is the theme of John Emerson Todd's *Emily Dickinson's Use of the Persona:* he distinguishes four, and might have named a hundred. The four are the "little girl"; lover-wife-Queen; the lyrist of death and eternity; and the persona which knows itself divided into soul and body. Todd quotes Coleridge's reference to the "sublime faculty by which a great mind becomes that which it meditates on." But the process by which Dickinson's imagination drives her beyond every experience given or invented is not meditative. The limitation of an invented experience is that, like a given experience, it coincides with itself, it has a formal or narrative presence, a perimeter. Dickinson's imagination is endless, like her desire: no particular form fulfils it even for the time being.

How we cope with such an imagination depends upon the liberality of our own. Blackmur called the marriage of the self with the self puerile because, I assume, it rejected every intervention of the world as a vile impediment. In Herrick, "the direct experience was always for the sake of something else to be found in the plenitude of God's creation of nature": one experience might be placed lovingly beside another which was all the better for being come upon as a gift of God. But Dickinson's imagination doesn't acknowledge anything as a gift. She does not suffuse a given object with the appropriate sentiments it has lacked: the best it can hope for is to be noticed by an imagination in a rush to transcend it or to defeat its importunity. If we want our poets to live, in their poetry, more daringly than we would choose to live, as by acting upon penury where we would look for riches, or rejecting mediation where we would welcome it, then Dickinson's imagination will do much of our living for us.

Robert Weisbuch's *Emily Dickinson's Poetry* offers to put her imagination under some degree of restraint by presenting it as the resultant of two conflicting attitudes. The first is Emersonian, a poetic of praise in which events and objects are italicized into symbols, "appearances rush toward essences, and possibilities never end." The second is what Dickinson called Veto, a vision reached by the negation of vision. Presumably what corresponds to the marriage of the self with the self, and to the refusal of mediation, is a *via negationis* as in certain theologies in which non-being is the ground of being. When Dickinson refers to Immortality, we are free to construe it as absolute zero which, desired as desperately as it is imagined, becomes All at the cost—if it is cost—of removing itself from time, place, and body.

Sewall's account of the biographer's problems does not refer to the first and last of them, the extent to which the artist is revealed in her work. Henry James observes, in the Preface to *The Tragic Muse,* that "any presentation of the artist in triumph must be flat in proportion as it really sticks to its subject—it can only smuggle in relief and variety—for, to put the matter in an image, all we then—in his triumph—see of the charm-compeller is the back he turns to us as he bends over his work." The successful artist can't have his cake and eat it, he can't have at the same time the privilege of the work and the privilege of the hero. "The privilege of the hero," James said, "belongs to him only as to the artist deluded, diverted, frustrated or vanquished; when the 'amateur' in him gains, for our admiration or compassion or whatever, all that the expert has to do without." Failure is therefore a richer biographical theme than success, since the first has never quite got into the work or it sprawls all around it, and the second is fully consigned to the work and there is no remainder. Walter Pater was one of James's instances, a minor one no doubt in his eyes, of the privilege of the work entirely removing that of the hero. Pater's mere life was nothing, the work being everything. But Dickinson's case is acute in a different sense. Much of the time, we see only the back she turns to us as she bends over her work, and when we peer over her shoulder for clues we find both true and false and can only scratch our heads. Now and again we see her going about her domestic chores, and we take the sight for what we think it is worth. Normally, we don't see her at all, for she is visible neither in chores nor in poems but only in the void between them. This is not because she is then, in James's sense, a failure or even a partial success, but because the feelings engaged transcend both success and failure. "Which of her forms has shown her substance right?" Yeats asks in "A Bronze Head," thinking of Maud Gonne. None of them, he implies, and he thinks of composite substance, a theory of "profound McTaggart," and Hegelian cosmology which may justify the notion. The void is where there is nothing but absolute desire, and the objects of desire have long since been overwhelmed by its endlessness.

It is natural, thinking of Dickinson, to wish that she had been mastered, not by one of her adored preceptors, Charles Wadsworth, Samuel Bowles, Higginson, Otis P. Lord, or another, but by a great subject, a theme which would not have taken no for an answer. "All her life," Blackmur said, "she was looking for a subject, and the looking was her subject." Instead of a subject she had a temper and an imagination, each sufficient to ensure that the looking would remain desperate and unappeased. Without a subject strong enough to master her desire, she could never be released from an aimless sense of "ourself behind ourself, concealed." There was no other authority.

The New England Puritanism which Sewall sketches as a context for Dickinson's poems offered her a range of Calvinist metaphors and, for her soul, a show of violence, but not the real thing, mastery. It was too late for that. Many years ago Allen Tate argued that Dickinson had the immense advantage, for a poet—whether or not it was an advantage otherwise for her soul—of living in New England at a time when its theocracy, damaged beyond repair as a compelling system of values, was still sufficient to be invoked as dramatizing the human soul. She was close enough to Hawthorne's conditions to know what sin meant and what redemption might mean; and she was far enough removed from Emerson's conditions, and from James's, so that she did not settle for the conversion of spiritual grace into the social graces, and sin into indelicacy. She could resort, as Emerson and James could not, to what Tate called "the entire powerful dumb-show of the puritan theology led by Redemption and Immortality." Emerson dissolved the drama by offering people the perfection of the Over-Soul in which conflict and tragedy have no place. Dickinson was not ready to think that her sensibility was of itself strong enough to defeat Nature and transfigure Death.

But her sensibility, like her taste, ran too free for its own good. Living chiefly on her nerves, she exacerbated every experience till she had wrung it nearly to death. Her typical passion issues from known or imagined pain, loneliness, loss, renunciation, dread, and the last conceit of death: even her exhilarations are predicated upon the loss of them. But each experience had not only to be imagined; it had to be imagined obliquely, according to an aesthetic of "slant," as if otherwise it would escape from her and revert to common life.

We keep coming back to the biographer's question of life and work. "Of few poets could the claim be made more confidently," Sewall maintains, "that her life was her work." I can't see any reason for confidence: the work, sublime as its total force is, does not extend to the circumference of her life, if my impression of life and work is sound. Indeed, I believe that much of what counted as experience to her never got into her poems, if only because her poetic procedures didn't accommodate them. I appreciate Sewall's desire to take the mystery out of Dickinson's life, and the romantic glamour out of its myth. He lists the stock notions which he hopes the biography will remove:

> that Amherst was no place for a poet to be born in; that Emily Dickinson was the lone star in a colorless and insignificant family; that her home was either a prison to her spirit or, at the other extreme, a cozy retreat irradiated (after July 1, 1856) by the attentions of a loving confidante; that she lived apart from the passions and bitterness that plague the rest of humanity and, not knowing such things first-hand, made them up for the purposes of poetry; that a love tragedy is the only way of explaining her withdrawal from society; that she spent her day "meditating majestically among her flowers."

Sewall is not convinced by the psychosexual interpretation of Dickinson's life, as in John Cody's *After Great Pain* (1971), which argues that Emily and Austin were each in love with Susan Gilbert, and that Emily was crushed when she lost Susan to Austin. Nor does he favour Clark Griffith's thesis, in *The Long Shadow* (1964), that Emily's entire life was distorted by fear of her dreadful father. Sewall finds her life natural and ordinary rather than weird, and he discounts the idea of a tragedy of love causing her withdrawal from the world. The withdrawal was in any case incomplete, and Sewall represents it as a gradual sequence. It is possible that a sufficient explanation is the fact that Dickinson's demands upon the people she chose to care about were extreme, and therefore extremely painful to her when they were refused. "After great pain a formal feeling comes," and a modest retirement from the social world seems a decent procedure to mark its formality. Faced with apparently bizarre evidence, Sewall tends to argue that it is not as odd as it appears, given a few simple circumstances in the background. But the problem with this tendency is that when you remove a mystery at one point it comes back at another. Besides, it is difficult to show how an extraordinary work issued from an apparently ordinary life, unless you claim that what was extraordinary was only the imagination in the case: a claim which solves a problem by enforcing a vocabulary that excludes it.

Sewall's biographical method arises from the fact that Dickinson's art shows no sign of having developed in any way that can be described. She remained, as an artist, what she was from the beginning. Sewall presents her life not as a linear narrative but as a structure of relations, taken one at a time; he trusts that an impartial portrait will emerge from the partiality of glimpses.

The method probably suggested itself when Sewall was working on the *Lyman Letters* (1965), tracing the relations between Lyman and the Dickinson family. In the first volume of the biography Sewall deals rather briskly with the general intellectual background, mainly Connecticut Valley Puritanism rather than the American Romanticism which he might have emphasized instead; and then he moves to the Dickinson family, beginning with Emily's grandfather Samuel Fowler Dickinson. Her father, Edward Dickinson, gets a better press than ever before and is found not guilty of tyranny. "Eminently the man of conviction, not feeling," Sewall concedes, and he accepts Emily's evidence that her father read "lonely & rigorous books," and those only on Sunday. But the dreadful anecdotes are set aside as improbable. Emily's mother is also promoted into a character, and rescued from the impression of loveless nonentity which has adhered to her. But the crucial member of the family, Sewall says, was brother Austin: "it was Austin and Emily against the world, a relationship of infinite importance to both." In 1856 Austin married Susan, and soon there was war between the houses. The marriage was a disaster. Susan hated sex, "low practices," and maternity: she had four abortions. She was a brilliant success in social life, a heavy drinker, incorrigibly extrovert: she had nothing to share with her husband. In 1862 Austin fell in love with Mabel

Loomis Todd, and she with him: when they became lovers, her husband, David, accepted the situation without fuss. Mabel continued to make herself sexually available to David, and besides, he was an assiduous philanderer, he wanted to be free to engage in his own diversions. Mabel resented his philandering only when the woman in question was low-class: otherwise the affair added interest to a situation already piquant. Emily seems to have felt that Austin's marriage was so dreadful that he was entitled to any joy he could find elsewhere. In 1877 she wrote of the married partners: "Austin is overcharged with care, and Sue with scintillation."

Emily, Austin, and Susan emerge as the leading characters in the biography, with the result that Emily's preceptors are displaced from the stage centre they usually occupy. Leonard Humphrey, an early figure in the list, is not crucial. Benjamin Franklin Newton is more important, "a gentle, yet grave preceptor." George Gould comes next, but Sewall doesn't accept the story that Emily's father forbade her to receive him and thereby ruined her young life. The Reverend Charles Wadsworth, "a man of sorrows," was necessary to Emily because he received her religious doubts and helped her, when she believed at all, "to keep Believing nimble." Emily was in love with Samuel Bowles for several years, but he was indifferent to her. Sewall thinks that the famous letters which Emily wrote to Bowles, probably in 1862, may have more bearing upon her vocation as poet than as lover. Bowles is not yet identified as the "Master" to whom Emily addressed three remarkable love letters, but Sewall thinks him a more plausible candidate than Wadsworth or anyone else. Higginson is somewhat roughly treated, I think. It is hard to blame him for failing to see that he had a genius on his hands. In 1892 Alice James, Henry's sister, wrote in her diary:

> It is reassuring to hear the English pronouncement that Emily Dickinson is fifth-rate—they have such a capacity for missing quality; the robust evades them equally with the subtle. Her being sicklied o'er with T. W. Higginson makes one quake lest there be a latent flaw which escapes one's vision.

Sewall does not pursue the question of a flaw. He thinks that Higginson should have brought his bewilderment, when faced with Dickinson's poems, to Emerson, Longfellow, Lowell, Bronson Alcott, or some other crony before acting upon his own good taste. Otis Lord was Dickinson's last love, and surely her greatest.

II

Emily Dickinson's reputation in poetry is now as secure as Hawthorne's in fiction and Emerson's in prophecy. She has poems which make one doubt whether their coyness and winsomeness are compatible with a major art, but her achieved work is substantial enough to justify the claims regularly made for her. It is clear that her poetry suffered from its amateur status; it is not exempt from the deficiencies characteristic of Sunday painting. But much of her work survives the uncritical circumstances in which it was written. What I have called her aesthetic of "slant" was established so powerfully that the conditions at hand damaged it only betimes.

Tate's argument, to which I have referred, seems valid to me, and compatible with a more particular relation to American Romanticism than he was willing to allow. Dickinson practised an aesthetic of slant by looking obliquely at spiritual forces officially given in allegorical forms. She chose to see those forces in statuesque terms, ominous indeed, and then to step aside from them. Stepping aside enabled her to disconnect her mind from their official status and to treat them as opposing forces in her domestic drama. The aim of many of her poems is to take at least some of the harm out of experiences by imagining them in advance. Premonitions instigated the poems, we may guess, and a technique of anticipation protected her, in advance of need, against one quality of a calamity which must befall her in the end: that quality was surprise, dismay, consternation:

> *I read my sentence—steadily—*
> *Reviewed it with my eyes,*
> *To see that I made no mistake*
> *In its extremest clause—*
> *The Date, and manner, of the shame—*
> *And then the Pious Form*
> *That "God have mercy" on the Soul*
> *The Jury voted Him—*

> *I made my soul familiar—with her*
> > *extremity—*
> *That at the last, it should not be a novel*
> > *Agony—*
> *But she, and Death, acquainted—*
> *Meet tranquilly, as friends—*
> *Salute, and pass, without a Hint—*
> *And there, the Matter ends.*

Yvor Winters complained of the change of sex between "Him" and "her," but the complaint is null. The irony in the first eight lines arises from the fact that the sentence is a standard document, it applies to everyone, like an official form in which the general matter is printed in advance and only the local details have to be filled in by hand. The jury votes, in the sense of giving a man a fair trial before hanging him: his guilt is taken for granted, but the form has to be gone through. The speaker-victim scans the page quickly to find the details—the date, the time, the place— "reviewed it with my eyes." The aim is to make the soul invulnerable to catastrophe by displacing the official form of its fall: death is not to be the end but a crossing between life and Immortality, hence accessible to cognition if we identify cognition with imagination. The future may be imagined just as richly as memory recovers or transfigures the past. The other may be imagined as continuous with the same, instants as if they had duration, fluidities as if they were fixities.

It is also characteristic of Dickinson that she represents dying as a domestic meeting with the figure of Death, as again in "Because I could not stop for Death." Dying is assimilated to the village ritual of meeting, in which much can be left unsaid, social amenity being what it is. The degree of intimacy is not specified: it is something between "acquainted" and "friends." "Without a Hint" is itself unhinted, left to spend itself in the dash at the end of the line. The pun in the last line on matter and form, matter and spirit, is justified because it doesn't enforce itself beyond the colloquial play of "And there, the Matter ends." Seeing death in this slantedly domestic way is a dry run, a rehearsal for the real thing. The poem is in the tradition of Donne's "A Valediction: Forbidding Mourning"—"As virtuous men pass mildly away"—but it is a brittle variant of it, rhetorically tight-lipped as Donne rarely is: no wonder it ends with "ends." I take this to mean that Dickinson's relation to the traditions she invokes can only be interrogative: everything depends upon the degree to which the interrogation of vulnerably residual traditions fulfils, without further ado, the demands of a subjective imagination.

I mean "subjective" in the sense which Harold Bloom clarified in a note on Elizabeth Bishop's poetry, where he distinguished between "a poetry of deep subjectivity"—as in Wordsworth, Stevens, and Bishop—and a confessional poetry, as in Coleridge and such modern American poets as Roethke, Robert Lowell, Berryman, and Jarrell. Bishop stands securely, Bloom said, in a tradition of American poetry that began with Emerson, Jones Very, and Dickinson, and culminated in aspects of Frost as well as of Stevens and Marianne Moore:

> When I read, say, "The Poems of Our Climate," by Stevens, or "The End of March," by Bishop, I encounter eventually the over-whelming self-revelation of a profoundly subjective consciousness. When I read, say, "Skunk Hour" by Lowell or one of Berryman's sonnets, I confront finally an opacity, for that is all the confessional mode can yield.

I take this to mean that in Lowell and Berryman the instigating events, real or imagined, have not been sufficiently transformed, or sufficiently converted into the idioms of a subjective imagination. That is: the events have merely been reported and are therefore still opaque. Bloom makes much of this distinction because he sees the activities of a subjective imagination as essentially American, Emerson their founding father, Stevens their supreme exemplar. Transformation is the American project in poetry: it is what guarantees the fellowship of poets otherwise as distinct as Whitman and Dickinson.

Bloom doesn't remark, a point equally crucial, that what amounts to conscientiousness in his favourite American tradition is the recognition that it must on occasion fail. The subjective transformation of reality is a project large enough for a major poetry, but only if it is attended by a scruple which recognizes that some facts of life can't be transformed. Stevens's scruple recognized that there are times in which the will demands that what it thinks be true; not just pleasurable. Dickinson gives herself every privilege in techniques of transformation, but she did not evade the fact that life is reluctant to be transformed and is often resolutely opaque.

Her vocabulary of numbness and blankness testifies to this dogged force in life:

> *The difference between Despair*
> *And Fear—is like the One*
> *Between the instant of a Wreck—*
> *And when the Wreck has been—*
>
> *The Mind is smooth—no Motion—*
> *Contented as the Eye*
> *Upon the Forehead of a Bust—*
> *That knows—it cannot see—*

Here the air of patient explication, the conceptual negotiation of differences between states close kin, marks Dickinson's refusal to yield to the experience or accept its tone. It is often said that her strength is in sensory images—"the thunder hurried slow"—but these depend upon the resilience with which she bodies forth against experience a concept, often an aphorism, strong enough to get the poem started and to lodge a claim for her poetry's kind of sense. She is not a thinker, she does not develop an elaborate argument, but her presence of mind is conceptual and discriminative. In this poem the reader is made to work through the difference between despair and fear by seeing that the terms of the comparison have been reversed, that fear is like the instant of the wreck and despair like its consequence. In "At Melville's Tomb," Hart Crane is loath to see in the wreck destitution so complete that no message can be constructed from its remains; so the scattered spars are hieroglyphs, signs, tokens. But in Dickinson's poems Nature's victory is indeed complete, except for the conceit of the unseeing eye that knows it can't see. The mind, like the forehead, is smooth: like the sea now, unwrinkled, beyond caring. The conceit of the stone eye knowing its blindness is enough to keep before us the other mind, Dickinson's, which expresses itself through that fancy. There is always an "as if." The discrimination with which the poem began is enhanced, at the end, by another one, the difference between what we know of stone and what Dickinson offers as a feasible sense of its sculptured life. "Contented" is slanted toward the doom the mind has learned to endure.

Dickinson achieves these dislocations because she never lets her

mind coincide with its object so fully as to accept an official or determin-
ing context. The slant of her imagination is her way of taking possession
of experience, if it is at all possible. Her emotions are those which make
dislocation possible; as desire turns the present moment toward a future it
projects, and a sense of loss turns it toward the past.

From (in part) *The Times Literary Supplement,* May 7, 1976.

HENRY ADAMS'S NOVELS

We are set to read *Democracy* (1880) and *Esther* (1884) in the context Adams provided for them, mainly his animadversions upon America, its history and institutions. It would be eccentric to enforce any other context, such as the history of English and American fiction, which would be much the same if Adams's novels had not been written. There is no embarrassment in admitting that we read the novels chiefly because he wrote them, and that for this compelling reason we are willing to follow whatever trail they suggest. The clearest trail leads into his other writings, before and after, where their preoccupations are held in common. Nor is it embarrassing to remark, to begin with, that the two novels amount to one, at least in the sense that each sustains, in effect if not by intention, the same story. *Democracy* turns upon a conflict between politics and morality, and *Esther* upon a conflict between the orthodoxy of religious belief and the rival truth of one's own feelings. But when we stand back a little from the details, we see that the two stories are indeed one.

One, somewhat along these lines. The story begins with vacancy; as a person might be vacant who has nothing much to do and can't be content to remain long in that state. Suppose the person in the case is a woman: in that event, having nothing to do would raise the larger question of what women have to do, or may be allowed to do, in a world ordained for the most part by men. The question would take a particularly acute form if it were to be posed by a writer preoccupied not only with the women he knew but with the idea of Woman as a force capable of unifying an entire society—medieval France, for instance—given certain favourable conditions. So the woman in question may well be presented as recently widowed, childless, and well-off: or a girl of twenty-five, not yet married, attending upon an invalid father soon to die. Vacancy, actual or impending, is enough to get the story under way. What is such a woman to do with her life, assuming she must do something and that she has desires, gifts of mind and feature, and a sense of what it means to be, in her time and place, a woman?

The readiest answer is: she should devote herself to some work or cause or interest. She should place herself where something worthwhile, or at least something interesting, is going on. If she paints, she may help to decorate a church; if she is drawn to political interests, she may move to Washington and see how power is exercised at the centre of things. How actively she takes up that interest depends on her relation both to vacancy and to the need of defeating it. If she is serious, the new interest is likely to be embodied in a man who controls its pace; a priest in one circumstance, a senator in the other. In Washington or New York a hundred years ago, a woman could hardly take a sustained interest in an engine without letting herself be attracted to the engineer. The man exerts a force of attraction, if only because he is the source of energy in the case: the woman subdues herself in his favour, at least to begin with, to the extent of making her will coincide with his. Her friends, at this pitch of exorbitance, are likely to be dismayed. But there is no merit in interfering, unless the case is desperate or a revelation of the man's true character will save the day. If a revelation is possible, so much the better. Otherwise the day can be saved only by the woman's will: she must find it humiliating, in the end, to subdue herself. She is not an American for nothing. In the end, she asserts the truth of her own values, chief among them being a conviction of her separate identity. She rejects the man, because she refuses the demands he makes upon her; even if it means returning to a new version of vacancy. At least she has been true to herself, after an interval of weakness, vanity, or bewilderment.

In *Democracy*, Mrs. Madeleine Lightfoot Lee, aged thirty, a stockbroker's widow, removes herself to Washington: she is bored with the commonplace interests available to her in New York, and the people who adhere to them. "Why will not somebody grow to be a tree and cast a shadow?" she asks of her New York friends. "She wanted," Adams says, "to see with her own eyes the action of primary forces; to touch with her own hand the massive machinery of society; to measure with her own mind the capacity of the motive power."[1] It is not clear whether she is content to see these things, for the gratification of understanding them, or insists on exerting her own pressure upon events. "What she wished to see, she thought, was the clash of interests, the interests of forty millions of people and a whole continent, centering at Washington; guided, restrained, controlled, or unrestrained and uncontrollable, by men of ordinary mould; the tremendous forces of government, and the machinery of society, at work." But the next sentence reads: "What she wanted, was POWER" (p. 8). The ambivalence is resolved, for the moment, by a new metaphor: Washington is a stage, the drama of politics is about to begin, the actors are ready to enter. Madeleine gets ready to watch the play.

But she also arranges her own play. She holds a salon in her rented house in Lafayette Square, where she lives with her sister Sybil, and assembles her players. A few of these are minor figures—Lord Skye, Count Popoff, Baron Jacobi, Mr. French, Nathan Gore, Hartbeest Schneidekoupan, Victoria Dare; but she also attracts to her presence men of larger scope, the lawyer John Carrington, Senator Clinton, and her largest catch, Senator Ratcliffe. The salon runs on the lines of the one Henry and Marian Adams ran in Washington, handsomely implied in Henry James's story "Pandora" (1884). In James's story the talk at the Bonnycastles' is mostly of social discrimination, the character of the new self-made girl, and of Washington itself, the talk "revolving about the subject in widening and narrowing circles, perching successively on its many branches, considering it from every point of view."[2] At Madeleine Lee's, the themes that matter are power, democracy, reform, party, the Presidency—who's in, who's out. Much of the sentiment provoked by these themes recapitulates Adams's own dismay, in "Civil Service Reform" and in other essays he published in *The Great Secession Winter of 1860–1861*. In those, he denounced the spoils system, and urged reformers "to trust neither to Presidents nor to senators, but appeal directly to the people."[3] At the beginning, Madeleine is drawn to Senator Ratcliffe because he

casts a shadow: she has misgivings about *Realpolitik,* but she acknowledges that an omelette can't be made without breaking eggs. She is a
reformer, and for a time she convinces herself that Ratcliffe will eventually do all the right things. Meanwhile, Carrington, a gentleman of the
old South, is in love with her, and implores her not to marry Ratcliffe.
She rejects his plea. In the end, he produces evidence that Ratcliffe has
taken a bribe of $100,000. Madeleine confronts Ratcliffe, and denounces
him. But she also rejects her own ambition, which now counts for vanity.
"As she lay, hour after hour, waiting for the sleep that did not come, she
had at first the keen mortification of reflecting how easily she had been
led by mere vanity into imagining that she could be of use in the world"
(p. 168). She asks Sybil to go abroad with her. "I want to go to
Egypt . . . democracy has shaken my nerves to pieces. Oh, what rest it
would be to live in the Great Pyramid and look out for ever at the polar
star!" (p. 182).

In *Esther* the heroine's vacancy begins in a church: she is there for
the wrong reasons. She is not a believer, she thinks of churches as mere
buildings and of the particular church—St. Paul's on Fifth Avenue—as an
opera house. Her associates include George Strong, a professor of
palaeontology who is content with his way of life because he doesn't
require it to matter; and Wharton, an artist, who would judge situations
by aesthetic criteria if he could find a style answerable to his time and its
feelings. But the force of attraction, in Esther's case, is exerted by the
priest, Stephen Hazard. Nearby also is Catherine Brooke, who is in the
story mainly so that Wharton can dominate her as Hazard dominates
Esther. The official business meanwhile is to decorate the church. Wharton
is in charge, but Esther is his apprentice, and Hazard takes up his brush on
one occasion. It is necessary to paint saints, but since saints can't now be
imagined, the artists must paint one another, so Hazard paints a likeness of
Wharton as St. Luke looking at Catherine Brooke, who is St. Cecilia.
Below the novel, but too far down to help, there is a diffuse sense of the
relation between sentiment and figure: Adams imagined it fully, not in
the novel, but in *Mont-Saint-Michel and Chartres.* In the novel, an equally
diffuse version of the sentiment alludes to the relation between Petrarch
and Laura, as it bears first upon Wharton's love of his wife, now estranged,
and then upon whatever relation we discern between Wharton and
Catherine.

Esther's father dies, and she accepts Hazard: the lovers talk of Hazard's theme, mysticism. To Esther now, "nothing seemed real except the imagination, and nothing true but the spiritual." As for Hazard in these conversations: "his great eyes shone with the radiance of paradise, and his delicate thin features expressed beatitude, as he discussed with Esther the purity of the soul, the victory of spirit over matter, and the peace of infinite love" (p. 265). But when Esther next attends church and listens to Hazard's sermon, she finds herself not believing a word of it. Privately, he urges her to put every question, and especially the question of faith, in his hands, "but the moment he was out of sight she forgot that he was to be the keeper of her conscience, and, without a thought of her dependence, she resumed the charge of her own affairs" (p. 275). She tells Hazard she can't marry him. To escape his fervour, she rushes off to Niagara for a few days, putting herself close to a more tolerable instance of power. Hazard follows her, but fruitlessly. She loves him, but she won't submit herself to his demand.

Reduced still further, the two stories amounting to one come out somewhat like this: a woman, to escape the vacancy a man's world has imposed on her, enters the world in the hope of sharing its force. For a time, she is exhilarated, her life seems to acquire density and reverberation. But gradually she recoils from it: it is not that the price is too high but that it is a price at all; she sees no reason why she should be required to pay anything or to bring to the occasion any gifts but her own. In the event, the price is found monstrous: she must submit to the man's terms, accept his values, believe in his God. Rather than yield to him, she withdraws into Egyptian vacancy.

Are we to convict these American women of naïveté? How could they have fancied that the world would yield to them, or admit them on their own terms? James's fiction, more than Adams's, takes up the challenge of these questions. Generally, James has his girls defeat the men at their own dreadful game, especially if the men are Europeans far gone in corruption, but the victorious girls are left wondering just what it is they have won. Keeping James close to Adams for the moment; in "Pandora," by charming the President of the United States, the self-made girl gets the spoils of office for her fiancé. But she doesn't rise, upon that success, to greater things: her fiancé, and not the new young man she has met on her way back from Europe, is the man she marries. This is as it should be: there is no reason to think that she will be abused by her husband or exposed to any misery. Husband and wife are as nearly equal as they well can be.

But the disappointment of Adams's heroines seems to need a larger context; grander ambitions have been stirred which could be satisfied by nothing less than a transformation of the world. Such a transformation is hardly to be imagined except by following Adams's imagination of it in "The Three Queens," the eleventh chapter of *Mont-Saint-Michel and Chartres.* He begins by quoting a passage from L. Garreau's *The Social State of France during the Crusades* to the effect that in the twelfth century there was a close resemblance between the manners of men and women and that the rule that such and such feelings or acts are permitted to one sex and not to the other was not yet settled: indeed, women were clearly superior to men in intelligence and thoughtfulness. Adams extends the account by saying that "the women ruled the household and the workshop; cared for the economy; supplied the intelligence, and dictated the taste" (p. 524). A few pages later he asserts that "the docile obedience of the man to the woman seemed as reasonable to the thirteenth century as the devotion of the woman to the man, not because she loved him, for there was no question of love, but because he was *her* man, and she owned him as though he were her child" (p. 533). Everything Adams goes on to say about unity and multiplicity, and the power of the Virgin, depends on his conviction that unity was possible only so long as women remained superior and dominant. "No one has ventured to explain why the Virgin wielded exclusive power over poor and rich, sinners and saints, alike" (p. 582). What Adams ventures to assert, if not to explain, is that the Protestant churches were cold failures because they rejected the Virgin. "If a Unity exists, in which and towards which all energies centre, it must explain and include Duality, Diversity, Infinity,—Sex!" (pp. 582–83).

In the context of these sentiments, Madeleine's outrage and Esther's recoil are not at all extravagant: we may suppose that because Adams invented these women, they retain something of his sense of the possibilities embodied in the Virgin, and that the declension from them must be understood as being historically inevitable though dismal still. Think of Esther when we read, still in *Mont-Saint-Michel and Chartres,* this passage:

In essence, religion was love; in no case was it logic. Reason can reach nothing except through the senses; God, by essence, cannot be reached through the senses; if he is to be known at all, he must be known by contact of spirit with spirit, essence with essence; directly;

by emotion; by ecstasy; by absorption of our existence in his; by substitution of his spirit for ours [p. 642].

The last two phrases point back not only to the axioms of medieval belief but to the terms Hazard tries to impose upon Esther. It is one thing if we absorb our own existence in God's, and substitute his spirit for ours: but it is another matter if we are obliged to make the same commitment to a mere priest. Hazard requires Esther to commit herself to him as if to God, and sacrifice her spirit in his service.

I would emphasize, then, the continuity between Adams's fiction and his work in history, politics, and autobiography: one story sustains and, in detail, exacerbates the whole. Between the fiction and *The Education of Henry Adams,* the continuity is especially clear. In the first chapter of *Democracy,* Madeleine is shown taking up one interest after another—German philosophy, philanthropy, a routine of charitable works, religion—only to drop each as more or less trivial. "Was she not herself devoured by ambition, and was she not now eating her heart out because she could find no one object worth a sacrifice?" (p. 4). What else is the *Education* but Adams's account of his own provisional interests, each of them taken up, assessed, and dropped in dreadful sequence, because none of them was worth a sacrifice? Not only the *Education* but the *History of the United States of America during the Administrations of Jefferson and Madison* told the same story. The questions Adams asked at the end of the *History* are the same questions he asked and answered, dismally for the most part, in *Democracy.* Here is the *History,* and the time in question is 1815:

The traits of American character were fixed; the rate of physical and economical growth was established; and history, certain that at a given distance of time the Union would contain so many millions of people, with wealth valued at so many millions of dollars, became thenceforward chiefly concerned to know what kind of people these millions were to be. They were intelligent, but what paths would their intelligence select? They were quick, but what solution of insoluble problems would quickness hurry? They were scientific, and what control would their science exercise over their destiny? They were mild, but what corruptions would their relaxations bring? They were peaceful, but by what machinery were their corruptions to be purged? What interests were to vivify a society so vast and uniform? What ideals were to ennoble it? What object, besides physical content, must a democratic continent aspire to attain? For the treatment of such questions, history required another century of experience.[4]

But Adams didn't wait another century to produce history's answer to some of those questions. At the end of *Democracy*, Madeleine adds a postscript to the letter Sybil is mailing to Carrington: referring to her rejection of the corrupt Ratcliffe, she says that "the bitterest part of all this horrid story is that nine out of ten of our countrymen would say I had made a mistake" (p. 184). In the fourth chapter Mr. Gore tells Madeleine that he believes in democracy "because it appears to me the inevitable consequence of what has gone before it":

> Democracy asserts the fact that the masses are now raised to a higher intelligence than formerly. All our civilisation aims at this mark. We want to do what we can to help it. I myself want to see the result. I grant it is an experiment, but it is the only direction society can take that is worth its taking; the only conception of its duty large enough to satisfy its instincts; the only result that is worth an effort or a risk [p. 40].

But what Adams felt, when he sat in the gallery of Congress in 1870 and listened to the announcement of Grant's Cabinet, was that the noble experiment had wretchedly failed. He described his sense of that failure in Chapter 17 of the *Education*. His brother Brooks gave the gist of it in his Introduction to Henry's *The Degradation of the Democratic Dogma*, that "Democracy is an infinite mass of conflicting minds and of conflicting interests which, by the persistent action of such a solvent as the modern or competitive industrial system, becomes resolved into what is, in substance, a vapor, which loses in collective intellectual energy in proportion to the perfection of its expansion."[5]

Esther's experience has the same result, though it is not clear that as an experiment it was fairly defined. The possibilities of the church as an institution are not justly embodied in Esther's experience with Stephen Hazard. She starts out not believing, tries to believe in response to Hazard's power of attraction, but when he, emotionally compromised, urges her to come to him, she blames the church for his errors of tact and rhetoric. "Why must the church always appeal to my weakness and never to my strength! I ask for spiritual life and you send me back to my flesh and blood as though I were a tigress you were sending back to her cubs" (p. 333). The rebuke is unfair, but it relates itself at once to yet another question Adams placed before American society at the end of the *History*: "could it produce, or was it compatible with, the differentiation of a higher variety of the human race?" Or, in the terms of Esther's rebuke, would it reduce culture to nature, and imprison people in its mere repetition?

The differentiation of a higher variety of the human race is a tall order, even at a time often drunk on talk of evolution and progress. It begins to appear as if Adams took to himself the task of setting American society tests he knew it couldn't pass. In *The Lion and the Honeycomb*, Blackmur said that "Adams used to argue that the great question was whether the American mind could catch up with American energy": "he doubted it, but thought a good jump might do it."[6] I don't think Adams had much faith in a high jump: on the contrary, he kept raising the mark, knowing that nobody could reach it.

It is common to argue that Adams's kinship with failure is easily explained by his failure to gain office or to be employed by any administration. My own prejudice is that his intimacy with failure was not contingent but constitutional and temperamental: it may have been hereditary. It is true that he saw failure begin in his own family with his grandfather John Quincy Adams. It is also true that his mother, as his older brother Charles Francis Jr. said of her, took "a constitutional and sincere pleasure in the forecast of evil: she delighted in the dark side of anticipation."[7] His own values were those of the Enlightenment and the eighteenth century which saw itself in those terms: the correspondence between Thomas Jefferson and John Adams may be taken as an exemplary text, as it was by Ezra Pound in the *Cantos* and Louis Zukofsky in "A-8" and other poems. The pathos of the *Education* is Adams's attempt to bring Enlightenment values to bear upon a society that has disowned them. Adams goes through the motions of sympathy toward his time; he is more hospitable than the time had a right to expect; but in the end the motions recoil upon himself and he calls them failure. He needed failure because he needed its tone. It is as if he had only one story to tell, and it must come out with failure as its moral.

I shall come back to the novels in the end, but I have to produce a few considerations at this point to justify my sense that failure in Adams was a constitutional necessity rather than a conclusion imposed by a train of events. The first is from Adams himself, the second from Blackmur's study of him, the third from a book that has nothing to do with Adams unless we choose to make it applicable.

The first comes from Chapter 24 of the *Education,* where Adams describes his meeting, in November 1898, with his friend John La Farge:

> One was never quite sure of his whole meaning until too late to respond, for he had no difficulty in carrying different shades of contradiction in his mind. As he said of his friend Okakura, his thought ran as a stream runs through grass, hidden perhaps but always there; and one felt often uncertain in what direction it flowed, for even a contradiction was to him only a shade of difference, a complementary color, about which no intelligent artist would dispute. Constantly he repulsed argument:—"Adams, you reason too much!" was one of his standing reproaches even in the mild discussion of rice and mangoes in the warm night of Tahiti dinners. He should have blamed Adams for being born in Boston. The mind resorts to reason for want of training, and Adams had never met a perfectly trained mind [p. 1058].

The second comes from far out in Blackmur's study of Adams, when he thinks of Adams and of James on the strength of their last conversations in Rye early in 1914, when Adams had long published the *Education* and James but recently *Notes of a Son and Brother:*

> Both men were concerned with experience as education, and to both the judgment of education called for a specialized form of autobiography in which the individual was suppressed in the act, only to be caught in the style. James imagined human reality always through dramatizing the bristling sensual record of the instance— almost any instance that had a story in it—and let the pattern, the type, the *vis a tergo,* take care of itself, which under the stress of the imaginative process it commonly did. Adams, on the other hand, tended in a given case to depend on his feeling for human type and pattern—for history and lines of force—as the source of drama, and

hence saw the individual as generalized *first:* so that whatever happened would fall into the pattern, if you only had the wit to see how—which Adams by the strength of his conceptual imagination did commonly see. To put it another way, Adams's set of intellectual instruments more or less *predicted* what he would discover; James resorted to instruments only to ascertain what his sensibility had *already* discovered.[8]

Blackmur thought James's way the better bet, as indeed it was and far better than Blackmur's statement of the case allows. You pay a penalty, he thought, for either way: in James, the penalty is "excess of feeling"; in Adams, "excess of consideration." But the penalties don't come to the same cost if your chief interest is in writing novels. The conceptual imagination brought Adams nearly as far as he had to go in the literary forms close to his talent; and let him down when, in the novels, he needed a talent for sensibility and drama. James didn't need the conceptual imagination as a separate attribute, since the gist of it operated quietly within his dramatic imagination, and he needed only its gist. If Adams's mind predicted what he would discover, it also vetoed anything inconsistent with the pattern, the type; which amounted to a lot of experience he couldn't have.

The third passage comes from a different setting, and without mentioning Adams has the merit of saying that the quality of mind we are attributing to him is one of the standard qualities and that it leans toward irony. I quote now two short sections of Gilles Deleuze's *Proust et les signes* and run them together:

> There is one aspect, however concealed it may be, of the logos, by means of which the Intelligence always *comes before,* by which the whole is already present, the law already known before what it applies to: this is the dialectical trick by which we discover only what we have already given ourselves, by which we derive from things only what we have already put there. . . . The Socratic demon, irony, consists in anticipating the encounters. In Socrates, the intelligence still comes before the encounters; it provokes them, it instigates and organizes them. Proust's humour is of another nature: Jewish humour as opposed to Greek irony. One must be endowed for the signs, ready to encounter them, one must open oneself to

their violence. The intelligence always comes after, it is good only when it comes after.[9]

This is to say, if we make it applicable, that Adams's mind was Socratic rather than Jamesian or Proustian. Excess of consideration was the quality of his determination that experience shouldn't take him by surprise. He practised it by learning, early on, how to construe an individual as a type, so that the boundary already marking the type would impose itself upon the individual. He knew this habit in himself. The mind resorts to reason for want of training. A trained mind would not be led or pulled by a train of thought already in motion: it would know itself as sensibility, and trust itself in that experimental capacity. But Adams's mind didn't: it trusted itself only for prediction and for setting the terms upon which experience would be received.

Think of the several passages in the *Education* where Adams's intelligence, desperately insinuating itself before any call for it, prescribed the terms of experience and gave it a character in advance: when he resorts to consideration of sequence, unity, and type, which have fixity above all in mind. Near the end, Adams's word for what the intelligence discloses by coming before the need of it is formula:

> Every man with self-respect enough to become effective, if only as a machine, has had to account to himself for himself somehow, and to invent a formula of his own for his universe, if the standard formulas failed. There, whether finished or not, education stopped. The formula, once made, could be but verified [p. 1151].

And, if verified, could only be applied in repetition: and to what end?

Kierkegaard said that the aim of irony is to enable the ironist to feel free. Free of what? In Adams's case, free of chaos, multiplicity, heterogeneity. There are minds which don't feel the need of this freedom: John Cage's mind, for instance, which enjoys heterogeneity and cultivates chance to provoke it. But Adams's mind needed to discover patterns, types, and sequences before it could enjoy their constituents. He was convinced that he had to understand forces and lines of force as if they had already supplanted the men whose actions they should merely chart in retrospect. It was Adams's fear that society could no longer be comprehended by understanding the motives of the men who composed it. (I am coming back to the novels.) In the *Education* he writes:

> The work of domestic progress is done by masses of mechanical power,—steam, electric, furnace or other,—which have to be controlled by a score or two of individuals who have shown capacity to manage it. The work of internal government has become the task of controlling these men, who are socially as remote as heathen gods, alone worth knowing, but never known, and who could tell nothing of political value if one skinned them alive. Most of them have nothing to tell, but are forces as dumb as their dynamos, absorbed in the development or economy of power. They are trustees for the public and whenever society assumes the property, it must confer on them that title; but the power will remain as before, whoever manages it, and will then control society without appeal, as it controls its stokers and pit-men. Modern politics is, at bottom, a struggle not of men but of forces [p. 1105].

Of the many quaking passages in the *Education,* this strikes me as the most terrible. I construe it as showing Adams's mind recoiling from the doomed attempt to understand society in the terms he set for understanding it. These were chiefly scientific terms. Adams couldn't see why a scientific understanding of society wasn't just as feasible as a scientific understanding of the operation of mechanics and couldn't yield laws just as lucid. His recourse to forces and lines of force is lurid because it has driven itself to the conclusion that society as such is incomprehensible. T. W. Adorno has maintained, in his essay "Society," that "this resistance of society to rational comprehension should be understood first and foremost as the sign of relationships between men which have grown increasingly independent of them, opaque, now standing off against human beings like some different substance."[10] Emile Durkheim's sociology is uppermost in Adorno's mind in that comment; especially Durkheim's rule that one should treat social facts as objects and renounce any effort to "understand" them. Adams wanted to understand them, but in practice he met at every point what Adorno called "the imbalance of institutions over men"; an imbalance he could deal with only by giving it the crass form of lines and diagrams. Men of power turned into heathen gods, alone worth knowing, but never known: they could only be known according to some abstract or mathematical model, now that gods no longer reside in our hills. A struggle not of men but of forces: so Adams's conceptual imagination occupied itself with types, representations, personifications; with the institutions that had supplanted the men who composed them.

If we think of the novels in this context, whether or not it coincides with Adams's, we see that failure is not the term we need. What *Democracy* and *Esther* show is not heroines who fail but heroines who refuse. Madeleine and Esther could easily have "won" in their societies. Instead, they refuse the only terms of success offered them. In politics as shown, the forces in the system have gone their own way, independent of the men who should have controlled them. The men of power—Grant, Senator Ratcliffe—have yielded themselves to the forces they should have exerted. Hazard's religion has turned him into a demigod, at fatal cost to his humanity. But Madeleine and Esther insist on coming to consciousness of themselves as subjects— Adorno's phrasing again—this is what their rejection of the institutions amounts to.

It is crucial that Adams's novels have heroines and not heroes because the social and political system which Madeleine and Esther reject is the work of men, to begin with, until it declares its independence of the men who established it and continues under its own monstrous power. Whatever we mean by self, identity, individuality is not something given to Madeleine and Esther: or if it is, they reject it. What they insist on is their right to exist separately—since this is what the situation has come to—from the institutions that offered them access to the spectacle of authority at the price of their souls.

Adams thought well of his novels, and especially of *Esther,* for reasons speculation can hardly take hold of. I think he kept fresh in his mind the association of the novels with his wife, and with Elizabeth Cameron, and through these with his more general sense of women and their superiority to men in every consideration that counted. We are not required to accept his fondnesses in preference to our own. Indeed, the novels are not so precious that it would be monstrous to defile them by asking such a blatant question as: why did he write them? Given the nature of his talent—conceptual, discursive, analytical, ironic—fiction seems the oddest recourse for it, unless drama were deemed odder still.

I suggest that Adams resorted to fiction in the hope of evading the marked character of his talent, and coping with its limitations. He knew precisely the kind of talent he had, and his want of training in all the other kinds. Fredric Jameson, referring to the mind's tendency toward illusions of its autonomy, describes a moment in which "there comes into being an illusion of transparency, in which the mind looks like the world, and we stare at concepts as though they were things." Adams knew that stare, and the specious fixity which defeated him when he determined to respect the character of life as process. It seems reasonable to think that he resorted to fiction in the hope of deflecting his tendency to see people as having only the force of their types. He wrote a political novel in the hope of seeing politics, for once, as a struggle not of forces but of men. He wrote a novel about religion in the hope of registering the feelings which the forms of religion merely organized and didn't fulfil.

But it was the defect of his program that his only access to fiction was by way of a few conventional forms which turned out to be useless to him. These were forms—melodrama, drawing-room comedy, the conversation piece—which he could only imitate, so they lay heavy on his project and represented only the intelligence that comes before its experience. He could do nothing with the conventional forms but accept their character and go through the motions they indicated. They, too, had only the force of the typical, with little or no allowance for forces still unrecognized and nameless.

NOTES

1. Henry Adams, *Novels (Democracy: An American Novel;* and *Esther: A Novel);* *Mont-Saint-Michel and Chartres; The Education of Henry Adams; Poems,* eds. Ernest Samuels and Jayne N. Samuels (New York: Library of America, 1983); *Democracy,* pp. 6, 7.

2. "Pandora," in Vol. V of *The Complete Tales of Henry James, 1883–1884,* ed. Leon Edel (London: Rupert Hart-Davis, 1963), p. 387.

3. Henry Adams, *The Great Secession Winter of 1860–1861, and Other Essays,* ed. George Hochfield (New York: Sycamore Press, 1958), p. 127.

4. Henry Adams, *History of the United States of America during the Administrations of Jefferson and Madison* (9 vols.; New York: Charles Scribner's Sons, 1889–91), IX, 241–42.

5. Brooks Adams, Introduction to *The Degradation of the Democratic Dogma,* by Henry Adams (New York: Macmillan, 1919), p. 109.

6. R. P. Blackmur, *The Lion and the Honeycomb* (London: Methuen, 1956), p. 3.

7. Quoted in *The Education of Henry Adams, and Other Selected Writings,* ed. Edward N. Saveth (New York: Twayne, 1963), p. xxxvii.

8. R. P. Blackmur, *Henry Adams,* ed. Veronica A. Makowsky (New York: Harcourt Brace Jovanovich, 1980), pp. 315–16.

9. *Proust and Signs,* trans. Richard Howard (New York: Braziller, 1972), pp. 94, 166–67.

10. "Society," trans. Fredric Jameson; reprinted in *The Salmagundi Reader,* eds. Robert Boyers and Peggy Boyers (Bloomington: Indiana University Press, 1983), p. 51.

———————

From *Nineteenth Century Fiction,* Summer 1984.

HENRY JAMES AND
The Sense of the Past

I

In the second chapter of *Ulysses,* Dedalus is teaching his class at Mr. Deasy's school in Dalkey: the subjects are history, to begin with, and poetry a little later. The first question touches upon King Pyrrhus. The boy Cochrane knows the date of the battle (279 B.C.) but not the place (Asculum). In the interval between question and answer, Stephen muses:

> Fabled by the daughters of memory. And yet it was in some way if not as memory fabled it. A phrase, then, of impatience, thud of Blake's wings of excess. I hear the ruin of all space, shattered glass and toppling masonry, and time one livid final flame. What's left us then?

Stephen's misgiving is turned upon Blake's excess. It may be true that Memory is inferior to Imagination. "Fable or Allegory," according to Blake's *Vision of the Last Judgment,* "is Form'd by the daughters of Memory. Imagination is surrounded by the daughters of Inspiration." Writing to

William Hayley on May 6, 1800, Blake said that "the ruins of Time build mansions in Eternity." In *The Marriage of Heaven and Hell,* he predicts that the whole creation will be consumed "and appear infinite and holy, whereas it now appears finite and corrupt." What's left us then, Stephen ruefully asks, the vision having only this disability, that no one will be there to appreciate it. It is enough for Blake that he sees the vision in the mind's eye, but Stephen wants to hold on to the present moment by holding on to the past. The battle of Asculum may not have taken place precisely as memory has fabled it, but it came to pass, Stephen assures himself, in some way.

On the next page, Stephen admits the mood in which history seems "a tale like any other too often heard," but he wants to retain historical events, even if nothing more than an approximation is possible:

> Had Pyrrhus not fallen by a beldam's hand in Argos or Julius Caesar not been knifed to death? They are not to be thought away. Time has branded them and fettered they are lodged in the room of the infinite possibilities they have ousted. But can those have been possible seeing that they never were? Or was that only possible which came to pass?

Stephen ponders these obscure questions by alluding to Aristotle's distinction, in the *Metaphysics,* between potentiality and actuality. The potential is what can be moved, the actual is what can't be moved because it has already come into being. The distinction corresponds to another in the *Poetics,* between history and poetry. History tells what has occurred, poetry the kind of thing that might occur. Julius Caesar was knifed to death. F. H. Bradley is free to ask who the real Julius Caesar was, but Caesar's death remains, an historical event: it is not to be thought away.

Several pages later, Stephen tells Mr. Deasy that history "is a nightmare from which I am trying to awake," and Deasy answers that "the ways of the Creator are not our ways ... All human history moves towards one great goal, the manifestation of God." Stephen's nightmare is presumably the lurid narrative of his life, embodying the destiny of having been born in that time and place and to those parents. He derives no consolation from Mr. Deasy's belief in the teleology of events or the epiphany of which believers live in hope.

I have adverted to this episode because it raises many of the questions which beset anyone who thinks about history. Is it a tale like any other, a form of fiction just as dependent as Nabokov's *Pale Fire* upon the concession of a few figures of speech and thought? Is every apparently historical narrative merely the fulfilment, as Hayden White has argued in *Metahistory,* of one or two of the "four master tropes" Kenneth Burke has elucidated? Or is history a tale unlike any other, as Mr. Deasy insists, the one story and one story only which has as its climax the manifestation of God?

The word "history" is commonly used in two senses. It refers to distinguishable events as they may be invoked in one's formal knowledge of the past. It also refers to human life as it may be represented in the mode of time, its tenses the past, present, and future, especially where the representation takes a narrative form, actual or implied. A painting is historical if it implies the precedence that makes its representations cohere.

It is generally agreed that we have inherited from the nineteenth century our preoccupation with history. Malraux claims, in *The Voices of Silence,* that "the crucial historical event of the nineteenth century was the birth of a new consciousness of history." But he doesn't remark, a truth not less, that the new consciousness arose from need and, specifically, from the emptiness caused by loss of confidence in human nature. Mr. Deasy transfers to history the privilege his ancestors would have deduced from an agreed sense of human nature.

But these remarks are premature. History is now the most ideologically blatant term in our vocabulary: it divides those who hold it immune to scepticism from those who think it just as liable to deconstruction as any other sentiment. "It seems history is to blame," as Haines says to Stephen; a sentimental Englishman, more Irish than the Irish, addressing a lapsed Catholic preparing to be a lapsed Irishman. But it is still possible to find, among the available attitudes toward history, not only Acceptance and Rejection, but acceptance with reservations and rejection with regret. I shall make a few notes on these positions.

Acceptance

1. To represent this sentiment, think of Aeneas carrying Anchises on his back, a motif that didn't begin with Virgil or end with Wallace Stevens. The past is a responsibility accepted, a burden willingly shouldered if

only because without it one's life seems weightless or otherwise trivial. (Examples: T. S. Eliot's advocated sense of tradition as discipline in "Tradition and the Individual Talent." Or Yeats's "Poetry and Tradition," in which the past is audible, and we are to listen to its voices as they reach us from our parents, the lore of what has happened in our place in other times.)

2. History as repetition, according to a disposition predicated upon the force of analogy. (Example from Benjamin's "Theses on the Philosophy of History": "Thus, to Robespierre ancient Rome was a past charged with the time of the now (*Jetztzeit*) which he blasted out of the continuum of history. The French Revolution viewed itself as Rome incarnate." And later:

> Historicism contents itself with establishing a causal connection between various moments in history. But no fact that is a cause is for that very reason historical. It became historical posthumously, as it were, through events that may be separated from it by thousands of years. A historian who takes this as his point of departure stops telling the sequence of events like the beads of a rosary. Instead, he grasps the constellation which his own era has formed with a definite earlier one.)

3. History as the narrative form of meaning, whether the meaning is construed in biological, evolutionary, familial, or otherwise enhancing terms. (Examples: Mr. Deasy on the manifestation of God. Lionel Trilling, commenting on Thomas Jefferson's *Notes on Virginia,* said that in proposing that the minds of children be formed upon matter chiefly historical Jefferson "did not doubt that the facts were to be known and that the narrative of them, which they themselves would dictate to any honest mind, would be the truth and, as such, unitary and canonical." Vico, Hegel, Darwin, and Marx agree with Mr. Deasy in finding a significant pattern among historical events: they differ only in naming the particular pattern each finds there.)

4. The Christian sense of history as significant because God sent his beloved Son to redeem mankind. (Text for this sentiment: Paul Ricoeur's essays on secular history and sacred history—the one, in which we all live our daily lives; the other, which is animated not by historical research but by faith. A Christian believes that secular history participates in sacred history and will eventually be found to coincide with it.)

5. The Marxist sense of history as the dimension in which social and personal life can alone be redeemed. (In *The Political Unconscious,* Fredric Jameson writes: "History is therefore the experience of Necessity, and it is this alone which can forestall its thematization or reification as a mere object of representation or as one master code among many others. . . . History is what hurts, it is what refuses desire and sets inexorable limits to individual as well as collective *praxis,* which its 'ruses' turn into grisly and ironic reversals of their overt intention." Jameson presumably thinks this experience, which does not entail any abject submission to Necessity, is the only one worth having.)

Acceptance, with Reservations

1. Suppose I were to think the past a burden, indeed, and mostly an intolerable one, but nonetheless worth trying to sustain. (Geoffrey Hartman says, in *The Fate of Reading,* that "the growth of the historical consciousness, its multiplying of disparate models all of which press their claim, amounts to a peculiarly modern burden. . . . To be aware of the past is to be surrounded by abstract potentialities, imperatives that cannot all be heeded, options exhausting the power of choice. A liberation, not of men and women, but of images, has created a *theatrum mundi* in which the distance between past and present, culture and culture, truth and superstition is suspended by a quasi-divine synchronism.") Surfeit, I suppose; a plethora. But every image has to wait for my attention. In *Ulysses,* Francis reminds Stephen of their years together at school:

> He asked about Glaucon, Alcibiades, Pisistratus. Where were they now? Neither knew. You have spoken of the past and its phantoms, Stephen said. Why think of them? If I call them into life across the waters of Lethe will not the poor ghosts troop to my call? Who supposes it? I, Bous Stephanoumenos, bullock befriending bard, am lord and giver of their life.

2. Call this an exemptive sense of the past. Hans Blumenberg has described the sentiment in which we give ourselves the history that sets us free of history; as if we could dispose of our problems by fabricating a

narrative that doesn't recognize them. ("But is was all so long ago"—
Finnegans Wake.)

3. The Nietzschean reservation, according to which three forms of
the historical sense are distinguished and acknowledged, but one of them
is most strongly recommended. In "The Use and Abuse of History"
Nietzsche describes the monumental, the antiquarian, and the critical
senses of history, differentiating the sentiments, desires, and satisfactions
that go with each. None of them is to be vetoed, but the crucial one to be
advanced is the critical sense, which interrogates the past and is always
ready to condemn it. Knowledge of the past is desired only in behalf of
the future. We seek, Nietzsche says, a past from which we might spring,
rather than that from which we seem to have derived. It is not the critical
historian's task to seek an origin in the hope of discovering the human
essence; but rather a local beginning which supposes, always available, a
beginning again, a new interrogation. Not being, but becoming, indicates the direction of intelligence, as Nietzsche insists in *The Will to
Power.*

Rejection

1. One version of this sentiment may be called Emerson, its motto his
assertion in "Self-Reliance"—"Life only avails, not the having lived." The
past is resented for the privilege it has been accorded, the immunity
granted to its forms. America against Europe; William Carlos Williams's
"reply to Greek and Latin with the bare hands."

2. Another version is revulsion against history for its pretension to
discover essence or meaning. Examples: E. M. Cioran has denounced
history as "nothing but a procession of false Absolutes, a series of temples
raised to pretexts, a depredation of the mind before the Improbable."
Foucault's "Nietzsche, Genealogy, History" goes beyond Nietzsche, and
replaces history by genealogy, which not only disavows the traditional
historian's interest in origin and essence but seeks to discover "that truth
or being do not lie at the root of what we know and what we are, but the
exteriority of accidents." The genealogist treats repetition as masquerade,
discovers the dispersal and dissipation of identity, and proposes "the
destruction of the man who maintains knowledge by the injustice proper
to the will to knowledge."

3. A third involves the denunciation of the past as the playground

of monsters, otherwise known as great men. Again from Benjamin's "Theses on the Philosophy of History":

> Whoever has emerged victorious participates to this day in the triumphal procession in which the present rulers step over those who are lying prostrate. According to traditional practice, the spoils are carried along in the procession. They are called cultural treasures. They owe their existence not only to the efforts of the great minds and talents who have created them, but also to the anonymous toil of their contemporaries. There is no document of civilization which is not at the same time a document of barbarism.

Hugh Kenner has remarked in *A Colder Eye*—expressing an evidently different philosophy of history from Benjamin's—that in Ireland "ruined castles, ruined houses, ruined towers round or square, mark achievement that flared briefly and flamed out, whereupon a few more stragglers shifted their ground."

But in any case history is the deeds of great men, a fact that Kenner (and Yeats) find acceptable.

Rejection, with Regret

1. In the Cyclops chapter, Leopold Bloom is arguing with John Wyse, the Citizen, and other cronies about injustice general and particular, hatred directed upon Jews being his case in point:

> But it's no use, says he. Force, hatred, history, all that. That's not life for men and women, insult and hatred. And everybody knows that it's the very opposite of that that is really life.
> —What? says Alf.
> —Love, says Bloom. I mean the opposite of hatred.

But Bloom can't remain long in the condition of rejecting anything; even his own history, which includes such dismal matters as the death, by suicide, of his father in the Queen's Hotel, Ennis, and of an infant son, Rudy. Indeed, the process of rejecting history, with regret, is hardly to be distinguished from that of accepting it, with reservations: in either case, Bloom puts the dismal image, so far as possible—though that is not far—out of his mind.

2. This version is more formal, and might be called Henry James: it features an artist's resentment of any consideration that threatens to preempt or otherwise thwart his imagination. History presents the past as that which doesn't need to be imagined and has only to be received. "Rejection, with regret" may not be the best formula for this sentiment in James. His autobiography, the Prefaces to his novels and tales, and the fiction itself show how willingly he found his provocations in the chance and choice of his own experience. But he was bound to reject anything that seemed opaque to his particular form of attention, and his criteria in that regard were severe.

This explains James's gruffness on the question of the historical novel. On October 5, 1901, he wrote a note of thanks to Sarah Orne Jewett for having sent him a copy of her historical novel *The Tory Lover.* James went through the motions of politeness, but in the end he brushed the civilities aside to explain why he thought such a novel misguided:

> The "historic" novel is, for me, condemned even in cases of labour as delicate as yours, to a fatal *cheapness,* for the simple reason that the difficulty of the job is inordinate and that a mere *escamotage,* in the interest of ease and of the abysmal public *naïveté,* becomes inevitable. You may multiply the little facts that can be got from pictures and documents, relics and prints as much as you like—*the* real thing is almost impossible to do and in its essence the whole effect is as nought: I mean the invention, the representation of the old *consciousness,* the soul, the sense, the horizon, the vision of individuals in whose minds half the things that make ours, that make the modern world, were non-existent.

The argument is difficult. It is impossible adequately to imagine an historical character, James is saying—as he has already said in his book on Hawthorne—because the materials available are so thin as to be futile and, besides, because our minds, complex of necessity, can't be forced to rid themselves of their complexity in deference to simplicities however engaging. Or forced—as James said in a review of J. A. Altsheler's *A Soldier of Manhattan*—to "the feat of completely putting off one consciousness before beginning to take on another." What James means by "*the* real thing" is the experience so far as it has been imagined and without any limitation other than the incorrigible ones which govern any transaction between the imagination and the means at hand. The historical novel offers to bring forward people and actions as if they didn't need to be imagined and had only to be recalled, as Stephen by merely recalling Pisistratus and Alcibiades would see them trooping to him. James resents the offer as an impertinence. So he doesn't give the historical novel either of the mercies he gives the novel of reality and the fiction of romance, in the Preface to *The American:*

> The real represents to my perception the things we cannot possibly *not* know, sooner or later, in one way or another; it being but one of the accidents of our hampered state, and one of the incidents of their quantity and number, that particular instances have 'not yet come our way. The romantic stands, on the other hand, for the things that, with all the facilities in the world, all the wealth and all the courage and all the wit and all the adventure, we never *can* directly know; the things that can reach us only through the beautiful circuit and subterfuge of our thought and our desire.

I assume, then, that James regarded "the historic" as what pretends to be knowable, given a little rummaging around the archives and nothing much in the exercise of imagination. His chief sentiment, faced by the pretension, was resentment at the implication that there is a form of reality which makes the imagination redundant.

II

James's relation to the past, so far as his novels are in question, begins with a preference for periods "far enough away without being too far," as he said in the Preface to *The Aspern Papers.* "I delight," he says, "in a palpable imaginable *visitable* past—in the nearer distances and the clearer mysteries, the marks and signs of a world we may reach over to as by making a long arm we grasp an object at the other end of our own table." "That," he continues, "to my imagination, is the past fragrant of all, or of almost all, the poetry of the thing outlived and lost and gone, and yet in which the precious element of closeness, telling so of connexions but tasting so of differences, remains appreciable." Beyond a certain point, the backward view is mostly of barriers. "We are divided of course between liking to feel the past strange and liking to feel it familiar; the difficulty is, for intensity, to catch it at the moment when the scales of the balance hang with the right evenness." But the poetry of the thing outlived, I will suggest, is given to it by the one who sees it; it is not in the thing itself, however arduously it may seem to be recovered. Perhaps I should approach this another way.

James's most explicit comment on his fondness for tales of the supernatural comes in the Preface to Vol. XVII of the New York edition, the one that contains "The Altar of the Dead" and other ghosts. He wrote such things to assert the claim of individual sensibility against "the densest and most materialized aggregation of men upon earth, the society most wedded by all its conditions to the immediate and the finite." He was bound, he said, to ask himself "what may not become of individual sensibility, of the faculty and the fibre itself, when everything makes against the indulgence of it save as a conscious, and highly emphasized, dead loss."

James's determination to refute the definition of reality in terms of the immediate and the finite joins with his insistence that the imagination must not accept such a restricted field. I take it that his exasperation puts him in league with other modern writers who propose "to reinvigorate the human capacities which have been blocked by modern social existence." I quote that sentence from an exceptionally acute essay by Marianne Dekoven, "History as Suppressed Referent in Modernist Fiction" (*English Literary History*, LI, No. 1, Spring 1984), which argues that while modernist literature, as a general thing, features "an art deliberately purified of history," there are works as different as "Benito Cereno," "In the Penal Colony," and *To the Lighthouse* which make us experience the historical referent "as an unassimilable, subterranean dissonance, denying us any illusion of clarity, mastery, or resolution." In James's ghost stories, I am now prompted to say, subterranean dissonance is maintained specifically to disturb the equanimity which supposes that reality consists only of the immediate and the finite. I would go further: ghosts—or what James in the same Preface to "The Altar of the Dead" called "some imaged appeal of the lost Dead"—are the only forms in which James is willing to allow the historical referent to intrude.

James's effrontery is clear enough. He insists that the past must be just as amenable to imaginative penetration as social existence is, and that it is to be admitted only on that understanding. It is not admitted if it holds itself opaque to the qualified imagination, either because it is too far gone—"with more moves back the element of the appreciable shrinks"—or because it in any other way presents a stony glare instead of an ascertainable countenance. But perhaps James's effrontery is only a more extreme insistence than Stephen Dedalus's in regard to Pisistratus and Alcibiades, ghosts too in their way. What is a ghost? Stephen asks: "one who has faded into impalpability through death, through absence, through change of manners." I note also that, as Ortega says in *The Revolt of the Masses,* "the past is of its essence a *revenant.*" If we add that James is far less taken with objects as in themselves they really are than with the observer's response to them, we have most of the constituents of his ghost stories to hand.

The Sense of the Past was started in the first months of 1900, taken up again in late summer of that year, and then set aside. The first two books and part of the third had been written at that point. In 1914 James went back to it, revised what he had done, and dictated about sixty-five pages of Notes, indicating what he had in view and how he wished to proceed. He then continued with the novel, working on it irregularly until the autumn of 1915, for about two hundred pages, and left off at the difficult point where "sweet Nan" Midmore is about to dislodge her brilliant sister from Ralph Pendrel's affections. The book was published in its unfinished state, and with the Notes in full, in 1917.

James's division of the novel into books is an arbitrary affair: it doesn't help us in divining the shape of the work he intended. It is better, I think, to regard it as consisting of these four parts. Part 1: Ralph Pendrel, an intelligent but rather epicene young man, has published a book, *An Essay in Aid of the Reading of History.* He wants to marry Aurora Coyne, recently widowed. She imposes a condition. He must take the risk of subjecting himself to the experience of Europe, indulge his remarkably keen sense of the past—the historic passion, the backward vision—and return to her, if he will, not reluctantly but "with desire." Aurora has become an Emersonian, and she wants to discover what the best is that Americans can turn out by themselves. Part 2: Ralph is to come into the possession of a house in London, bequeathed to him by a distant relative who has read the *Essay* with admiration. The house will minister to Ralph's "sense of close communication with the old." It is no complication at all that the house has regularly been let, for the few weeks of the season, to Mrs. Midmore, her two daughters, and her son Perry. Ralph, in this respect as different from James as could well be, "was by the turn of his spirit oddly indifferent to the actual and the possible; his interest was all in the spent and the displaced, in what had been determined and composed round-about him, what had been presented as a subject and a picture, by ceasing—so far as things ever cease—to bustle or even to be."

> It was when life was framed in death that the picture was really hung up.

His notion is "to recover the lost moment, to feel the stopped pulse," but to do this by becoming the person who had once lived the moment and felt the pulse. One night he goes to the house, and spends hours wandering through its rooms: gradually he senses that he is in touch with "a conscious past, recognising no less than recognised." This sense is provoked especially by a portrait, the face of a man turned away from the painter and the viewer, and Ralph comes to imagine that the face is his own. The following day he goes to see the American Ambassador, and tells him that he and the man in the portrait are to exchange personalities and experiences. He—Ralph—is to enter upon the experience of the past, and the man in the portrait upon that of the future. (In the event, the exchange doesn't quite take place. Ralph, in becoming the other self, never entirely gives up his own.) The Ambassador accompanies him to the house, where they part. Ralph enters the house, crossing the threshold into the past.

Part 3: The past is 1820. Ralph enters, however partially, upon the experience of his exchanged self, and in that capacity is engaged to marry Molly Midmore. This third Part consists of a sequence of conversations between Ralph and Molly, her mother, her son, their friend Sir Cantopher Bland—who is in love, apparently, with Nan—and finally Nan arrives unexpectedly from the country. In effect, this Part tells the story of the Wrong Sister being displaced by the Right Sister. But it also shows Ralph and the Midmores gradually feeling that sinister forces are at large. James describes this as malaise in a letter of August 9, 1900, to Howells:

> The "central figure," the subject of the experience, has the terror of a particular ground for feeling and fearing that he himself is, or may at any moment become, a producer, an object, of this (for you and

me) state of panic on the part of others. He lives in an air of malaise as to the malaise he may, woefully, more or less fatally, find himself creating.

James was mainly interested in this Part of the novel, and especially in the exchange of panic between Ralph and the Midmores. It is also the Part which most clearly interested T. S. Eliot, who, in "The Hawthorne Aspect," compared *The Sense of the Past* with *The House of the Seven Gables:*

> James's situation is the shrinkage and extinction of an idea. The Pyncheon tragedy is simple; the "curse" upon a family a matter of the simplest fairy mechanics. James has taken Hawthorne's ghost sense and given it substance. At the same time making the tragedy much more ethereal: the tragedy of that "Sense," the hypertrophy, in Ralph, of a partial civilisation; the vulgar vitality of the Midmores in their financial decay contrasted with the decay of Ralph in his financial prosperity, when they precisely should have been the civilisation he had come to seek. All this watched over by the absent but conscious Aurora.

Not a word about the man in the portrait, we note.

The novel, in this Part, is indeed bizarre. The exorbitance of inter-pretation to the signs interpreted is so extreme that Yvor Winters thought Ralph—and James, too—virtually insane. In *Maule's Curse* he refers to "the feeling that James is nearly as hallucinated as Pendrel; it is a kind of pushing of James's passion for subtle distinctions of manner to something resembling madness." But James, in this Part, has to do several mutually excruciating things. He has to show that Ralph's determination to enter the past is perverse. He has tempted himself, and yielded to the temptation, to cross the threshold; not merely to imagine the past, but to constitute it, to *be* it. Part of the story is the treachery Ralph commits against the present, a sin he must be brought to repent. James has then to show how the social scene with the Midmores starts in a mood of elegance and brio, only to end in grimaces of terror and revulsion—and this without anything hap-pening which could be called an event. Moods and tones have to turn upon minute disclosures, avowals not absolutely convincing, little gaps and fissures where only a seamless web of goodwill and fervour would suffice.

Part 4 was never written. James's Notes show that he knew it bristled with difficulties. He had not only to show the right girl ousting the wrong one—no wonder the house is in Mansfield Square—but he had to show the relation between Nan and Ralph developing to the point at which she would sacrifice herself and let him return to the present—now "his own original precious Present." The difference between Nan and Molly is that Nan prefigures the modern sensibility, and Molly doesn't even sense that there might be such a thing. Indeed, one of the morals of the story is that we can sense, of the past, only such forces as anticipate our own and lead to us. In the end, Aurora would come over to London and rescue Ralph, but he would have to be shown wanting to be rescued. The past must be shown to be a fine place for a visit, but James wouldn't want any of his people to live there. So he insists, in the Notes, upon "Ralph's insuperable and ineffaceable margin of independence, clinging taint of modernity"; again upon his "unspeakable homesickness for his own time and place." But Ralph is only as modern as he can't help being. At this point his yearning for modernity coincides with James's prejudice in its favour; as in nearly every reference to Hawthorne, James would only patronize the past, and condescend to its penury.

But there is another emphasis we have to make. *The Sense of the Past* is also an allegory of the artistic imagination which comes upon its matter by a hunch so imperative that it feels like the touch of destiny. The artist enters upon his subject as Ralph enters the house of the imaged dead in Mansfield Square, as if something were already there, waiting for his talent. Thereafter, he proceeds upon no official plan but by a kind of tact. James calls it improvisation. Ralph in the world of 1820 comes upon whatever he needs to know as if by instinct: at one point he needs a miniature portrait of Molly if he is to produce evidence of his integrity, and when he puts his hand into his pocket, lo, he finds it there. Each improvisation, as James says, "gave way without fear to the brightening of further lights." Ralph grew many of his perceptions and possibilities "from moment to moment." The motive, which should in the normal way precede its fulfilment in action, is in Ralph's case "constituted so much more after the fact than before it." Where do these intimations come from, if not from the experience of an artist who doesn't especially know what he is doing until he has done it? James speaks of it, several times in this novel, as legerdemain, or the happy tact that made an object in Ralph's pocket "respond to the fingers suddenly seeking it." On one occasion, James pushes the analogy of the artistic process quite home:

> Aren't we perhaps able to guess that he felt himself for the ten elapsing seconds the most prodigious professor of legerdemain likely ever to have existed?—and even though an artist gasping in the act of success.

He is the artist doing the work as if naturally or by instinct, and watching himself doing it.

But the analogy is even more particular. The artist implied in the analogy is not a novelist but a painter, master of spaces and surfaces. Hence, I think, the recurrence of James's emphasis upon the theme of produced surfaces, impressions, ornaments, and appearances which don't have to be completed by any suggestion of corresponding depth. At one point James refers to "breath after breath and hint after hint—though whence directed who should say?—so spending themselves upon the surface of his sensibility that impressions, as we have already seen, were successively effaced and nothing persisted but the force of derived motion." It is this force which effaces, in an earlier passage, the distinction between ornament and use. The ornamented person is Mrs. Midmore, and Ralph is brought to understand "that he was apparently now to see ornament itself frankly recognised as use." Or later, when Ralph is somehow drawing out from Perry's face an intelligence for which there is otherwise not the least evidence:

> Violating nature, as might fairly seem, in the face before him, what was such a glimmer intelligence *of?*—this he asked himself while he watched it grow and while, into the bargain, he might have marvelled at the oddity of one's wanting to be impressive without wanting to be understood. To be understood simply as impressive—it was this that would best consort . . .

In yet another passage Mrs. Midmore's sensibility is identified with "her social surface," and Ralph is made to feel that he, too, will have to conduct himself and win through by force of his maintained manner, even though his deployment of a manner would imply, but only to himself, that his true self, whatever that might be, would be located behind the manner:

> It wouldn't of course always be the same, nor would he wish it to, since that would represent the really mad grimace; but the vision of it was precious in proportion as he felt how, so remarkably, in fact so unaccountably, he should need always to work from behind something. . . .

Behind what?—a manner, a mask, a surface, in keeping with the fact that a ghost has only visual existence and can do nothing but appear. Working behind a succession of manners is James's way of showing that Ralph retains enough independence to bring him back to modernity.

James's sense of the past, then, is opportunistic rather than devout. He does not look to the past in search of some human essence, some mythical origin in which the whole human story is deduced from something taken as the germ of it. Metaphysically incurious, he is far more concerned with the possibility, given an inch by nature, of making an ell of it by imaginative enlargement. He wants to be able to visit the past, the more passionately to return to his precious present. The past in itself was never allowed to engage an intrinsic interest. Eliot may have had this in view when he said that Hawthorne's sense of the past "exercised itself in a grip on the past itself," but that in James "it is a sense of the sense." In this, James is a characteristic American, if William Empson is right in thinking that American writers are continually exploiting their styles to effect an escape from their subjects. James's later style, according to Empson, was "sweetly funny in its way, but a patent attempt to cheat"—to cheat, I presume he means, by drawing the reader's attention away from the mere subject and concentrating it on the complexity of the linguistic surface. James was quite open about this, though he didn't call it cheating; he never claimed that his first loyalty was to the subject, or that he would sacrifice any nuance out of deference to it. The past, it appears, was just another subject to him, in no respect privileged: what counted was, as always, what he made of it. English writers feel dogged about this, because they would claim that they sacrifice much of themselves and a lot of their cleverness in favour of the subject; and that the past, among subjects, is especially worth sacrificing your virtues for.

What English writers mostly claim is that they respect the past by registering the weight of it in their language. F. R. Leavis was being typically English in claiming that you have to be English to appreciate all the historical experience that the language has gone through, and to write it accordingly. The claim was charmingly absurd, made at a time when most of the great writers in English were American or Irish. Leavis always thought Eliot, Pound, Yeats, and Joyce disabled by being foreigners, mere tourists, in English. F. W. Bateson brought much the same charge against Eliot's poetry, and insisted that English be kept up. It is only in very extreme cases that an American critic is found complaining that an American poet has deprived English words of most of their meaning so as to have them mean only the little he wants them to mean—Blackmur's essay on Cummings is a case in point. When Marianne Moore deprived English words of their weight and density so as to enhance their mobility—which she cultivated at some cost—Hugh Kenner praised her for doing so. But that was because he likes poetry to be American rather than English, and doesn't like to see bracelets of bright hair about the bone.

What this seems to suggest is that James's style, when once he had settled into it, told him what he would be free to think about such a big subject as the past. He didn't think about it at all except as offering a particular opportunity for the exhibition of a style he cared far more about. What *The Sense of the Past* says is that you should deal with the past only by first planting your feet on the ground of the present. All the better if you enforce a prejudice, that nothing in the past is as interesting as the mind with which you construe that interest.

From *Salmagundi*, Nos. 68–69 (Fall 1985–Winter 1986).

ON "GERONTION"

I have been reading "Gerontion" along with two books which make a lively context for the reading: Ronald Bush's *T. S. Eliot: A Study in Character and Style* and Alfred Kazin's *An American Procession.* Kazin's comments on "Gerontion" are not meant to be a full analysis but to trace a line of dismalness, on the question of History, from Henry Adams to Eliot. I have also been looking at a few older readings of the poem, including passages from Yvor Winters and John Crowe Ransom; and an especially far-reaching essay, which I didn't know until Bush quoted it, by Sherna Vinograd.

I should begin with a remark or two about the text of the poem. The epigraph from *Measure for Measure* (III.i.32f.) should read: "Thou hast nor youth nor age, / But as it were an after-dinner's sleep, / Dreaming on both . . ." William H. Marshall's essay "The Text of T. S. Eliot's 'Gerontion'" (*Studies in Bibliography,* Vol. IV, 1951–52) notes that Eliot approved three emendations which haven't yet been made: line 1, to delete the final comma; line 35, to read "And issues;" making it clear that he thought of "issues" as a noun going with "corridors" and not a verb going with "deceives"; line 37, to add a final comma. Line 8: some editions have "jew," some "Jew." Line 19: "juvescence" probably started as

Eliot's mistake for "juvenescence," and has been retained, perhaps for metrical preference. Line 40: "or if still believed" appears in some printings as "or is still believed," probably a printer's error. Line 42: Ransom pointed out that "Gives too soon / Into weak hands, what's thought can be dispensed with" is ungrammatical, and should read—if grammar were King—"what it's thought." Line 52: "concitation," meaning rousing, stirring up, agitating, has been obsolete since the seventeenth century.

The main allusions in the poem are well known, but I'll refer to three of them. The first two lines are adapted from a striking sentence in A. C. Benson's *Edward Fitzgerald* (1905): "Here he sits, in a dry month, old and blind, being read to by a country boy, longing for rain." The most famous allusion comes from Chapter 18 of *The Education of Henry Adams,* the first paragraph about Washington in spring:

> Here and there a negro log cabin alone disturbed the dogwood and the judas-tree, the azalea and the laurel . . . No European spring had shown him the same intermixture of delicate grace and passionate depravity that marked the Maryland May. He loved it too much, as though it were Greek and half human.

George Monteiro has noted, too (*Explicator,* Vol. XVIII: Item 30, February 1960), that Chapter 21 of Adams's *Education* seems to have given Eliot material for the poem's dying fall. Adams describes how he came back from the South Seas with John La Farge:

> Adams would rather, as choice, have gone back to the east, if it were only to sleep forever in the trade-winds under the southern stars, wandering over the dark purple ocean, with its purple sense of solitude and void.

The remaining allusions are clear enough: the New Testament, Lancelot Andrewes, *The Revenger's Tragedy, The Changeling.* Even if the allusions are ignored, the reading needn't be interrupted, except perhaps for one difficult passage:

> *And it is not by any concitation*
> *Of the backward devils.*

The devils seem to be evil spirits prompting Gerontion to backslide—
Ransom's interpretation is reasonable—and the backsliding is that of
prying into history for excitement: the source is probably *Inferno* XX,
where Dante's soothsayers and false prophets have their heads twisted
backwards. Readers may be reminded of a passage in "The Dry Salvages":

> *Men's curiosity searches past and future*
> *And clings to that dimension.*

So to the readings. On the whole, "Gerontion" has been sensitively
construed. Some early readers were troubled not by the words but by the
gaps between them. Blackmur (*Hound and Horn,* Vol. I, March 1928) felt
that Eliot hadn't quite "completed" the poem but had left the reader to
complete it for him. In *Primitivism and Decadence* (1937), Yvor Winters
was irritated by what he called "pseudo-reference" or "reference to a
non-existent plot": each of the figures named in the poem—Mr. Silvero,
Madame de Tornquist, Fraulein von Kulp, and Hakagawa—"is denoted
in the performance of an act, and each act, save possibly that of Hakagawa,
implies an anterior situation, is a link in a chain of action," but we have
"no hint of the nature of the history implied." (I'll come back to this
question.) But in *The Anatomy of Nonsense* (1943), Winters, while still
severe on Eliot's work generally, was clearly impressed by "Gerontion."
The poem, he said, "is the portrait of an individual from whom grace has
been withdrawn, and who is dying of spiritual starvation while remem-
bering his past; it is thus a prelude to *The Waste Land,* a portrait of a
society from which grace has been withdrawn and which is dying of its
own triviality and ugliness." This interpretation, or something like it, has
been pretty generally accepted. In *An American Procession,* Kazin brings
Eliot and Adams together on the ground of "Gerontion":

> Both suffered the inaccessibility of God. That is the deepest strain in
> "Gerontion": it is easier for God to devour us than for us to partake
> of him in a seemly spirit.

But Kazin forces the comparison of Eliot and Adams to the point of
asserting that what Eliot valued was religion, not faith, and that he
valued religion for the "culture" it leaves; so, apparently, did Adams,
to whom "religion is culture rather than belief, religion is literature

that attests the unbelief Adams never denied and was even sardonically proud of."

The title of the poem is satiric: not Newman's Gerontius, a respectably aged man, but a little old man—Adams, by the way, was tiny—ripe for satire. The epigraph that follows from *Measure for Measure* is a piece of mockery: the Duke, disguised, urges Claudio to adopt a perspective so lofty that his current interest in the fate of his mere life will appear of no account. But it gives the "figure" of the poem: "age" and "youth," constituents of reality, float adrift, removed at every moment by the unreality Gerontion's ego enforces. Wasted, as Kazin says, by history in which he has played no part, Gerontion is transfixed between a real action he is not resolute enough to take and the vacant gesture that mocks it.

Eliot wrote "Gerontion" in the spring and early summer of 1919. If we read the other things he wrote about the same time, including "Hamlet and His Problems," the review of *The Education of Henry Adams,* and "Tradition and the Individual Talent," we find him wrestling with a problem of peculiarly personal insistence, the exorbitance of emotion to any object that supposedly provokes and justifies it. Think of "Gerontion" and then of these sentences from "Hamlet and His Problems":

Hamlet (the man) is dominated by an emotion which is inexpressible, because it is in *excess* of the facts as they appear. . . . Hamlet is up against the difficulty that his disgust is occasioned by his mother, but that his mother is not an adequate equivalent for it; his disgust envelops and exceeds her. It is thus a feeling which he cannot understand; he cannot objectify it, and it therefore remains to poison life and obstruct action.

Later in the same essay he refers to Hamlet's buffoonery, "the buffoonery of an emotion which can find no outlet in action." What corresponds to this buffoonery, in "Gerontion," is Gerontion's unmoored eloquence.

The problem of the exorbitance of emotion to any occasion it meets compelled Eliot to formulate further questions. What would "adequacy" entail in a relation between the inner and the outer world? Is it possible to prescribe relations between the experiences we designate as knowledge, feeling, emotion, ideas, and images? The answers to these questions involved Eliot in elaborate philosophical definitions, most of them glosses on Bradley and Royce. Briefly and inadequately: Eliot insisted that one's sentient experience be understood as a continuous development and refinement of feeling, on the assumption that feeling or immediate experience is what one starts from. Thereafter consciousness, the construction of a subject, the discrimination of subject and object, emotions, ideas, and so forth should be construed as different stages in the history of one's feeling. The life of one's feeling should be continuous. As for adequacy: the emotion attendant upon any occasion should enable one to understand it and therefore to survive it. It should not be "in excess of the facts as they appear"; as they appear, I assume, to one's intelligence, which seeks, in any experience, coherence and comprehensiveness.

These are my words, not Eliot's, but it wouldn't matter if they were even less accurate than they are, because I mean them to indicate rather the site of a problem than its solution. My suggestions for a solution are nearly random; no matter, because the only "solution" that counts is punctual to our reading of "Gerontion"—nothing of further scope is in question.

I agree with those critics who say that Adams is the most pervasive presence in "Gerontion," but not when they affirm, as Kazin does, that "the Adams whom Eliot reviewed with so much distaste could only have been the speaker in 'Gerontion.'" The poem discourages this notion by starting with two lines which couldn't be attached to Adams in any reader's sense of him. It is not necessary to know that they refer to Fitzgerald: the only confirmation provided by reading Benson's book is such as to strengthen the sense, in the two lines, of spiritual lassitude. Fitzgerald's defect, according to Benson, was moral debility to the degree of disgrace: he couldn't or at least wouldn't shake himself up to an interest in anything. His life documents the "gifts reserved for age," according to the list the familiar compound ghost of "Little Gidding" supplies, starting with

> *the cold friction of expiring sense*
> *Without enchantment, offering no promise*
> *But bitter tastelessness of shadow fruit*
> *As body and soul begin to fall asunder.*

But Adams, too, was spiritually defective, though in ways which require a different description. In Eliot's review of *The Education of Henry Adams*

(*The Athenaeum,* May 23, 1919), Adams is presented as a type of the New England mind: he is compared, as an American patrician, to George Wyndham, the English Romantic aristocrat on whom Eliot commented, in *The Sacred Wood,* that he "had curiosity, but he employed it romantically, not to penetrate the real world, but to complete the varied features of the world he made for himself." Adams was always busy, but "busy with himself." A great many things interested him, "but he could believe in nothing."

> Wherever this man stepped, the ground did not simply give way, it flew into particles; towards the end of his life he came across the speculations of Poincaré, and Science disappeared, entirely. He was seeking for education, with the wings of a beautiful but ineffectual conscience beating vainly in a vacuum jar.

(I don't know how far the reader is meant to bother with Eliot's allusion to Arnold in that last sentence, or Arnold's reflection upon Shelley: it may be just a vivacity on Eliot's part. Anyway, to continue:)

> His extreme sensitiveness to all the suggestions which dampen enthusiasm or dispel conviction may be responsible for what one feels in him as immaturity, indeed as a lack of personality; an instability.

At this point Eliot comes to the question I've touched on, the ideal continuity of feeling. Adams is defective again:

> For the immaturity there may be another reason. It is probable that men ripen best through experiences that are at once sensuous and intellectual; certainly many men will admit that their keenest ideas have come to them with the quality of a sense-perception; and that their keenest sensuous experience has been "as if the body thought." There is nothing to indicate that Adams's senses either flowered or fruited: he remains little Paul Dombey asking questions.

Finally, Eliot made a brief contrast between Adams and Henry James, in James's favour, to enforce the point that "it is the sensuous contributor to the intelligence that makes the difference."

The difference, to put it more explicitly than Eliot puts it, is that feeling, in James, was indeed continuous: his ideas were distinguishable moments or phases of his feeling, inseparable from its life. Adams had an idea, and then he had another, but his ideas were disjunct from his feeling. He was like Tennyson and Browning, as Eliot described them in "The Metaphysical Poets":

> Tennyson and Browning are poets, and they think; but they do not feel their thought as immediately as the odour of a rose. A thought to Donne was an experience; it modified his sensibility.

Or, to try another contrast, Adams didn't have the power that Eliot attributed to Yeats, of preserving the liveliest emotions of youth "to receive their full and due expression in retrospect"; "for the interesting feelings of age are not just different feelings: they are feelings into which the feelings of youth are integrated."

Suppose, then, we were to think of Gerontion as a familiar compound ghost, compounded mainly of Adams and Fitzgerald; a fragmented figure in whom ideas have long since lost connection with the experience of smelling a rose; a figure spiritually febrile, vain enough to think that history must be corrupt and the world incomprehensible upon no better evidence than that his spiritual *anomie* requires these notions. Vanity, in such a case, would issue in a self-regarding style, for which the readiest examples are available in Jacobean smoke and sulphur, the revenge tragedies of Webster, Tourneur, and Middleton. Nearly any smoke and sulphur would do, provided they provoked the vaunting eloquence which works as a substitute for the action it should accompany and define.

The epigraph from *Measure for Measure* establishes a motif—that of fracture and dissociation—which remains throughout the poem. A second epigraph with a similar emphasis, Bush reports, appears in an early typescript of the poem: two lines from *Inferno* XXXIII—"Come 'l mio corpo stea / nel mondo su, nulla scienza porto" ("How my body stands in the world above, I have no knowledge"). Fra Alberigo is saying that because he betrayed his guests, his soul was taken while he lived.

So the poem begins, with Benson's sentence transposed from third to first person.

Lines 1–16: "Wasted by history" is Kazin's note on both Adams and Eliot. But for the moment it is enough to say that the speaker is dissociated from whatever he would acknowledge as reality: an epic style of it, indeed, the effect of references to Thermopylae and cutlasses being to disengage the poem from its modern sources. Or even from its modern application. Not to have fought at the Marne would have the same bearing. What the lines mainly establish is Gerontion's self-regard, especially in the elaborately suspended syntax between "Nor fought . . . " and "Bitten by flies, fought."

"A dull head among windy spaces": Bush makes a telling point about wind, which he takes as the dominant element of the poem, a Dantesque cold wind, as he describes it, embodying "a ceaseless randomness which cannot find an end and yet cannot die." The point is fulfilled in the later reference, "Vacant shuttles / Weave the wind." Bush's phrase, "Gerontion's windiness," makes a firm connection between the element and its corresponding rhetoric.

Lines 17–20: The Pharisees couldn't recognize the Messiah, demanded a sign to stimulate their conviction. The first words of St. John's Gospel, developed in Lancelot Andrewes's sermon for Christmas Day 1618, testify to silence as the wordless Word. Eliot's coined word "juvescence" calls up its opposite, the well-established "senescence." "Came Christ the tiger": I like Ransom's gloss, that "the lamb who came to be devoured turns into the tiger when Gerontion has forgotten the lamb."

Lines 21–32: The line from Adams's *Education* starts off a Black Mass of images and figures. Bush treats these and other pseudo-references as dream-play, arising from Gerontion's guilt. I am content with that, especially as it accommodates the sacrilegious and blasphemous gestures—"to be eaten, to be divided, to be drunk / Among whispers." But I am more fully persuaded by Sherna Vinograd's argument ("The Accidental: A Clue to Structure in Eliot's Poetry," *Accent,* IX, No. 4, Summer 1949). The question is: how are we to deal with Mr. Silvero, Hakagawa, and the rest, who apparently have lives which are given to us only in their shadow-play—caressing hands, bowing among the Titians, shifting the candles, and so forth? Arrested gestures are invariably sinister in Eliot's poetry, but each is sinister in a different way. Self-awareness, egotism, the self-preoccupation that Eliot feared perhaps because he saw it in himself: it is easy to attribute such a motive to these figures, and to regard them as alike involved, with Gerontion, in the vanity of restlessness and curiosity. Sherna Vinograd's essay concentrates on these figures which inhabit the poem without disclosing themselves: they are drawn over into the drifting movement of the poem, in ways hard to account for. But she makes this suggestion:

> Of course, any poem which subdues hard fact or sharp concrete image to its drift gives a sense of mastery to poet and reader. When, however, the poem's drift lies implicit somewhere between arbitrary image, symbol and an irony extended to the point of allegory, we move with the poem in the tension and terror of a world nearly but not wholly revealed.

Such a world would have the terrible, because specious, stability of the dreaming which holds it in place: we revert to Claudio's prison of self. "I have no ghosts," Gerontion complains or confesses: ghosts, I assume, would be for him genuine possessions, authentic memories, integrities of spirit.

Lines 33–47: Up to this point, Gerontion may be taken as talking to himself, musing the obscure. But he moves into a different tone, more discursive and argumentative, as if he accosted his conscience. Now that it is too late to play a part in history, all he can propose—like Adams—is to understand it. Adams thought of understanding it in terms of unity and multiplicity, order and chaos. Gerontion, projecting his guilt upon history, resents it; personifies History—"she"—the better to resent its force; and construes that force on the analogy of sexual power and the caprice with which women exert it. The motif of dissociation persists: nothing is given at the right time; "the giving famishes the craving"; we are not saved even by our virtues.

I take it that History, in this passage, is the modern substitute for the large meaning traditionally offered by religion: it includes the ambition and the vanity in a range of speculation from Hegel to Adams. It is a commonplace that the nineteenth century established History to take the place of Providence, and set about trying to discern its *Geist* as believers tried to construe their God. Gerontion's History seems as arbitrary as the most wilful God: destiny is diminished to caprice. "These tears are shaken from the wrath-bearing tree," but also from Gerontion's Jacobean network of whispers and vanities.

Lines 48–60: The main difficulty here is to construe "you" and "your." I don't see any need to give them a personal form. Gerontion can still be regarded as communing with his conscience, the communion now being more intense, more intimate. Eliot says, in his review of Adams's *Education,* that "conscience told him that one must be a learner all one's life . . . " To be intimate with one's conscience is a quality of the New England mind. Something along this line is probably enough to give "you" and "your" sufficient point.

It is in this passage of the poem that we smell the Jacobean smoke and sulphur. But the passage as a whole recalls the self-justifying swagger of Othello's last major speech. Compare Gerontion's:

> *Think at last*
> *We have not reached conclusion, when I*
> *Stiffen in a rented house*

with Othello's:

> *Set you down this;*
> *And say besides, that in Aleppo once . . .*

The rhetorical brag in the stretching between "I" and "Stiffen" is just as assertive as Othello's claim upon the record of history. "Cheering himself up," Eliot called it, in "Shakespeare and the Stoicism of Seneca":

He is endeavouring to escape reality, he has ceased to think about Desdemona, and is thinking about himself. Humility is the most difficult of all virtues to achieve; nothing dies harder than the desire to think well of oneself. Othello succeeds in turning himself into a pathetic figure, by adopting an *aesthetic* rather than a moral attitude, dramatising himself against his environment. He takes in the spectator, but the human motive is primarily to take in himself.

So, too, Gerontion cheers himself up by making words give him the splendor and the grand appearance History has denied him. But there is a difference. Othello wants to see himself looking well accoutred in pathos. Gerontion claims that it is his virtue that has destroyed him:

> *I that was near your heart was removed therefrom*
> *To lose beauty in terror, terror in inquisition.*

If he is talking to his conscience, the claim in "inquisition" is that his analytical scruple has defeated him, it has cut him adrift from the sensuous power of his old life. He then gets petulant:

> *I have lost my passion: why should I need to keep it*
> *Since what is kept must be adulterated?*

So the poem moves toward its end.

Lines 61–75: Not as easy as they seem. "These," the first word, may be taken to refer to the five senses Gerontion has just been listing. But that doesn't work well with the divergence between "membrane" and "sense":

> *These with a thousand small deliberations*
> *Protract the profit of their chilled delirium,*
> *Excite the membrane, when the sense has cooled,*
> *With pungent sauces . . .*

Better to take it as saying: "these large deliberations, and a thousand small ones, are the sort of thing I go in for to keep me going." Gerontion is explicating the "concitation" he disavowed ten lines back. I take this last section as representing the moment in which he detects himself and his self-dramatization, as if to say, "Well, who cares, what difference does my posturing make, I'm not fooling anyone, I'm not even fooling myself." This change of mood then leads naturally enough into

> *What will the spider do,*
> *Suspend its operations, will the weevil*
> *Delay?*

Otherwise put: "What does all this matter? Those who have something to do will do it. Even the insects have more talent for conviction than I have. The spider will keep going about his business: the weevil will keep on worming into the corn."

> *De Bailhache, Fresca, Mrs. Cammel, whirled*
> *Beyond the circuit of the shuddering Bear*
> *In fractured atoms.*

Who these people are—though Vinograd's comments are still valid—is less to the point than what happens to them. The phonetic trajectory of "whirled," "circuit," and "Bear" sends them, as Hugh Kenner has remarked, into the void. The void is the place where those go who are ignored by History: it is the secular name for Hell. The Bear came, as Kenner also says, from Chapman's *Bussy D'Ambois:*

> *fly where men feel*
> *The cunning axle-tree, or those that suffer*
> *Under the chariot of the snowy Bear.*

No astronomical fact requires "shuddering": it comes from the "whirling," the vortex:

> *Gull against the wind, in the windy straits*
> *Of Belle Isle, or running on the Horn.*

A reversion, this, to the epic grandeurs and pretensions with which the poem begins—a mariner's Thermopylae—and a desperate gesture to fend off History's dire intentions:

> *White feathers in the snow, the Gulf claims,*
> *And an old man driven by the Trades*
> *To a sleepy corner.*

Edward Fitzgerald's Stoicism; Adams's, or anyone's, desire to let go. The last lines are hardly necessary:

> *Tenants of the house,*
> *Thoughts of a dry brain in a dry season.*

"Thoughts" is a word of poor repute in Eliot; it is quite distinct from "thinking," because it marks the moment at which the mind, wearied, is prepared to settle for the easy victory of ideas rather than continue to explore its feeling.

That Henry Adams is one of the ghosts of the poem can hardly be doubted: much of Gerontion's feeling is continuous with Adams's sense, in the *Education,* that "Chaos was the law of nature; Order was the dream of man." But it is my impression that Yeats, just as much as Adams, represented the egotism and vanity the poem tries to repudiate.

On July 4, 1919, Eliot reviewed in *The Athenaeum* Yeats's *The Cutting of an Agate.* He maintained that Yeats was "not of this world," that his mind was "independent of experience." It was a mind "in which perception of fact, and feeling and thinking are all a little different from ours." There was no difference, Eliot maintained, between dream and reality in Yeats's work: they were identical, because each was equally independent of experience. Eliot insisted that Yeats's mind was "extreme in egoism, and therefore crude." The defect of Yeats's mind was not, in Eliot's view, that it was inconsistent, illogical, or incoherent, but that the objects upon which it was directed were not fixed: "as in his portraits of Synge and several other Irishmen, we do not seem to get the men themselves before us, but feelings of Mr. Yeats projected." In 1934 Eliot included Yeats in the parade of heretics surveyed with notable asperity in *After Strange Gods,* and he deplored the fact that "so much of Yeats's verse is stimulated by folklore, occultism, mythology and symbolism, crystal-gazing and hermetic writings." Eliot's opinion of these stimulants was no higher in 1934 than in 1919 when he wrote "A Cooking Egg" and reflected upon the instruction to be received from Madame Blavatsky in the Seven Sacred Trances. He thought Yeats's supernatural world "the wrong supernatural world," not a structure of spiritual significance but "a highly sophisticated lower mythology summoned, like a physician, to supply the fading pulse of poetry with some transient stimulant so that the dying patient may utter his last words." Where Yeats should have bowed his head in humility and penitence before a divinely revealed body of truth, he merely indulged himself in "dissociated phases of consciousness." The revelations given in those states could neither be confirmed nor denied. It is clear that Eliot thought Yeats's procedures mostly vain, a blatant example of egoism.

If we hold in our minds, while reading "Gerontion," not only Adams but Yeats, we come more vividly upon a crucial force within the form—an appalled sense, on Eliot's part, of the availability of words to provide us with specious worlds in which we may take refuge. That Eliot himself was susceptible to those worlds, and to the character of language which created them, is sufficiently documented by his relations to Poe, Tennyson, and Mallarmé. But "Gerontion" recognizes that mere words have to be redeemed, converted into the Word of God, for which silence is the only decent analogy. Thereafter, purified, the words can participate in a correspondingly authenticated world, verifiable by experience. If the words are not converted—if they persist in being their mere selves—they remain signs of our egoism, and Yeats's work is their example. In their vanity, they are doomed to indulge themselves in explosions of eloquence, arbitrary because unmoored—

> *whirled*
> *Beyond the circuit of the shuddering Bear*
> *In fractured atoms.*

—exciting the membrane with pungent sauces but coinciding with no respectable truth. Such explosions have the status of the dreadful little gestures Hamm and Clov make in Beckett's *Endgame* to give themselves the illusion that they exist, gestures which are succeeded at once by relapse into nothingness.

Of "Gerontion" as a whole, and by way of summarizing the general argument: the poem forces a certain mentality to give itself away. The mentality is what Eliot, in "Shakespeare and the Stoicism of Seneca," calls *bovarysme,* "the human will to see things as they are not." What made the poem possible was the capacity of certain styles to create the semblance of worlds other than this one. But Eliot was not a disinterested critic of that capacity. As a poet, he was addicted to such styles, especially to the style of lurid incantation which he found just as conveniently in Poe and Tennyson as in Donne, Webster, and Chapman. Eliot—again as poet; I don't speak of him in any other sense—was deeply susceptible to the ease of mind, the release of spirit, in styles which smoothed his passage beyond empirical provocations. What gives "Gerontion" its extraordinary resonance is the fact that it detects a mentality which Eliot had to recognize as partly his own—so far as the character of his poetry could be felt as evidence—and forces it, against the pressure of equivocation, to disclose itself.

From *The Southern Review,* Vol. XXI, No. 4 (October 1985).

STEVENS'S GIBBERISH

The poem goes, according to Stevens in "Notes Toward a Supreme Fiction," "from the poet's gibberish to / The gibberish of the vulgate and back again." Perhaps it moves to and fro; perhaps it is "of both / At once":

> *Is it a luminous flittering*
> *Or the concentration of a cloudy day?*
> *Is there a poem that never reaches words*
>
> *And one that chaffers the time away?*

To flitter is to fly about, casually as birds seem to fly or as people seem to talk. Luminous seems to say that the speech is adequate, as most instances of common speech are. If it is the concentration of a cloudy sky, it seems to involve more than one tone, as poetry tries to be more than common speech. To glance at the other choice: a poem that never reaches words is one so sublime or so abysmal that the reaching of words would amount only to half measures. Poetry that chaffers the time away would be poetry of the common life, good of its kind and while it lasts.

It seems to be agreed, on Frank Kermode's suggestion, that in "Notes" Stevens has Valéry's theory of poetry in mind, especially some passages from *Eupalinos,* "Pure Poetry," and "Poetry and Abstract Thought."

The passage from *Eupalinos* is one in which Socrates tells Phaedrus that if an altar were to be raised in honour of the diverse character of language, it should have three faces. The first face, almost unformed, would signify the common speech which dies almost as soon as it is born, consumed in its immediate use; it is transformed at once into the bread we ask for, the road we are shown, the anger of someone who suffers an insult. The second face would pour from its rounded lips a clear fountain of everlasting water; it would show the noblest traits, eyes large and sublime, and the strong, distended neck that sculptors give the Muses. As for the third face: it would be necessary to show an inhuman physiognomy, with those traits of severity and fineness which only the Egyptians have known how to give to the faces of their gods.

In the passage from "Poetry and Abstract Thought," Valéry writes:

Think, too, that of all the arts, ours is perhaps the one that co-ordinates the largest number of independent parts or factors: sound, sense, the real and the imaginary, logic, syntax, and the double invention of content and form . . . and all this by means of a medium essentially practical, perpetually changing, soiled, a maid of all work, everyday language, from which we must draw a pure, ideal Voice, capable of communicating without weakness, without apparent effort, without offense to the ear, and without breaking the ephemeral sphere of the poetic universe, an idea of some self miraculously superior to Myself.

The third passage is from "Pure Poetry," where Valéry says that common language

is the fruit of the disorder of life in common, since beings of every nature, subjected to innumerable conditions and needs, receive it and use it to further their desires and to set up communications among themselves. Whereas the poet's language, although he necessarily uses the elements provided by this statistical disorder, constitutes, on the contrary, an effort by one man to create an artificial and ideal order by means of a material of vulgar origin.

The passages are not entirely commensurate. Two of them are content to make a distinction between ordinary speech and poetic speech; which corresponds to a distinction between a local communicative purpose and an ideal act of composition; between the accidental disorders of ordinary life and an ideal order issuing in an ideal Voice; between one's ordinary self and a self uncannily superior to it; and finally between the crowd of people who speak and the one man, the poet, who differs from ordinary people by that sole virtue. The passage from *Eupalinos* goes further, and proposes a third face or mode of expression in which language seems to go beyond itself and is fulfilled only by inhuman or divine forms: these don't correspond even to the superior type of expressiveness or communication featured by the second face.

There isn't much ordinary speech in Stevens's poetry, though there are lines one might imagine someone saying in thoughtful circumstances:

> *It may be that one life is a punishment*
> *For another . . .*

Even in jaunty weather, Stevens is a majestic poet: he found it hard, and rarely tried, to forget Milton, Wordsworth, Emerson, and Pater. Whatever he meant by the gibberish of the vulgate, it didn't come naturally to him.

The second face of language was more congenial to him, its demands were those he would in any case have made: high speech, a voice not the same as his own but a superior version of it, dictions reluctant to be consumed in their use:

> *Two things of opposite natures seem to depend*
> *On one another, as a man depends*
> *On a woman, day on night, the imagined*
> *On the real. This is the origin of change.*
> *Winter and spring, cold copulars, embrace*
> *And forth the particulars of rapture come.*

Cold copulars: copular is an adjective made to embrace a noun, copula being in logic and grammar "that part of a proposition which connects subject and predicate." In Roman law, copula meant sexual union. The analogy keeps us among ordinary desires, but the phrase itself is majestic.

The third face is seen in Stevens's poetry when he recognizes, brave humanist as he is, that the human imagination did not create the world:

The clouds preceded us

> *There was a muddy centre before we breathed.*
> *There was a myth before the myth began,*
> *Venerable and articulate and complete.*

There is little to be said about the clouds that preceded us, or about the divine power that created them, but the face must be recognized as divine or otherwise inhuman.

Even if we keep to the first two faces, which correspond respectively to common speech and poetic speech, we find differences between Valéry's theory and Stevens's. Valéry supposes that common speech is adequate to its occasions; it says what is required, and disappears. Poetic speech wants to remain after the occasion that incited it has lapsed: it claims a character or quality of interest beyond its mere usefulness. But Stevens says that common speech and poetic speech are both gibberish; though he thinks of each, I assume, at some pitch of extremity where it discloses not its mundane but its essential nature. He doesn't say that they are the same gibberish. Nor does he say, as Valéry does, that common speech is adequate as far as it goes and that it is willing to be consumed in its use. Stevens's linguistic theory is more radical than Valéry's; he doesn't accept that common speech coincides at every point with the needs it serves. He is closer in that respect to William Carlos Williams, who says, in the first Book of *Paterson,* that people die incommunicado because "the language, the language / fails them." The language "is divorced from their minds."

R. P. Blackmur has made two comments on Stevens's lines. Where Stevens says that the poet

tries by a peculiar speech to speak

> *The peculiar potency of the general,*
> *To compound the imagination's Latin with*
> *The lingua franca et jocundissima*

Blackmur takes the imagination's Latin to mean "the 'received,' objective and authoritative imagination, whether of philosophy, religion, myth, or dramatic symbol." Presumably Blackmur has in mind whatever it is, still available as belief or animating lore, which the poet can allude to as authoritative: all the better that he can't claim to have invented it. Latin had this force in Christendom for many centuries and in the Roman Catholic Church till recently: it testified to an order of truth and observance, a common possession free from the disorder of one's particular self.

In "Notes Toward a Supreme Fiction" the poet seeks a complete poetic speech by bringing together two constituents: "the imagination's Latin" presumably he knows already, and we may construe it as tradition, so far as it is alive; and he must complete the Latin with "the gibberish of the vulgate," otherwise the lingua franca et jocundissima.

Vulgate is printed in lower case. Superior case, the Vulgate is the Latin version of the Bible as made by St. Jerome in A.D. 406, a translation moving toward commonness and community by comparison with the Hebrew, even though by comparison with every vernacular language it is unyieldingly grave. It is not surprising that the pull of "vulgus" brought the Vulgate first into lower case and finally made it refer to common speech, the ready vernacular on ordinary occasions. But the equivocation of the word allows us to think that just as there is an esoteric Hebrew behind Jerome's Latin, and a Logos behind the Hebrew, so there is a complete speech, transparent to itself, behind both the common speech and the exalted forms of poetry. This is the poetry that never reaches words. The imagination's Latin is the little of such poetry that has been translated; that is, received as tradition.

Blackmur's second comment is that

> gibberish is not a frivolous word in the context; it is a word manqué more than a word mocking. One gibbers before a reality too great, when one is appalled with perception, when words fail though meaning persists: which is precisely, as Mr. Eliot suggested in a recent number of the *Partisan Review,* a proper domain of poetry.

The reference is to "The Music of Poetry," where Eliot speaks of a situation in which "the poet is occupied with frontiers of consciousness beyond which words fail, though meanings still exist." Presumably Eliot has in mind that particular words fail by not being enough, or that words as such fail at those frontiers, as the imagination's Latin fails before the Hebrew, and the Hebrew fails before the Logos or before an ultimate Heideggerian silence. Or the failure may be constitutional, according to Shelley's *A Defence of Poetry*, where "the mind in creation is as a fading coal," and "when composition begins, inspiration is already on the decline." In any case, gibberish testifies to a failure not local or incidental but categorical: it is merely the best that can be done with words, and it is not enough.

But there is another gibberish which corresponds not to words that fail but to words that drive meanings beyond their rational forms into a void or a vertigo. It is by taking the chances offered by words—their arbitrary sounds and contingent senses—that the poet drives meanings ahead of anything he would recognize as his prior intention.

We have now to ask whether failure, according to Stevens, coincides with the general complaint of modern poets that the words are not right, the language is woefully corrupt; or that the success of words, its particular form, is disgusting to hieratic poets like Stevens. Is Stevens making the complaint we hear in Eliot's *Four Quartets,* that the words we speak are already last year's and therefore useless for present need? Or has Stevens a complaint of his own?

There is a chapter in James Guetti's book *Word-Music* which bears upon the question. Guetti proposes to show that Stevens's poems never stay long with the rational or cognitive procedures they seem to favour: the poems engage in these procedures only to veer from them, as if upon a change of heart. It is as if, "after exercising one faculty, we were then prepared to exercise another." Stevens's view of reality, according to Guetti, "does not depend upon a nostalgic model of a world without intelligence but upon the continuing dynamic of the intelligence exhausting itself in order to achieve images beyond itself." At the end of such a process we see "the uprising of things arresting beyond our intelligence of them." We see what Stevens calls "the palm at the end of the mind."

We could develop this argument in two ways. We could say that the palm at the end of the mind is the irrefutable but incomprehensible reality to which gibberish is the only testament. Or that when Stevens comes to the end of cognitive processes, it is because he remembers, not a moment too soon, his tenderness for the irrational, the unpredictable. A gaunt version of this sentiment would be Valéry's third face, that of Egyptian divinity. Stevens sees the palm in two moods; in one, he resents his sense of having come to the end of the mind; in the other, a far less frequent sentiment, he is pleased to acknowledge that the world is indeed as it appears to be without our ministry. To be at the end of the mind in the latter mood is to commit oneself, like Alain Robbe-Grillet, to the bareness of denotation: in the other, to let words run beyond themselves or beside themselves into gibberish.

The poem "Man Carrying Thing" has an implication for the argument. It begins:

> *The poem must resist the intelligence*
> *Almost successfully*

and goes on to illustrate the aphorism by way of a scene in a landscape or in a painting:

> *A brune figure in winter evening resists*
> *Identity. The thing he carries resists*
>
> *The most necessitous sense. Accept them, then,*
> *As secondary (parts not quite perceived*
>
> *Of the obvious whole . . .)*

The poem moves between two levels of motivation. According to one, the mind imposes its choice categories upon experience, and declares them authoritative. That is the level represented by identity, "the most necessitous sense," the primary free from doubt because the mind would have it so. On the same level we have the storm as distinct from the first hundred flakes of snow which it includes, and at last the bright obvious which is such because the mind enforces the conclusion that it is. According to the second motive, the poem is the form resistance takes; it secretes or acknowledges the brune figure and the thing he carries. These are secondary things, not required by an insistent intelligence: they are good precisely because theirs is the poetry of what is uncertain, floating like a hundred flakes of snow. The storm is primary in our sense of it, and the snow and the other constituents of the storm are secondary because it is intelligence which gathers all these sensory events together and names them as a storm. The failure of the poem's resistance to the force of intelligence begins with "a horror of thoughts that suddenly are real";

because the thoughts have ousted the earlier constituents of reality, and that is their horror. The degree of failure is shown by the motionlessness of the bright obvious. The two levels of motivation have now been reduced to one, the secondary overwhelmed by what the intelligence declares to be primary. Stevens returns to his aphorism once more in his "Adagia": "Poetry must resist the intelligence almost successfully." That is: poetry must exceed, if necessary to the degree of scandal, the forms which intelligence prescribes; presumably by yielding to chance, association, dream, the irrational.

What then does Stevens want? Not the satisfied prescriptions of intelligence, however much he reveres intelligence; because it excludes too much. But he is not willing to hand himself over to irrationality—as Surrealists do—because that would also exclude too much. What he seems to want is either that the mind will transform itself, and run so wildly beyond or beside its official forms as to include the irrational in its processes. Or else that the mind, coming to the end of its processes, will point beyond itself toward images it cannot predict or specify, images corresponding to "the hum of thoughts evaded in the mind."

There is some evidence for these possibilities in "The Irrational Element in Poetry," an essay in which Stevens maintains that "what interests us is a particular process in the rational mind which we recognize as irrational in the sense that it takes place unaccountably." Put like that, it has to include inspiration, the gift of tongues. But Stevens allows, too, for the wilfulness by which a poet of a certain tradition may deliberately open himself to the irrational. He quotes, in an eccentric translation, the famous letter in which Rimbaud says that "it is necessary to be a seer, to make oneself a seer. The poet makes himself a seer by a long, immense and reasoned unruliness of the senses. . . . He attains the unknown." Unruliness isn't quite as accurate as disordering, which is an act rather than a condition. However, it leads Stevens to brood upon the relation between the unknown and the known. He says that

> there are those who, having never yet been convinced that the rational has quite made us divine, are willing to assume the efficacy of the irrational in that respect. The rational mind, dealing with the known, expects to find it glistening in a familiar ether. What it really finds is the unknown always behind and beyond the known, giving it the appearance, at best, of chiaroscuro.

This would undermine the parable of the palm at the end of the mind, except that the poetic imagination can't be equated with the rational mind and doesn't suffer from its pedantry. The discovery of the palm is the prize to be won by the poetic imagination, a gift of the gods.

As an occasion on which Stevens thought of the mind as transforming itself to include the irrational and to traffic with gibberish, I quote a passage from "Notes," "It Must Be Abstract," section three, where the poet's strongest desire is to find thought going back to its beginning, taking up the quality of Firstness—in C. S. Peirce's vocabulary—the sense of a state of being or existing independent of anything else—as if thinking could be felt in the blood and along the heart. The section begins with a proposition:

> *The poem refreshes life so that we share,*
> *For a moment, the first idea . . . It satisfies*
> *Belief in an immaculate beginning*
>
> *And sends us, winged by an unconscious will,*
> *To an immaculate end.*

Poetry, Stevens here implies, is still an act of the mind, but an act performed in such association with a sense of immaculate beginning that thinking is indistinguishable from intuition. Having provided the theme, he gives the first variation upon it:

> *We say: At night an Arabian in my room,*
> *With his damned hoobla-hoobla-hoobla-how,*
> *Inscribes a primitive astronomy*
>
> *Across the unscrawled fores the future casts*
> *And throws his stars around the floor. By day*
> *The wood-dove used to chant his hoobla-hoo*
>
> *And still the grossest iridescence of ocean*
> *Howls hoo and rises and howls hoo and falls.*
> *Life's nonsense pierces us with strange relation.*

Stevens informed a puzzled Hi Simons that "the Arabian is the moon" and the unscrawled fores "the unformed handwriting." The primitive astronomy is, I assume, a peremptory destiny inscribed upon a future otherwise indeterminate. The difficulty is that Stevens was ready to find resemblances where another man would see only differences. Or he was ready to declare a resemblance between two things on the evidence of their having even a minor attribute in common. In "Three Academic Pieces" he construed resemblance as the first principle which makes possible not only likeness but relatedness and appearance. Bearing in mind that the wood-dove or stock-dove is the amorous bird of Venus, and that Stevens has an early poem in which the poet's "golden strings"

> *Resound in quiet night,*
> *With an Arab moon above,*
> *Easing the dark senses need,*
> *Once more, in songs of love.*

Harold Bloom has interpreted the Arabian passage on the assumption that "the Arabian is the moon as erotic stimulus to a poet aged sixty-three, who reacts with a necessary bitterness." The whole passage is then a reverie on the failure of the erotic imagination, the voice of the turtle "not a hoobla-hoo, but a hoobla-how, the 'how' crassly referring to one's own sexuality." Once one lived an erotic life by day, but now "vain desire rises to torment one only by night." The Arabian moon has potency to spare, to waste, to throw about one's room: the ocean ceaselessly rises and falls as if it spoke the gibberish of erotic powers equally possessed.

Readers who haven't been told or aren't much illuminated by being told that the Arabian is the moon may choose to see in him a shadow of the Arabian Nights, or of the Arabian bird, the phoenix, or of the Arabian sect whose members believed that the soul dies with the body and rises again with it at the Resurrection. The relation between hoo and hoobla-how and hoobla-hoobla-hoobla-how is, to say the least and the most of it, a relation of resemblance, which Stevens in "Three Academic Pieces" was careful to distinguish from identity. "Both in nature and in metaphor," he said, "identity is the vanishing-point of resemblance"; and further, that the prodigy of nature "is not identity but resemblance and its universe of reproduction is not an assembly line but an incessant creation." So, in the poem, there is resemblance between the Arabian, the wood-dove, and the ocean as forms of power no longer available to the nocturnal speaker. Intelligence may not respect the resemblance, or it may think its casualness a scandal: it is gibberish, but which gibberish? But that only shows why "the poem reveals itself only to the ignorant man"; it is the ignorant man who appreciates, without being too intelligent about it, that "life's nonsense pierces us with strange relation."

Hugh Kenner, determined not to take Stevens's poems as seriously as he has taken Pound's and Eliot's, has quoted this one to make a case for reading Stevens as a Nonsense poet, "the most insouciant of all Nonsense poets, apotheosis of an honored métier, he for whom even a Carroll or a Lear came but to prepare the way." Kenner's authority on Nonsense is Elizabeth Sewell, whose *The Field of Nonsense* ascribes to Carroll and Lear what Kenner calls "the impulse to use words as counters in an arbitrary game whose criteria are pattern, symmetry, and elusive quasi-sense." In Kenner's version, the aim of Nonsense is "to detach the rituals of high poetry from their normal structures of meaning, and to draw more or less explicit attention to their self-sufficiency as rituals." The formula isn't entirely accurate: rituals can't be self-sufficient, they summarize and articulate a force of sentiment which coincides with a force of belief. Detached from this double force, they become something else. But if, while attending upon the procedures of French Symbolism, you chose to disown their portentousness, you might reasonably resort to Nonsense for an escape clause.

It shouldn't be hard, in that spirit, to get from Nonsense to gibberish with the aid of two of Sewell's sentences which Kenner hasn't quoted. The first: "In Nonsense all the world is paper and all the seas are ink." The second: "Nonsense can only engage the force towards disorder in continual play." But if you think Kenner's reference to elusive quasi-sense misleading, as I do, you may turn again in the more feasible direction of Eliot's "The Music of Poetry" and find that Lear's non-sense, as Eliot describes it, "is not vacuity of sense: it is a parody of sense, and that is the sense of it." "The Jumblies" is "a poem of adventure, and of nostalgia for the romance of foreign voyage and exploration." "The Yongy-Bongy Bo" and "The Dong with a Luminous Nose" are "poems of unrequited passion—'blues,' in fact." We enjoy the music, which is of a high order, Eliot says, "and we enjoy the feeling of irresponsibility towards the sense." This is closer to what we need. Nonsense poetry acknowledges particular traditions of making sense, but releases the reader from the piety the traditions expect of him; as Stevens's early poems release the reader, for a while, from the claims of reason's click-clack which he will have to yield to in the end. Gibberish is superior to any official syntax in its testimony to the unknown behind the known; and it has only this disability, that it denies us the gratification of construing it. We can spend a vacation in it, but we can't live there. What can be construed has a different disability. E. M. Cioran has remarked that "it is the indigence of language which renders the universe intelligible." The difference between the poet's gibberish and the gibberish of the vulgate is that the latter is regularly mistaken for adequate speech by those, including Valéry, who so use it; the former is known, at least to poets, both for what it is and for the desperation with which it makes gestures toward what can't be known. When the mood of those gestures changes and turns both desperation and resignation into comic buoyancy, we have Nonsense. Corresponding turns in painting may be seen in Chirico, Klee, and Matisse.

The poet's gibberish arises, then, from a mood of debonair irresponsibility toward accredited meanings. It may be found wherever one set of values displaces those of rationality; as in Anselm's formula *fides quaerens intellectum,* which scandalizes rationalists by turning upside down a conventional order of privilege. Or when the Fool holds King Lear back from delirium by pestering him with conundrums. Or when language is used not as an instrument of communication but intrinsically, as in Mallarmé's assertion that speech has merely a commercial relation to reality and that the poet should hand over the initiative to words as such. Or when Elizabeth Sewell says, in her study of Valéry, that "words are the mind's one defence against possession by thought or dreams."

> Words made into poetry, the prophetic ornamented discourse, carefully chained lest too much freedom should let in the powers of darkness—these will effect such resolution as can be achieved between the logical and the irrational functions of the mind.

So, too, when we refer to language as such; when we treat the signifier as palpable and the signified as a shadow; when we let connotations overwhelm denotations; then we cultivate gibberish as the form of our desire, endless by definition.

Rhyme, for instance. The fact that "wrist" rhymes with "Pyrrhonist" is of no interest to a speaker of English who wants to get on with whatever he's doing. It is a phonetic coincidence merely. But I recall from

Blackmur's essay on *Crime and Punishment* a striking defence of coincidence. Far from belittling the probabilities, Blackmur said, "the use of coincidence in art, like the sense of it in life, heightens the sense of inevitability; for coincidence is the artist's way of representing those forces in us not ourselves." Coincidence "creates our sense of that other self within us which we neither can ever quite escape nor quite meet up with." The application to rhyming words is not exact, and is the better for that consideration. The plethora of coincidences in *Romeo and Juliet* may indeed make us feel that there is a mischievous spirit at large thwarting our best designs. But the fact that "wrist" rhymes with "Pyrrhonist" is a happy chance that needn't be acted upon; it arises from the limited though large number of phonetic relations in English, and it lies dormant till a poet pays attention to it. It has nothing to do with need. Blackmur's remark about coincidence is applicable if we choose to make it so, but it depends upon a choice: to regard "those forces in us not ourselves" either as the fate lying in wait for us or as opportunities which will stay till we call upon them. In "A Lot of Night Music," Anthony Hecht took them as a congenial gibberish which he could just as easily have let lie dormant:

> Even a Pyrrhonist
> Who knows only that he can never know
> (But adores a paradox)
> Would admit it's getting dark. Pale as a wrist-
> Watch numeral glow,
> Fireflies build a sky among the phlox,
>
> Imparting their faint light
> Conservatively only to themselves.

The poem is under way, picking up phonetic offerings which, outside the poem, would have seemed improbable but, inside, quickly seem to have the force of destiny. It's hardly likely that Hecht began with Pyrrhonist and wrist. He may have started with the sense of things metaphorically getting dark; then found an apt figure in the wristwatch that glows in the dark only as far as itself. Fireflies among the phlox may have suggested themselves as a companionable figure. And the thought that we can't be sure, and that we nevertheless act as if we were, implies a Pyrrhonist as the professional mind that proceeds thus. But this suggests a line of thinking, as if it could go on independently of words, for which the right words are by good fortune found. It may not have happened that way. For all I know, Hecht may have begun with the phonetic coincidence of Pyrrhonist and wrist and set about finding a rational process to make use of it.

There is also the gibberish of syntax, which Kenneth Burke described in *Counter-Statement* as qualitative progression; where the transition in, say, a poem from one moment to the next is effected not by rational or official development but by association or contrast. The progression is psychological in the sense that a surfeit of one mood suggests another mood as relief: the only law governing such transitions is natural or constitutional.

If we transfer to the reader the faculty of gibberish hitherto ascribed to the poet, we offer him the latitude of reading which Roland Barthes proposed; not the duty of interpreting, moment by dutiful moment, the words on the page, but the pleasure that goes its own playful way. Barthes urged readers to act wilfully, running to excess in whatever directions they chose; anything, rather than accept the official rhetoric evidently enforced by a poem or novel. According to Barthes, there is no single privileged interpretation: the text is an occasion for being wilful.

In this respect, Barthes's recommendation coincides with Derrida's, especially in the well-known essay in which Derrida distinguished two kinds of interpretation and called one of them play. A sober interpretation is the result of trying to discover in a book a truth or an origin which is independent of the play of signs. Play, the adversary kind of interpretation, is indifferent to the privilege of stability or meaning; it scorns the search for a reassuring source of authority. Derrida's play is the reader's gibberish. But James Hans has pointed out, in *The Play of the World,* that Derrida's play is constrained in two respects; "first, the beginning of play is always necessarily connected to a foreproject, to a series of prejudgments that are at issue in the activity of play itself; and second, the result of play is a structure, a framework or order that has been confirmed by the play." It is this structure, according to Hans, which "will become part of the structure of prejudgments that will affect future play." The point is contentious. Derrida's rhetoric, as he well knows, is subject to the same constraints that apply to every post-Nietzschean form of thought: they are parasitic upon the very structures they would destroy.

But the versions of gibberish I have mentioned are enough to indicate the desire to evade the imperatives of reason. I have not mentioned dreams or delirium, mainly because the attempts to assimilate dreams to the structure of language seem to me to have confused a valid issue; and I find it disgusting to try to endow madness with the glamour of visionariness, as David Cooper did in his introduction to Foucault's book on madness. I don't believe that madness is "a form of vision that destroys itself by its own choice of oblivion in the face of existing forms of social tactics and strategy." By its own choice!

Reverting to Stevens's poem: the poet's gibberish points toward an Utopia of language, in which, the poet's dealings with fictiveness being what they are, the possible is accorded just as much authority as the actual. There has never been a strong reason for considering the two gibberishes to be the same; if the poem goes from one to the other, it is because it can't for long remain with either of them. Movement between the two traces the bohemian poet's dealing, however ruefully, with the common speech he regards as bourgeois. Does the poet evade us? Stevens asks. He would if he could; if he had a language so occult that it would keep the poet in a private Utopia of the sublime.

The poet, a few lines later, is the speaker "Of a speech only a little of the tongue"; mainly, I think, because Stevens believed that the mind can go further in thought than the tongue can say. There is a jotting in his "Adagia" to that effect: "The eye sees less than the tongue says. The tongue says less than the mind thinks." It is an unfashionable belief. But more to the point is the next assertion in the poem, that what the poet seeks is the gibberish of the vulgate. Presumably if he were to discover it, it would not be what it seemed to be at the start; the poet's finding it would mean that he had reached an accommodation between his own desires and vulgar desires: an improbable felicity, except that there must be occasions on which poets don't want to differ from other people.

I have to quote again the final passage in which Stevens says of the poet:

> *He tries by a peculiar speech to speak*

> *The peculiar potency of the general,*
> *To compound the imagination's Latin with*
> *The lingua franca et jocundissima.*

The lines have drawn a good deal of comment, notably from Harold Bloom, who disapproves of them. Stevens, he says, weakly misreads Valéry by insisting "that the poet is beyond language, a Transcendentalist and very American dream."

> Yet Stevens moves us here by the very honesty of his own doubt. It is wholly Emersonian that Stevens posits an oratory at our "bluntest barriers," our ultimate limitations, which is a kind of speech opposed to poetry-as-writing, a speech indeed of the direct will and so "only a little of the tongue." This is the Emersonian emphasis upon the poet as transcending his own poetry, upon an ideal or possible orator who will destroy all limitations. What is least convincing is the declaration in the canto's final lines, where Stevens speaks of himself as if he were Whitman (or, in our time, Williams), when in fact he was wholly of those who speak "the imagination's Latin."

But it is not a matter of Stevens as Whitman or as Williams. He had moods in which kinship with Whitman was vigorous, as in "Like Decorations in a Nigger Cemetery," and his review of Williams shows that the two had much in common, including access to a lingua franca. What is at issue is Stevens's desire, on behalf of the poet as such—the poet as the idea or paradigm of poetry and therefore indeed beyond his mere poems—to outdo his characterization of himself: a Latinist, no doubt, if only one characterization were allowed, but in the present mood desiring to complete his Latin with a lingua franca et jocundissima. The big dictionaries say that lingua franca is a mixed language used in the Levant, consisting largely of Italian words deprived of their inflections; and, more generally, any mixed jargon formed as a medium of communication between people of different native languages. A rough-and-ready lingo, it has only one purpose, to get business transacted. If it were to be, in addition, jocundissima, it would be a nonchalant language, free of scruple and misgiving. A language compounded of the imagination's Latin and such a lingo would be wonderfully complete; it would testify to a way of being present in the world more complete than any way in which Stevens could have construed himself as present. So I take these last lines as a celebration of the central poet, invoked as fully by Shelley as by Emerson, the poet who exists only in the idea of such a being, and the desire that he should exist. The lingo is the opposite of gibberish in one respect, while it sounds gibberish to a Latinist: it doesn't gibber, as before a reality that exceeds it; it is entirely adequate, subject only to the limitations of its local business, limitations which for the time being aren't thought to count.

Bringing these considerations together: when I first read Stevens's poems, I took him at his word and assumed that he was chiefly a philosophic poet, heir to Lucretius, Wordsworth, and Goethe. Knowledge was his category: even if his epistemologies seemed wayward, they could be construed within a philosophic tradition continuous from Plato to Santayana and William James. Realism and Idealism provided the necessary terms. I tried, as many other readers of Stevens did, to ascribe to him a formal position in epistemology. It was difficult: he seemed careless by comparison with the strict philosophers. Gradually I started thinking that his contradictions issued not from errors of logic but from varieties of mood and humour. Now I think his moodiness such that it undermines the category itself. Knowledge is only the interest of a mood among many moods. Or if we insist on retaining it as a privileged category, we have to set up Pleasure to take the rigour out of it. I would now read Stevens's ostensibly philosophic poems as poems of pleasure; exalted pleasure, indeed, as when a mind circulates among its possibilities, only one of which is the consideration that the only emperor is the emperor of ice cream.

It is not necessary to maintain a strict distinction between eating ice cream and reading Valéry. Both of these experiences can be regarded as forms of knowledge. But we become better readers of Stevens, better in the sense of unhaggling, when we take both experiences chiefly as forms of pleasure. Not a philosophic poet, then, but a resourceful epicurean, waiting upon life's nonsense just as attentively as upon its sense.

TRILLING, MIND, AND SOCIETY

There is a passage in *Matthew Arnold* in which Lionel Trilling, pondering "The Scholar Gypsy" and "Empedocles on Etna," reflects upon the source and provocation of those poems in Arnold's sensibility: "The great truth that Arnold is now to keep ever before him and to develop with increasing explicitness is that all human values, all human emotions, are of social growth if not of social origin. His poems do not rest in the statement of his individual emotion; they are always hinting a cause. Understanding what the human individual must do for himself, Arnold knows how much of what man does for himself depends upon what society allows him to do." Trilling's preoccupation with society arises from the same cause: knowing that people cannot live or act in a vacuum, he asks whether the air provided by society sustains or poisons them. But he puts the question with a notable difference. It was common for critics to maintain, during the years in which Trilling wrote his major books, that the relation between the individual artist and society was a relation between virtue and vice, or at least a relation between the highest aesthetic purity and the worst conditions which an indifferent society would impose upon a pure intention. Society was deemed to be a bourgeois conspiracy of the worst to thwart the best: the artist was regarded as a holy man in the degree of his victimage. Artist and critic were supposed to huddle together for comfort in the storm, since their motives were equally noble. The storm was a monster compounded of money and aggression.

Trilling was never persuaded by these common assumptions, and he turned their rhetoric upside down. I do not imply that he put his talent at the disposal of a mass society or that he tried to take the harm out of the standard social purposes; but he did not encourage the artist to take spiritual comfort from the grossness of material conditions or to regard himself as a victim of social alienation. Trilling did not interpret the relation between artist and society in terms so favourable to the artist that society could only be construed as barbarism and the artist as a tragic hero. He continued to urge upon the artist a concern for social consequence even when the particular society in question merited every rebuke it received. He did not turn away from society or from the values of responsibility, companionship, and mutuality which the concept of society almost desperately entailed. He never encouraged the artist to think that he might dispense with society, despise its purposes, and find within himself a sufficient moral authority. Trilling did his major work during years in which he felt that the idea of a society was breaking down: not merely societies at large, the relationships and institutions which constitute their substance where they have substance, but the instinctive respect for social aims, the purposes certified by the sentiment of *societas,* the responsibility of one to another. We may leave aside for the moment the question of this sentiment in Trilling himself: it is possible to maintain that he had to persuade himself of the validity of the sentiment before he could convince others. It is a commonplace that the American imagination is inclined to be disappointed by the fruits of society and civilization and that it guards itself against disappointment by withholding expectation: it does not put its trust in societies. It is hardly to be expected that Trilling would always feel himself immune to this distemper or would always find his informal sentiments in accord with his official argument. I speak of hints and guesses and would find it hard to offer proof. For the moment it is enough to say that Trilling set out to attach to the sentiment of society an aura of conscientiousness and value. He described the idea of society as if it had, by comparison with the individual people who compose it at any moment, not of course historical priority but logical priority; not priority of time but privilege of idea and feeling. He persuaded his readers to find even in the imperfections of society a perfection lost, abused, but not destroyed. The mind engaged in the understanding of society is encouraged to see, even in the monstrous lineaments offered to its attention, a sequence of human possibilities. At a time when other critics were repudiating the idea of society as a source of value because particular societies were demonstrably corrupt, Trilling kept the lines of communication open.

Indeed Trilling was ready to withhold himself from some of his own possibilities and set a limit upon his produced insights, lest his mind break the connection between individual feeling and purposes socially communicable. Blackmur said of Trilling that he cultivated "a mind never entirely his own, a mind always deliberately to some extent what he understands to be the mind of society, and also a mind always deliberately to some extent the mind of the old European society taken as corrective and as prophecy." The mind Trilling insisted upon using was not the furthest reach of his powers but his choice of attributes: the choice testified to his scruple as well as ministering to his temper. He thought it decent to restrain his own will before urging his readers to observe a similar degree of decorum. Trilling used not the general mind of society but a particular mind compounded of his own major purposes and the purposes he ascribed to the best intentions of a possible society rather than the particular society in question and in force. Such a mind could not be entirely American, since it would not release itself from the hope of living in an answerable society and making a home for itself in forms domestic, moral, and historical. A hundred reasons prevented the mind from being entirely European, reasons of responsibility and temper, despite the attributes which enabled Trilling to keep the peace somehow between Arnold and Freud. We are free to call his mind artificial if we redeem the character of artifice and emphasize the motives which made it, in Trilling's case, judicious: he would have found it easier to use a mind entirely his own than to rely upon the particles of general intelligence which might still be redeemed.

The sentiment I have quoted from Trilling on Arnold is now well established, even commonplace. Every structuralist is ready to assert that we are determined in our inner lives by the social and linguistic codes we think we have mastered: what we feel and say is merely felt and said through us: we are instruments rather than subjects. The argument is familiar, and I suppose we do in part believe it. But Trilling's urbanity of choice and restraint is not commonplace. I cannot think of any structuralist who has Trilling's sense of the cost of a human act, his conviction that the question of mind and society is morally crucial. It is possible to say that the individual mind is constituted by the codes it ostensibly uses; it is also possible to make the announcement in virtually any tone we choose, doom-laden, rueful, ironic, or bland. The intonation makes a difference because it expresses our sense of the considerations we have to set aside before we come to a conclusion: we are blunt if we do not register misgiving along with the conclusion.

It is my impression that Trilling insisted upon the validity of mind as an integral force and held himself aloof from the necessitarian argument. The idea of society, like the idea of mind, was a matter of conviction; if you released yourself from responsibility, you insisted upon providing the force of conscience from your own moral resources, perhaps enriched by your aesthetic sense. If you acted upon the assumption that mind is merely a function of the governing codes, you chose slavery in preference to freedom. Trilling was severe upon these motives: they were either abject or arrogant; they pretended that mind could float free from society or that the least evidence of a movement of mind was a delusion. In the passage I have quoted on Arnold, Trilling goes on to speak of the mind's dependence upon society and to say that "only the greatest minds can even seem to be free of this dependence—and they but seem to be." But while it is probably true that "all human values, all human emotions, are of social growth if not of social origin," there are certain intellectual processes which arise from a refusal to obey this truth. I have in view the act which Arnold feared and distrusted, "the dialogue of the mind with itself," a dialogue which began when "the individual, absorbed in separate interests, withdrew from the service of the commonwealth" (a phrase from S. H. Butcher which Trilling quotes with admiration in his book on Arnold). The modern version of that dialogue often issues as the mind's attendance upon the heuristic possibilities of language, since these arise from the grammatical and phonetic character of the language rather than from circumstances directly social or political. The names of Beckett, Borges, and the Joyce of *Finnegans Wake* stand for such possibilities. Trilling's sympathy did not embrace those activities, presumably because he distrusted their claim upon the ostensibly unconditioned character of language. A self-engendered style is always wilful. Trilling disapproved of self-sufficiency, which he considered "the classic advice of philosophy in a disorganized society." It meant, in another formulation, "self-cultivation in loneliness, in the face of the degeneracy of the world, with reference to some external but ill-defined idea." Trilling also distrusted that action without end or purpose which is sometimes promoted as role-playing: he thought it a bogus abundance, a wilful setting out to look for life, as though there were not enough life already to hand. Sceptical of anything we do or any experience we seek merely for the sake of knowledge, Trilling valued consciousness as a human power, but only as a means to another end. He was not one of those critics who represent consciousness as the supreme act, the sublime form of intelligence, an act more opulent than any end it might propose. In Trilling's work consciousness is respected as a means, an instrument, but the end is given as social consequence. If knowledge must be distinguished from power, Trilling accepts the necessity, but he associates literature with power and responds to it in that way: he did not need to be told by Hazlitt that the language of poetry naturally falls in with the language of power. The act of consciousness often appears self-indulgent, pursued for the frisson it provides, but power is a public act which lives upon consequence. Trilling's mind distrusted the temptation to aspire beyond the finite condition to a state of being that is absolute, unconditioned, peremptory, detached from public consequence: he urged the reader's mind to make a virtue of the necessity of living in time and place. When we mark the importance Trilling ascribed to society and history, we mark his patience, the grace with which he accepted the mind's finitude; his distrust of angelic pretensions was instinctual.

Perhaps this explains why Trilling's mind was especially sensitive to the moment in which a person's feeling moves from one level of awareness to another, registering new and heavier burdens: acknowledgement of different levels, as of different burdens, entailed assent to temporal conditions and mediations. In his fictions, Trilling was particularly inclined to represent moral decisions as movements from one level of awareness to another. In "The Other Margaret" there is a moment in which the young girl recognizes for the first time the fact of responsibility; it marks her entry upon the moral life. I read the recognition as a private intimation corresponding to the public act by which one participates in politics and society, the burden of *The Middle of the Journey*. Indeed there is a paradigm in Trilling's novel which points to the crucial moment in which one phase of feeling turns into another. I call it the "almost" moment, and I come upon it when John Laskell hears a voice outside his window: "But it said nothing. For the sounds were not words although they fell just short of words." Later, when John is in bed, conscious but conscious of nothing in particular, we are told that "he lay through the day, drinking in the light that filled the room, and experienced something just short of an emotion": "It had great delicacy and simplicity, as if the circulation of his blood had approached the threshold of his consciousness and was just about to become an idea. It was as if being had become a sensation." The temporal equivalent of this is the bearing of the present tense upon the future. John is associated with the present in its emergence from the past: if he is all sensibility, this is what his sensibility engages as its special responsibility. Arthur Croom is associated with the near future, and with the art of administration, which is congenially engaged with the near future; it cannot do anything with the past, and it leaves the far future well or ill alone. The man of the far future is Gifford Maxim; his time is "the bloody, moral, apocalyptic future that was sure to come." The strain of these characters, one upon another, is tested when each finds himself impelled to become something else, to take the risk of new choices and powers. In these ways we are made to feel the continuous line of force between private and public life. John Laskell's fixation upon the rose testifies to the perennial attraction of living to oneself, but the morality of the novel calls upon him to resist.

I have remarked that Trilling is a critic not of consciousness but of power, and for the same reason he insists upon referring to consciousness as mind. He does not take pleasure in the latitude, the mobility, the imperative nature of consciousness: he is not a critic of, say, the persuasion of Georges Poulet, who regards the act of consciousness as the ultimate human sign. Poulet's account of consciousness is always expansive: he does not care what consciousness does so long as it does not die. Trilling's understanding of consciousness is more pragmatic, more administrative, turned toward the near future in which urgent work must be done. He is interested not in the possibilities of mind but only in its consequences. There is a revealing passage in *The Middle of the Journey* in which Emily is described: "She sat there with her face made intelligent by grief, which, because it subordinated all facts to one fact, is so like an act of intelligence that it gives to the face of sorrowing people, for a short time, the look of wisdom." I do not fault the description but I find it strange that this is what we are to suppose an act of intelligence as doing, subordinating all facts to one fact. A critic devoted to consciousness would resent the assumption and would be reluctant even to agree that this is what intelligence does in the organization of public life. He would concede that the work of administration involves the application of intelligence to the matter in hand, and the subordination of all facts to one fact; but he would find the proposed account of intelligence itself sordid rather than edifying. He would not be appeased upon hearing that Trilling was chiefly concerned with the bearing of intelligence upon the public world rather than upon the internal state of the individual mind or the role of consciousness in private experience. Trilling thought of mind as concerned with the imposition of order upon general experience, the reduction of multiplicity to unity, and the determination of choices. He judged mind upon its results.

A few years ago I entered into correspondence with Trilling upon this point. In April 1972 he gave the Thomas Jefferson Lecture in the Humanities—"Mind in the Modern World." The lecture was notable for its patience, the care and consideration for which Trilling's work is admired. On that occasion, as often earlier, he addressed himself to a fundamental question in the life of society, reflecting upon the insecurity with which the values of mind are now proposed when they are proposed at all. Trilling maintained that our contemporary ideology reveals a disaffection from history, as if amnesia were a virtue. The mind, he said, is increasingly discredited on the grounds that its activity is necessarily indirect: "It cannot be in an immediate relation to experience, but must always stand merely proximate to it." Thus far the theme is fairly common. The philosopher Merleau-Ponty, for instance, has spoken of certain great works in this century which express "the revolt of life's immediacy against reason." Trilling spoke, near the end of his lecture, of the "contemporary ideology of irrationalism" which celebrates "the attainment of an immediacy of experience and perception which is beyond the power of rational mind." "In our day," he argued, "it has become just possible to claim just such credence for the idea that madness is a beneficent condition, to be understood as the paradigm of authentic existence and cognition." I share Trilling's sense of a crisis in modern society as a perturbation in the relation between mind and experience, but I wonder to what extent Trilling's argument was forced upon him by his settling upon a certain terminology. I suggested to him that by speaking of mind in the modern world and by assuming that the typical act of mind is the subordination of all facts to one fact, he was bound to discover that the modern world has turned away from this sense of life. Would not the report be substantially altered if the question were put in terms not of mind but of imagination? It is well established that Trilling associated mind with the idea of order and even with the idea of hierarchy, "the subordination of some elements of thought to others." He put the force of his authority in favour of objectivity, meaning "the respect we give to the object as object, as it exists apart from us," the fullest recognition of "the integral and entire existence of the object."

It is not surprising, then, that he was deeply suspicious of those forms of consciousness for which the word "mind" seems blunt, and for which we find ourselves resorting to the more daring concepts "imagination" and "genius." We want an understanding of consciousness which takes risk in its stride. Trilling was suspicious of those powers not chiefly in themselves but in their consequences at large: he did not think they would provide the authority of a valid culture. He would admit them, I feel, only as a critical force bearing upon the administrative function of mind, keeping its orders and hierarchies lively by keeping them under scrutiny. He spoke of genius as "a unique originating power of mind," and showed himself responsive to its manifestations when they appeared in literature as action and power, but he did not include its qualities in the ideal form of a true society. I assume that he wanted to think of a society's intellectual resources as held to some extent in common rather than in a few exceptional people. He wanted the artist to embody the highest form of the common mind, including a degree of critical force and scruple found in the common mind only on its strenuous occasions. He did not want the artist's mind to differ in kind from the common forms of intelligence: he thought it an advantage, for example, that an artist's mind could maintain a consecutive argument just as scrupulously as the mind of a scientist, a philosopher, or a schoolmaster. It is also probable that Trilling's recourse to the terminology of mind rather than of imagination was a reaction against the extreme rhetoric of imagination offered by the main tradition of European Romanticism. That tradition, on the whole, does not align itself unequivocally with order, reason, hierarchy, and consecutive argument. The order it proposes comes late rather than early, and is often opaque to common forms of sense. It may be that Trilling thought imagination, viewed as a possible principle of organization in society, was seriously compromised by the rhetoric of two centuries in which it dominated European thought as a justification of will and subjectivity. It is possible that he blamed the rhetoric of imagination and genius for the situation he described in his Jefferson lecture. According to such a judgement the rhetoric undermines knowledge of "the object as in itself it really is," proposes intuition as a more profound attribute than knowledge or method, and sponsors the ideal of a direct unmediated access to experience rather than the distance imposed by rational categories. The idiom of mind was more congenial to Trilling than the idiom of genius and imagination because mind could be translated into practical terms and put to work in society; imagination and genius could not be put to work, or could be only indirectly and in forms too wayward to be trusted.

This marks a crucial difference between Trilling and Blackmur. Blackmur's essays in *The Lion and the Honeycomb* show that his later work was directly concerned with the relation between intelligence and society, but he did not believe that a sense of society should be invoked to curb the excess of an individual imagination (as Eliot proposed to bring a sense of tradition and orthodoxy to bear upon the same unpredictable force). Blackmur thought that "the politics of existing states is always too simple for literature; it is good only to *aggravate* literature," so he did not attach to politics in practice or even in principle the aura of conscientiousness which we find in Trilling's account. Blackmur felt that the excess of energy over intelligence presented a major social and cultural problem, but he could not bring himself to find the answer in the mere promotion of thought. "It is the radical defect of thought," he argued, "that it leaves us discontented with what we actually feel—with what we know and do not know—as we know sunlight and surfeit and terror, all at once perhaps, and yet know nothing of them. Thought requires of us that we make a form for our knowledge which is personal, declarative, and abstract at the same time that we construe it as impersonal, expressive, and concrete." Thought was premature or belated; either way it was not a true form of energy. So Blackmur resorted to the idiom of imagination and pressed so hard upon it that he tortured the theme and drove his readers to vertigo. He was a critic of the Sublime, cousin to Longinus; and he revelled in great literature not for its use or application but for the rush of its energy beyond all of its predictable forms: as when Ophelia said, "O to have seen what I have seen, see what I see." The sublimist is alive only to the moments in which spirit rushes free of matter and substance is transfigured, become all spirit. This was Blackmur's most impassioned concern, and the other concerns came later and with an effort of will and responsibility. He knew that there was a world outside the text and that he must take account of its force, but his temper kept him fascinated by those acts and gestures in literature which seem to be caused by nothing but an aboriginal energy leaping forth as perception, a force for which society could not provide a word of explanation. He delighted to find evidence in such moments that the blow of imagination is beyond prediction. So he was a verbalist in criticism, not chiefly because he thought words wiser than their poet but because he felt in the momentum of words and never in the momentum of society the true rush of energy. "Words bring meaning to birth," he said, "and themselves contained the meaning as an imminent possibility before the pangs of junction." I quote Blackmur's sentence partly to say that Trilling would have blushed to own it. Trilling was content to think of words as instruments, the strongest and best, rather than as constituents of poetry: he did not propose to reify Language or establish it as a power somehow prior to the mind of its poet. Blackmur and Trilling would have agreed that "no order remains vital which has lost its intimate contact, at some point, with the disorder or the unknown order which gave it rise"; but Trilling's agreement would have been rueful, Blackmur's nervous and exultant. Trilling thought that an unknown order was an order not yet known; Blackmur thought it an order beyond knowledge. Blackmur was excited by the violence of perception, and content to know that it could not be explained. Trilling hoped that it might still be explained. Occasionally, as in his account of Di Grasso's leap in the story by Isaac Babel, Trilling was driven beyond himself to admire the grace of violence; but his sense of social consequence inhibited him as a rule. To Trilling the hardest question turned upon the presence of will in society: he did not favour an ethic of inertia, but he could find a justification for will only when its defeat, in the long or the short run, was inevitable; then it might be entertained as critique, lest the official purposes of society weary of themselves. Generally, however, that which lies beyond knowledge terrified him as deeply as that which overwhelms order. Even in *The Opposing Self*, where the self's opposition is the theme, his feeling often leans toward those who yearn to be released from will as from society and culture; Wordsworth's leech gatherer, Flaubert's ascetics. I think Trilling's favourite virtue was patience; Blackmur's, quirkiness.

I have been maintaining that Trilling's theme is the mutual bearing of mind and society. Society is never represented as a mere aggregate of philistines; mind is never represented as if its freedom were absolute and its activity unconditioned. The happiest situation is one in which spirit and matter, self and circumstance, make a harmony together and mind acknowledges its responsibility to society. This situation rarely obtains, as Trilling knew when he referred in *The Liberal Imagination* to "the chronic American belief that there exists an opposition between reality and mind and that one must enlist oneself in the party of reality." He resented the common assumption that reality is merely "external and hard, gross, unpleasant," and that mind is respectable only when it resembles that reality and reproduces the sensation it affords. Trilling refused to make the mind a sacred object or to think it omnipotent. Belsen and Buchenwald testified sufficiently to the ultimate failure of mind to respond, with any degree of adequacy, to such evidence. But he was not daunted by an inevitable and ultimate failure: there were valuable things to be done before the end. Short of ultimacy, Trilling thought so well of the relation between mind and society that he ascribed high value to its consequences. In *The Liberal Imagination,* for example, he proposed as a crucial theme in principle the organization of society into ideological groups: a theme which turns out to be the burden of *The Middle of the Journey,* the relation between conscience and ideology in America in the middle of the twentieth century.

It is time to ask what precisely Trilling meant by his cardinal terms, and to show that his recourse to them became more rueful in his later books. In his early essays he invoked mind with some confidence; he could not believe that a society would deprive itself of the power embodied in consecutive thought, the relation between one image and another, the response of a practical intelligence to the facts of a case. But in later essays he felt that society was indeed depriving itself of this power and of the security of purpose it certified. In *Beyond Culture,* he referred to the idea of mind, "that faculty whose ancient potency our commitment to the idea of culture denies":

To us today, mind must inevitably seem but a poor gray thing, for it always sought to detach itself from the passions (but not from the emotions, Spinoza said, and explained the difference) and from the conditions of time and place. Yet it is salutary for us to contemplate

it, whatever its grayness, because of the bright belief that was once
attached to it, that it was the faculty which belonged not to professions,
or to social classes, or to cultural groups, but to man, and that it was
possible for men, and becoming to them, to learn its proper use, for
it was the means by which they could communicate with each other.

Trilling's understanding of mind presents it, therefore, as the distinctively
human attribute, the disinterested act of intelligence propelled by a sense
of experience held in common, the speech of people who share the
common experience. It is not the dialogue of the mind with itself, since
that dialogue has lost or set aside its sense of general human nature and
the universal conditions in which life is lived. Mind is the power used by
"a man speaking to men" about the continuities of shared experience in
the hope of understanding it. Trilling was aware of the exorbitance of
mind, "the desiccation of spirit which results from an allegiance to mind
that excludes impulse and will, and desire and preference." But he refused
to disown mind for that or any other reason. In fact his later essays are
designed to circumvent the low repute in which mind is held and to
ensure that the work of mind is carried out by resorting, if necessary, to a
more congenial terminology. The new word is "culture."

But the word we need at once is "society." In *Sincerity and Authenticity,*
Trilling refers to society as "an entity whose nature is not to be exactly
defined by the nature of the individuals who constitute it." Society is "a
concept that is readily hypostatized—the things that are said about it
suggest that it has a life of its own and its own laws. An aggregate of
individual human beings, society is yet something other than this, something other than human, and its being conceived in this way, as having
indeed a life of its own but not a human life, gives rise to the human
desire to bring it into accord with humanity." The repetition of "human"
and "humanity" reflects the desperation in Trilling's rhetoric, the need to
recite these syllables as if to recite them were to make them tell upon our
consciences. Trilling is referring to the modern meaning of "society," for
the moment, and taking for granted the low repute in which it is held. In
that sense the laws which originally reflected the fellowship and mutuality of people living together are now deemed to have forgotten their
origin and become forces in themselves, independent and therefore
monstrous. Conventions which were once amenities have lost their
responsiveness: they are now chains. Raymond Williams has pointed out

that when the idea of society as an object somehow maintaining a life of its own came to be fairly generally held, it became natural to present as a problem the relation between man and society and to assume that man's purposes and society's directions do not coincide. The word "system," as applied to society, brings this sentiment into focus. We have the same feeling in regard to bureaucracy, administration, government, the state, economic laws, multinational corporations: we think of these things very much as Blake thought of the House of Commons and the House of Lords, "something else besides human life." Trilling does not repudiate this sentiment: he allows the word "society" to attach to itself the charge that it has become "something other than human"—Blake's charge and almost his words. But Trilling has not changed his position: he has merely altered his strategy, fallen back upon another line of defence. Society has lost its humanity, granted; but it can still be redeemed by recourse to Culture, because Culture is precisely the effort to bring society "into accord with humanity." Trilling assumes that mind has always known its human bearing and that the temptation to release itself from the chains of feeling, impulse, and will is merely occasional: generally this knowledge makes mind what it is and keeps it true to its vocation. Culture is the process by which a forgetful society is reminded of its human responsibility and recalled from the monstrous forms it has taken. Hans-Georg Gadamer has spoken, in *Wahrheit und Methode,* of the work of Culture as turning an event into an experience (*Erlebnis*), and he has quoted Georg Simmel to the effect that the important thing about the concept of *Erlebnis* is that "the objective does not only become, as in knowing, an image and idea, but an element in the life process itself."

I am not sure that Trilling's understanding of Culture registers this distinction, or that the idiom he uses is adequately sensitive to that "life process." It seems to me that when Trilling speaks of society's being brought into accord with humanity, the evidence he produces is invariably an image or an idea or a set of ideas. Ideas are certainly the chief instruments of the cultural process in Trilling's version: "By culture we must mean," he writes in *The Liberal Imagination,* "not merely the general social condition to which the novel responds but also a particular congeries of formulated ideas." If the work of Culture were to be successful it would establish the presence of ideas in society as having about the same authority as that of beliefs and doctrines in religion. Society would authenticate its conscience by virtue of its ideas: it would be a secular version of the City of God. In *Beyond Culture,* Trilling describes the work of Culture as the attempt to "make a coherent life, to confront the terrors of the outer and the inner world, to establish the ritual and art, the pieties and duties which make possible the life of the group and the individual." The energy of Society must be transformed into human images: events must become experiences. The criterion is not aesthetic consciousness or the proliferation of self-delighting fictions. If Trilling's terms seem to be compromised by their dealing with the public world, they are purified again by the grace with which he attaches to them an aura of conscientiousness and scruple. In *Sincerity and Authenticity,* Trilling approaches the same argument by way of another terminology. Society is not true, or is rarely felt to be true, since social life compels people to play merely social roles. When Society is false, Culture is the effort to make it true again; true, that is, to humanity, to human feeling in its natural form. The work of Culture is an effort to move behind, beneath, or beyond the impersonations which Society imposes upon people, and to allow them to disclose their true selves. Trilling has no doubt that each of us has a true self: "It is through our conscious certitude of our personal selfhood that we reach our knowledge of others." Of Rousseau, Schiller, and Wordsworth he writes that they are not concerned "with energy directed outward upon the world in aggression and dominance, but, rather, with such energy as contrives that the center shall hold, that the circumference of the self keep unbroken, that the person be an integer, impenetrable, perdurable, and autonomous in being if not in action." Finally Trilling describes being as "the gratifying experience of the self as an entity."

It is clear that by Culture Trilling meant High Culture, an action with ideas as its content and an urbane style as its form and bearing. The actions of Popular Culture are not observed, presumably because Trilling thinks them of little interest or imperfect and fitful in their bearing upon society, effecting only a simpleminded and perhaps corrupt transformation of society. I assume that there is a direct relation between his insistence upon High Culture and his equal insistence upon the unbroken circumference of the self: in both cases Trilling's tone is severe because he is maintaining a position under continuous attack. In the past few years it has become unfashionable to speak of the self as a circle defined by an irrefutable centre. Trilling's insistence was widely taken as proof that he was dismally out of touch with contemporary ways of feeling. His insistence is still unfashionable. The current mood is more accurately embodied in such critics as Leo Bersani and Richard Poirier than in Trilling. Poirier's *The Performing Self* is an attack upon the identification of Culture with High Culture and of both with Literary Culture, the politics of the Book. In his *A World Elsewhere,* Poirier argues that "there can be no such thing as a successfully imperial self in literature . . . , because literature and the nature of language are so efficient in disposing of such selves." Literature is repressive and not at all liberal in its dealing with impulse, desire, and aberration: "think of the impulses literature represses, continually, in the interests of form." Bersani, in *A Future for Astyanax,* regards the idea of a legible and ordered self as a sinister conspiracy on the part of society, an attempt to neutralize desire and domesticate every independent impulse by assimilating it to a cosy narrative of development and growth. Bersani treats this conspiracy with contempt, and he withholds from desire and its manifestations the slightest criticism: desire is presented not as a social danger but as an indisputably personal value. Bersani speaks of desire with as much exaltation as Trilling brings to his account of the integrity of self: desire is placed beyond criticism. The reader is not even encouraged to reflect upon the fact that in desire he is enslaved to its object: the rhetoric of desire is drawn from the idiom of freedom, energy, creativity. Trilling reflected, especially in his later books, as much in anger as in sorrow upon the immodesty of will which he found rampant in modern literature: what he treated as dangerous Bersani treats as the only form of life worth the trouble of defending.

It may be useful at this point to represent Trilling's major books in a narrative sequence, because they reveal a certain development, not a change of attitude on his part but a more explicit set of strategies to cope with a changing situation. It has been alleged that he merely turned Tory and adopted the morality of inertia rather than participate in the spirit of the age. The truth is more complex. In his early essays Trilling maintained the hope of a mutual relation between society and the individual mind. He took for granted the integral self, and he considered its highest form disclosed in mind: the most serious acts of the mind were directed upon the public objective world and took their morality from the universally respected good of society. Mind acted upon reality: reality was not merely given—it was received by mind and modified by the spirit of that reception. The pure of heart were those who maintained a social conscience and did not merely cultivate their sensibilities. The grand themes were social, personal, historical, political; the most pressing arguments were ideological. Ideally there would be a fine adjustment of pressure between mind and society. But in frequent practice the adjustment was disturbed, mind was intimidated by society, browbeaten by institutions, conventions, impersonations, monsters of the marketplace. But there remained another possibility: mind could define itself and establish its character by opposition to the imperatives of society. This is the official theme of *The Opposing Self*, in which Trilling reflected upon the self which emerged at the end of the eighteenth century, exhibiting an "intense and adverse imagination of the culture in which it has its being." I do not understand why Trilling speaks of "culture" rather than of "society" in that sentence, since culture is the action of mind rather than its context or circumstance. Trilling endorses the mind in this relation because a conflict between mind and society certifies both terms and guarantees the integrity of each. Mind is still a subject of pure intention; society is not yet gone beyond redemption. Keats is the hero of *The Opposing Self* because he is the purest example of that conflict, holding in balance "the reality of self and the reality of circumstance." Mutual support is the best condition, but mutual tension even to the degree of opposition and conflict will answer nearly as well, because it keeps both terms alive. In *The Opposing Self*, Trilling praises the adversary mind in Keats, Tolstoy, Dickens, Jane Austen, James, and Orwell. He is not distressed to find the self quarreling with society, because the quarrel is good for each participant.

In his later books, especially in *Beyond Culture*, Trilling was dispirited to see that the hard-earned achievements of an opposing self were now mass-produced and sold in cheap plastic imitations, the rhetoric of a counterculture which he could not help despising. The rhetorical flourishes of the counterculture seemed cheap, glib in their easily acquired alienation, their borrowed sentiments. I think that Trilling was outraged by the vulgarization of a motive which he sometimes felt in himself, the dream of freedom representing itself as a rage for unconditioned spirit. He protested against unconditioned spirit, and perhaps protested so vehemently because he had to resist its temptation in himself: in any case he rebuked those who went the low road by simply disengaging themselves from the daily concerns of society. Officially Trilling was far more strenuously concerned with spirit as it strives to live in the rough banal conditions available in the ordinary world. He was sceptical of those minds which established conditions so favourable to spirit that they hardly counted as conditions at all. He could not see how such minds could represent man's tragic fate, if the conditions they set might be easily transformed into spiritual terms. In *The Opposing Self,* he adverted to "our preference for the apocalyptic subject and the charismatic style," not with any implication that he was bored with the subject and irritated by the style but with a firm suggestion that we are facile in our dealing with both. We go through the motions of subject and style without having earned the right to either; we are merely role-playing, impersonating our betters. Trilling was suspicious of an adversary stance taken in advance of its provocation, and he was scandalized by those, mainly university teachers of English, who encouraged their students to adopt such a stance without suffering the experience of earning it.

Disengagement from society was to Trilling a grave scandal even though it was a natural temptation, offering a holiday in reality. There is a passage in "On the Teaching of Modern Literature" in which he expounds the implications of modern literature in these terms and represents it in ways which are, I think, misleading. Trilling quotes Thomas Mann as saying that his fiction could be understood as an effort to free himself from the middle class. He then goes further: the aim of modern literature as a whole is "not merely freedom from the middle class but freedom from society itself." "I venture to say," he continues, "that the idea of losing oneself up to the point of self-destruction, of surrendering oneself to experience without regard to self-interest or conventional morality, of escaping wholly from the societal bonds, is an 'element' somewhere in the mind of every modern person who dares to think of what Arnold in his unaffected Victorian way called 'the fulness of spiritual perfection.'" Up to this point the argument seems to me sound, but Trilling goes on to warn the teacher that "if he is committed to an admiration of modern literature, he must also be committed to this chief idea of modern literature." "I press the logic of the situation," he goes on, "not in order to question the legitimacy of the commitment, or even the propriety of expressing the commitment in the college classroom (although it does seem odd!), but to confront those of us who do teach modern literature with the striking actuality of our enterprise." I think he presses the logic exorbitantly. Even if we grant that the end of modern literature is to achieve freedom from society, the end is never reached. Poirier's argument here is persuasive: literature's interests are vested notoriously in eventual orders, resolutions, and symmetries. In any case the chief idea to which Trilling refers is merely an idea, and it must make its way in the world against the force of other ideas and interests and against the more sullen dogged force of those states of being which do not entertain ideas at all. Besides, the idea abstracted from a novel or poem is not the same as the idea when it is involved in the texture, density, and organization of the work: an idea is nothing more or less than a motif when it is implicated in the structure of the work. And since Trilling was anxious about the consequences of his idea in the world at large, it is necessary to remark that a reader of a novel or poem does not go out into the world and act upon an idea, even a chief idea, he has encountered in his reading. He is much more likely to act upon his prejudice, habit, routine, all those persuasive imperatives which he has received without the labour of taking thought. An idea in literature is likely to tell upon a reader's life more as a scruple, a misgiving, a conceit, a fantasy, a consciously held fiction than as a plan of action or a program. It is simply untrue that people live, in that sense, by literature. Literature is not important for what it can do: it cannot cure a toothache. In the idiom of action, literature never goes beyond gesture: it is always a play, or a play within a play; its intensities are always virtual, a mime of passion. But literature is not reduced or humiliated by this consideration: the fact that it keeps itself within parentheses and refuses to compete in any direct sense with the forces engaged in society means that it stays true to its nature as a vision of life—not life as lived but life as seen, known, felt, imagined, understood. It is my impression that Trilling pressed his logic too far on this occasion not because he misunderstood the action of ideas in literature but because the idea in question was this particular one. The notion of escaping from society into a state of ostensibly unconditioned spirit was uniquely disturbing to him precisely because it placed at risk the only source of obligation and authority he could regard as having any hope of success in the world: if that failed, failure was complete.

The occasion on which Trilling expounded these matters most directly was the essay "Hawthorne in Our Time," in which he distinguished not so much between Hawthorne, James, and Kafka as between our diverse understanding of their tempers and achievements. He maintained—not very convincingly—that we have lost interest in James because we have turned against his conviction "that the world is *there:* the unquestionable, inescapable world; the world so beautifully and so disastrously solid, physical, material, 'natural.'" We have decided that

James is not one of us, after all, because he does not share our intransigence; he takes undue pleasure in the world, and yields to it for that reason. I find this argument unpersuasive not because I do not recognize a feeling at large in the world which is indeed what Trilling describes it as being but because I cannot see any evidence that James has fallen in our esteem for any such reason. If we no longer feel, while reading James, the first excitement of discovery, it is because we know that we are reading a classic, and we take his presence for granted. Trilling's account of Hawthorne is questionable for another reason. Hawthorne too suffers in our eyes, according to the argument, because "he always consented to the power of his imagination being controlled by the power of the world." It seems to me on the contrary that Hawthorne was interested in the given or received world only to the extent to which it might be "spiritualized"—it is his word—by the imagination. He felt that most of what we meet as "the world" was merely society's perversion of nature and that only by an immense effort of imagination could we break our chains.

In Trilling's argument, Kafka is the modern hero because he refuses to yield his imagination to the apparent intractability of the world. Kafka gives very little recognition to the ordinary world "as we know it socially, politically, erotically, domestically": he does not concern himself with the relations between one person and another, or with cases of conscience, or with morality. The modern consciousness requires, according to Trilling, "that an artist have an imagination which is more intransigent than James could allow, more spontaneous, peremptory, and obligatory, which shall impose itself upon us with such unquestionable authority that 'the actual' can have no power over us but shall seem the creation of some inferior imagination, that of mere convention and habit." We are preoccupied by "the ideal of the autonomous self." Trilling is outraged by modern wilfulness, our alleged contempt for conditions and circumstances, the "angelism" with which we insist upon direct access to spirit and essence. Essence means, in that insistence, the immediacy of our experience, and spirit is the attribute that makes the insistence what it is, our autonomous identity. Trilling is pointing to a force that is undoubtedly active in contemporary feeling. But I wonder why he finds it necessary to represent Kafka in such terms. Kafka is not interested in miming our daily activities, but he does not ignore "the actual" or encourage us to ignore society. It is an essential principle of his art to conceive social institutions at such an advanced stage of reification that they are already congealed in their monstrous forms: they are systems rather than *societas*. Trilling admires Kafka's art, but with reluctance, I think. I suggest that the reason is not that Kafka scorns the actual detail of our lives but that he does not hold out the possibility of redeeming the monstrous forms of society. Trilling hated to think that social institutions were beyond redemption; it was never too late to attempt the work of culture, invoking a *sensus communis* still alive, bringing social institutions into accord with humanity. Kafka's art is terrifying because it represents the damage as already complete; in the penal colony called society it is too late to call upon intelligence, mind, goodwill with any confidence that their response will make a difference.

Kafka is crucial in Trilling's criticism because he represents an outer limit of his sympathies. Consider these sentences in which Trilling reflects upon "the extraordinary aesthetic success which Kafka consistently achieves": "Aesthetically, it seems, it is impossible for him to fail. There is never a fault of conception or execution, never an error of taste, or logic, or emphasis. As why should there be? An imagination so boldly autonomous, once it has brought itself into being, conceives of nothing that can throw it off its stride. Like the dream, it confronts subjective fact only, and there are no aesthetically unsuccessful dreams, no failed nightmares." It is a revealing passage, starting with that "aesthetically" in which the adverb imposes a limiting judgement while its official assertion is appreciative. Trilling drives a wedge between aesthetics and morality by associating the first with dream and nightmare, irrefutable but narrow activities, and by implication associating those values to which Kafka is indifferent with nearly everything of density and substance in a serious life. Kafka's imagination has "brought itself into being," presumably by contrast with other imaginations which have been produced by a more humane engagement of intelligence with certain daily conditions in which it is maintained. Kafka's imagination "conceives of nothing that can throw it off its stride" because it refuses to take any obstacles into account. The force of Trilling's sentences ascribes to Kafka a degree of virtuosity in the aesthetic mode which is entirely compatible with spiritual arrogance and penury of interests. Trilling invariably uses the word "aesthetic" with a limiting intention: it means an inordinate concern for those procedures which are chiefly characterized by their offering little or no resistance to the exorbitance of will. These procedures are deemed to be brittle, inhuman, self-regarding. I have in view especially such procedures as the deployment of Language in a self-delighting or heuristic mood and of Form in its insistence upon autonomy.

To resume a long argument: I have been maintaining that Trilling was unwilling, even in a grim time, to find the poetic experience in dissociation from the texture of society and that he insisted upon attaching even to an imperfect society an aura of inherited value. But if nearly every social institution harbors corruption, where is a scrupulous image of society to be found? He can hardly say, with Plato's disputant in *The Republic,* "not here, O Adeimantus, but in another world." And yet there is a sense in which, given such desperate conditions in practice, Trilling points beyond them not to any particular society but to the idea of a society, an idea sustained only by his need of such a thing. He can also point in another direction, toward Language: or, rather, toward a certain kind of language, a certain style, *eloquentia.* This is "the mind of the old European society" to which Blackmur referred, "taken as corrective and as prophecy." It is a corrective by virtue of the tradition it embodies, at once a rhetoric, a poetic, and a politics: it is a prophecy by virtue of its persistence as a working possibility. But of course it is beautiful only in its potentiality.

Normally we do not think of Lionel Trilling as a critic of language in the sense in which we apply that description to Blackmur, Leo Spitzer, or Erich Auerbach. Close intensive reading of a text is never the substance of Trilling's work, though it may have occupied his preparatory hours: he disposes of a poem's language before he deals with it in any explicit way. The poetic experience reaches him of course in language, but he does not settle upon it professionally until the language has ventured into the public world in the form of ideas. Indeed it may be one of the limitations of his criticism that its author is content with a strictly instrumental theory of language and that he has circumvented the questions raised by modern linguistics and hermeneutics. But the explanation is probably simple enough. Trilling values in language chiefly its self-forgetful character, the nonchalance with which it sometimes takes its nature for granted and turns toward something more interesting, the ideas and attitudes which make for life and death. He suspects any manifestations of language which call attention to themselves as constituents rather than as instruments, or which appeal to a particular class of reader rather than to readers in general. What Trilling values in language corresponds to what he values in society: reasonable energies at work, fair purposes and consequences, more nonchalance than self-consciousness, and just enough tension to foster and maintain vitality. For the same reason Trilling distrusted every version of formalism: the forms he valued were transparent rather than opaque, functional rather than problematical. A form offers itself as a problem when its motives are not sustained by forces in the world at large and the available analogies are deemed useless. In both language and form Trilling values those procedures which can be construed as corresponding to a certain way of life, reasonable, culti-vated, urbane. The rhetorical function of criticism is to maintain the correspondence.

From *Sewanee Review,* Vol. LXVIII, No. 2 (Spring 1978).

CONRAD AIKEN

The Selected Letters of Conrad Aiken, edited by Joseph Killorin.

Conrad Aiken and T. S. Eliot were together at Harvard in 1908 as editors of *The Harvard Advocate.* Eliot was a year older than Aiken, and wiser in every visible way. They remained friends, in some fashion, for the rest of their lives; friends, but not close. They saw each other when occasion made the seeing easy. Aiken reviewed Eliot's books, judiciously, justly, but not enthusiastically. Eliot did not return these favours, but on the other hand he was not, like Aiken, a professional reviewer. Aiken suspected that Eliot prompted or even wrote the damaging review of *Blue Voyage* which appeared in *The Criterion,* anonymously, in July 1927. The novel, according to Anon., was heavily indebted to Joyce and exhibited "a deliberate indulgence in the prolix and fragmentary." Anon. was right, incidentally, especially about the prolixity. However, the friendship weathered the occasion. Aiken admired Eliot, and knew that his early poems were original, but he admired lots of people and thought that in poetry there was room for everybody. Or nearly everybody: he made an exception in favour of Frost, whom he disliked, and extended the dislike to Frost's anthologist, Louis Untermeyer. But generally he found something to praise in nearly everything he read. In 1913 he wrote to the editor of *Poetry* scolding Ezra Pound for his severity and asserting that Pound was neglecting Masefield,

Drinkwater, de la Mare, James Stephens, Bottomley, W. H. Davies, Abercrombie, Rupert Brooke, Gibson. There was nothing wrong with poetry, given a reader's goodwill.

But Aiken's instincts were sounder than his discrimination. In the summer of 1914 he put Eliot in touch with Pound. He knew what people needed, and went far out of his way to make it available. He helped Malcolm Lowry, and you can see from these *Letters* what the word "help" could mean, in such a case. At one point he even took over Lowry Sr.'s responsibilities, legally, morally, in relation to Malcolm. For years he tried to prevent John Gould Fletcher from going mad. With his own life, he did the best he could: he tended to fall in love with younger women, and he suffered the consequences without learning anything from the experience that he could use next time. He was a big, generous, ebullient man.

Meanwhile he wrote reams of verse and prose. He had no great difficulty in getting the stuff published. He won prizes: his curriculum vitae makes an impressive document. But he has never been taken seriously. Graham Greene has somewhere committed himself to the view that Aiken "is perhaps the most exciting, the most finally satisfying of all novelists." I have transcribed those superlatives from the jacket of the English edition of Aiken's *Three Novels,* the three being *Blue Voyage, Great Circle,* and *King Coffin,* and I have read the three. Well, there's no accounting for superlatives, but Greene's encomium seems to me ludicrous. Aiken's novels are blowsy things, blatantly verbose, extraordinarily tedious. Aiken convinced himself, while still at Harvard, that he was by nature a philosophic poet, and he was encouraged by Santayana's *Three Philosophical Poets* to believe that philosophical poetry was the best kind. So he went prowling around the universe to find support for his ambition. Listening to Richard Strauss, he convinced himself that he should go for the big stuff, write "verbal symphonies," set down leitmotifs at carefully casual intervals. And then there was Melville, blowing the biggest prose of all. Who could survive such temptations? Aiken thought he had a talent for narrative, large compositions containing ideas, characters, incidents, more ideas, then opinions, philosophic hypotheses, every damn thing under the sun; so long as it were verbal. He had words for every occasion, adjectives to burn. He turned everything into an epic. To get a character through the door of an apartment in Cambridge, Massachusetts, he invoked the entire Ciceronian tradition:

Here you go, outstripping with speed of mind the speed of this train. You are already in Cambridge, you are already noiselessly letting yourself into your flat in Shepard Street, you are already standing, just inside the door, and listening to hear if your excellent wife Bertha is at home. Not a sound—not a whisper—not the creak of a board. You cast a furtive look at the chairs in the hall: what is that you are expecting, or even almost hoping, to see? A hat? A man's hat? No, you avert your eyes from the thought.

That, for the record, is from *Great Circle.* The poetry is similarly blighted by redundancy: the narrative poems are interminable, as if Aiken wanted to get into some *Guinness Book of Records* for the longest something-or-other in American poetry. The 1970 edition of his *Collected Poems* runs, very slowly indeed, to 1,049 pages, but it's not just the length, it's the prosiness, the repetitiveness, the grinding on and on through boring narrative waste. When *The Waste Land* came out, Aiken thought that Eliot's poem owed a lot to Aiken. "Am I cuckoo in fancying that it cancels the debt I owed him?"

> I seem to detect echoes or parodies of *Senlin, House, Forslin:* in the evening at the violet hour etc., Madame Sosostris etc., and in general the "symphonic" nature, the references to music (Wagner, Stravinsky) and the repetition of motifs, and the "crowd" stuff beginning "Unreal city." However, that's neither here nor there: it's the best thing I've seen in years.

Aiken could fool himself with these notions, but he could not see that Eliot's verse, whatever its further merits and defects, was concentrated rather than diffuse; it was not, like Aiken's, garrulous.

It may be a question of space. I thought about this recently when reading, or failing to read, the Complete Works, in effect, of Charles Olson: another big, generous, garrulous man. And again the sprawling verbiage: as if he wanted to clear a space for himself commensurate with the space of America. Olson had a theory about space, that Space rather than Time is the American category. Enough of that. But Aiken, too, seems to have felt that he must write at large, for space, echoes, reverberation. Some of his poems read like exercises to discover how many ostensibly varied lines you could get from a few words. The poem

"Thee" gives itself the words Thee, Thine, and Thou, and the privilege of doodling with them until their possibilities are exhausted.

Of course, he was a nice man by all accounts. Everybody, or nearly everybody, liked him. Allen Tate, Blackmur, all sorts of people warmed to Aiken, but when they had finished complaining about the neglect of his poetry they went on their several ways without adverting to it. When his name comes up, people agree that he has been shamefully neglected, but nobody has been able to think of any compelling reason for changing that situation. If you call him a Man of Letters, you can say that he wrote novels, poems, essays, reviews, but you can't say that your life would be the poorer if he had not written at all. So I'll try again. Aiken, let us agree, had many virtues as a poet but not the virtues that make a poem memorable: his work is easy to forget. People have to remind one another that it exists.

Prolix, The Criterion's word, is inescapable. I have enjoyed Aiken's letters more than his poems or novels, because the letter is the right place for sprawl, high jinks, goodwill, and gossip. Aiken was a great gossip, a chatterbox of affection with all the warmth in the world. The mother of his children accused him of abandoning them, and the charge is fair, but he nearly made up for it with his letters to them. Many a duly domiciled father never gave his children as much. Not the puns, they're easy; but the gaiety of affection, tenderness. The man who wrote these letters may have been silly and raucous, but he was never constricted, niggardly in care. Mr. Killorin estimates that Aiken wrote about 12,000 letters. About 4,000 of them have survived: 3,500 have been read for this selection, which prints a mere 245. There are letters I prefer, among the modern American poets. William Carlos Williams's letters are richer, Kenneth Burke's (I have warm reason to know) more provocative, Hart Crane's are more informative about the poetry. But Aiken's letters are charming, they testify to a certain grandeur in him which never got into the poems or novels. He could be discriminating, too. He said of Middleton Murry's criticism that it could be very good if he paid "less attention to his own shadow as it falls across the page he reviews, or perhaps I should say, if he liked it less." Some of his reports on Lowry are brilliant: like Lowry's own prose, too long to quote, I'm afraid. On Eliot, Aiken's letters are wary: he never quite knew what to make of Eliot, and he never got beyond the stage of being fascinated by his manner, his appearance, his voice. He had no trouble reviewing Eliot's books, but the man himself left him bewildered. When Aiken told Eliot that he had called his review of *The Waste Land* "An Anatomy of Melancholy," Eliot said, "There's nothing melancholy about it—it's nothing but pure calculation of effect." But most of his epiphanies of Eliot came from social occasions, including one in 1930 when Aiken went to lunch with Eliot and a man called Gordon George:

> Vivien, said Tom, had been much disappointed at being unable to join us, but as she was having a massage at four thought it easier to stay in bed. Gordon George was a kind of high church or catholic fairy who had written an article on T and was submitting it to him: Tom said that when revised he would himself send it to the Bookman. After the first course, Vivien appeared, shivering, shuddering, a scarecrow of a woman with legs like jackstraws, sallow as to face. She examined me with furtive intensity through the whole meal: flung gobs of food here and there on the floor: eyed me to see if I had seen this: picked them up: stacked the dishes, scraping the food off each in turn; and during everything constantly directed at T a cold stream of hatred, as he did (so it seemed to me) toward her. George said something about pure intellect. Tom, giving his best pontifical frown, said there was no such thing. Vivien at this looked at me, then at Tom, and gave a peacock's laugh. Why what do you mean, she said. You argue with me every night in your life about pure intellect, don't you.—I don't know what you mean, says Tom. —Why don't be absurd—you know perfectly well that *every* night you tell me that there *is* such a thing; and what's more, that *you* have it, and that nobody *else* has it.—To which Tom's lame reply was You don't know what you're saying.—And thereupon I banged with my fists on the table and said Hear hear and more more, and the hate subsided.—Now isn't this a dainty dish?

That letter was sent to Theodore Spencer, then a bright young don at Harvard. Aiken sent such dainty dishes only to people he knew would appreciate them. So he gave Robert N. Linscott, an editor at Houghton Mifflin, an elaborate account of a night on the town with Edwin Arlington Robinson, another sprawling poet, incidentally, given to long narrative poems but a far more powerful because more dramatic poet than Aiken.

The best way to read the *Letters* is to take them as companion pieces to Aiken's *Ushant* (1952), the autobiographical essay which has regularly been applauded, though the applause has been, I suspect, merely manual. Many incidents in *Ushant* are also recited in letters; including a bizarre episode involving Aiken and Eliot, called Tsetse in *Ushant.* Textual scholars may wish to have the two versions. First, from *Ushant:*

> ... that evident streak of sadism in the Tsetse's otherwise urbane and kindly character, which now and then, as D. [Aiken] well knew, he enjoyed indulging. "You don't know the meaning of words," he had once remarked to D., in a sudden such thrust; and on a subsequent occasion, when D., acknowledging from his hospital bed in Fitzroy Square the Tsetse's latest book, and, writing in great pain, the morning after an operation, and with his head still full of ether, had praised the book with that kind of drunken fulsomeness which can perhaps sound a little false, even though based on genuine and envious admiration, the Tsetse had replied, not with a letter, but with a printed page torn out of *The Midwives' Gazette,* on which he had underlined in ink certain words and phrases—"Blood—mucous—shreds of mucous—purulent offensive discharge." That was all—no comment or signature. The bite of the tsetse, and no mistake.

The version in the *Letters* is much more opulent, in a letter to Linscott: it gives Aiken's thank-you note, quite nice really, to Eliot, then Eliot's reply, and finally Aiken's retort direct. It's all too long to quote, but I'll transcribe enough of it to convey its delicacy:

> The reply to this, after a few days, with a french postmark, was a page torn out of the Midwives Gazette: instructions for those about to take exams for nursing certificates. At the top, T.S.E. had underlined the words *Model Answers.* Under this was a column descriptive of various forms of vaginal discharge, normal and abnormal. Here the words *blood, mucous,* and *shreds of mucous* had been underlined with a pen, and lower down also the phrase *purulent offensive discharge.* Otherwise, no comment.—The recipient was unable to sleep for mortification and pain. He replied the next day: "Have you tried Kotex for it? Manufactured by the Dupont Powder Co. Absorbent, Deodorant, Antiseptic, *Inflammable.* A boon to women the world over. The problem of disposal—that bugbear to all sensitive women—a thing of the past. LADIES! YOUR ALLURE! *Some* days! Can you

wear your lightest frocks, your daintiest silks and satins, with perfect security? KOTEX. Used with success by Blue-Eyed Claude the Cabin Boy"... Three days later Tom called: a little flustered and embarrassed, a little at a disadvantage, but excessively friendly. There was no reference to his communication to me, and only a passing reference by me to my suggestion of Kotex, a suggestion for which he thanked me.

From *The New Review*, Vol. V, No. 2 (Autumn 1978).

MARIANNE MOORE

The Complete Prose of Marianne Moore, edited and
with an introduction by Patricia C. Willis.

L arge as it is, *The Complete Prose of Marianne Moore* is not complete.
It doesn't contain the Ford Correspondence, in which she offered
Ford's marketing research director, Robert B. Young, many won-
drous names for the car eventually called Edsel, or the waywardly
informative interview with Donald Hall. These items have appeared in
A Marianne Moore Reader (1961). Some juvenilia remain unrescued
from the *Carlisle Evening Sentinel,* to which she contributed, according
to her "Subject, Predicate, Object" (1958), "woman's suffrage party
notes."

The book begins in 1907, when Moore, in her junior year at Bryn
Mawr, started writing stories, sketches, subdued melodramas, drawing-
room episodes, the dialogue aphoristic and in other respects neo-Wildean.
The remark that "angels are not happier than men because they are better
than men, but because they don't investigate each other's spheres" is well
and characteristically met by the response: "You don't separate pedantry
from art, I see." Already, Moore had a mind inclined to make itself up. In
1908 Ford Madox Ford's *The English Review* showed her several of
the discursive forms available to an untimid intelligence. But she was
slow in getting started. Although her first poems were published in

The Egoist in May 1915 and later in *Poetry,* her work was much rejected, and she withdrew from occasions of disappointment. "I do not appear," she informed Ezra Pound in January 1919, as if she were Emily Dickinson.

But she was returning to authorship, encouraged by Alfred Kreymborg and his companions in the magazine *Others.* When Scofield Thayer and J. S. Watson took *The Dial* upon themselves in 1920, she contributed reviews—of T. S. Eliot's *The Sacred Wood,* William Carlos Williams's *Kora in Hell,* Wallace Stevens's *Harmonium,* and many minor works—in a style equably responsive to procedures she did not choose to emulate. Welcoming Eliot's appreciation of Swinburne's genius, and receiving the point that appeal from Swinburne's words to the objects supposedly denoted by them is not in general rewarding, she went beyond Eliot to say that "there is about Swinburne the atmosphere of magnificence, a kind of permanent association of him with King Solomon 'perfumed with all the powders of the merchants, approaching in his litter'—an atmosphere which is not destroyed, one feels, even by indiscriminate browsing—and now in his verse as much as ever, as Swinburne says of the Sussex seaboard, 'You feel the sea in the air at every step.' "

Moore became acting editor of *The Dial,* and took first responsibility for the issue of July 1925. She was not, on the whole, a daring editor. In matters of style and structure, she trusted her judgement more than anyone else's. Without hesitating, apparently, she turned Hart Crane's "The Wine Menagerie" into a new poem, "Again," and published it under his name in May 1926. "His gratitude was ardent and later his repudiation of it commensurate—he perhaps being in both instances under a disability with which I was not familiar," she loftily reminisced in 1960. But she never published anything she thought might displease Mr. Thayer and/or Dr. Watson. In 1926 she let the opportunity of publishing Joyce's "Anna Livia Plurabelle" recede, even though Watson told her he thought its publication in *The Dial* would not trouble Thayer. She disagreed.

Moore thought well of criticism. "A genuine achievement in criticism is an achievement in creation," she said, and in the poem "Picking and Choosing" the reflection that "the critic should know what he likes" is prefaced by considerations that tell the critic the particular temptations to overcome:

Literature is a phase of life. If one is afraid of it,
the situation is irremediable; if one approaches it familiarly,
what one says of it is worthless.
The opaque allusion, the simulated flight upward,
accomplishes nothing.

Those who in criticism accomplish something are typified by Gordon Craig, "so inclinational and unashamed," and Kenneth Burke, "a psychologist, of racoon-like curiosity."

The Dial elicited many of Moore's most formidable essays, and established not only her assured presence but the particular form of her probity. She required of herself, and therefore of other writers, selfless attention to the matter in hand. The choice of matter was rarely questioned; enough that she disliked coarseness and revered Henry James. Not "daft about the meaning," and hardly preferring one theme to another, she consulted a poet's diction, the brio of phrase without which no theme mattered. Reviewing *Harmonium,* she didn't think it necessary to say what the book was about: she concentrated on indicating how Stevens chose his words and how opulently he moved among them. Her commentary placed beside Stevens's poems unvying sentences celebrating the poet's "immunity to fear":

> The riot of gorgeousness in which Mr. Stevens' imagination takes refuge recalls Balzac's reputed attitude to money, to which he was indifferent unless he could have it "in heaps or by the ton." . . . One is met in these poems by some such clash of pigment as where in a showman's display of orchids or gladiolas one receives the effect of vials of picrocarmine, magenta, gamboge, and violet mingled each at the highest point of intensity.

At which point Moore quoted a passage from the second part of "The Comedian as the Letter C" to remark of it not what it is or what it is doing there but the excitement it provides "of proximity to Java peacocks, golden pheasants, South American macaw feather capes, Chilcat blankets, hair seal needle-work, Singalese masks, and Rousseau's paintings of banana leaves and alligators."

The *Complete Prose* verifies the sense one has of the *Complete Poems,* that Moore's chief companions were Pound and Williams. Literary historians are justified in seeing her work in some relation to Objectivism, which Williams described as a development of Imagism concerned with "an image more particularized yet broadened in its significance," but Moore never allowed her temperament to settle upon any of the categories available to it. She was drawn to Pound and Williams, rather than to Yeats or Eliot or Stevens. Yeats's majesty she admired from a distance; she reveled in Stevens's poems without for a moment thinking that his pagan spiritedness pointed a direction she should take, and she raised the question of producing "a fangless edition of *Prufrock and Other Observations*" which, by arranging Eliot's poems in a milder order, would mitigate the impression "of ungallantry, the youthful cruelty" of his "Portrait of a Lady." She was much happier with Eliot's middle poems, especially with "Marina" and "Ash-Wednesday," their method

> lean cartography; reiteration with compactness; emphasis by word pattern rather than by punctuation; the conjoining of opposites to produce irony; a counterfeiting verbally of the systole, diastole, of sensation—of what the eye sees and the mind feels; the movement within the movement of differentiated kindred sounds.

But Pound and Williams were her companions in style, especially in the quality of her poems which Williams praised as rapidity, "a swiftness that passes without repugnance from thing to thing." Her respect for surfaces, including unpestered appearances, was unconditional: to merit her attention, an object was not required to plead that it had more within—an essence or pure spirit—which surpassed its showing. So she admired the acknowledged "pressure of business" that modified self-consciousness, as in the writings of natural scientists, geologists, ornithologists. Her exemplars were not only Thoreau for his curiosity, Henry James for his accessibility to experience, and Pound for unfussy precision, but Darwin, Audubon, Ruskin—did she forget Agassiz?—for their "faithfulness to the scene—to the action and aspect of what makes the scene important, alive or stationed there."

In such men, the grace of paying attention to the matter in hand creates an informal morality. But it doesn't follow that in Moore's poems and essays a visual imagination, however acute, is the only means of grace. It is sometimes maintained, as if the duty of looking hard and selflessly at something needed an extreme logic, that Moore's poems were written to be seen rather than heard or spoken; as if their character were most fully expressed as a phalanx of neatnesses and deliberations enabled by her typewriter, appealing to the eye and enacting the probity of unbiased seeing before reaching the inner ear. This seems implausible. I am willing to be informed that she composed on a typewriter, though in the *Complete Prose* she speaks of marking the end rhymes and internal rhymes of her poems in different colored pencils. But the acoustic value of her poems is quietly enforced: her favoured practice of rhyming an accented and an unaccented syllable—fan/an, egg-shell/jewel, known/illusion—doesn't register on the retina, but in the voice. The rapidity that Williams described in Moore's poems must be sensed in a voice trying to keep up with it. The difficulty of the relations between the words shouldn't be eased by letting the eye slide across printed lines. Tongue, throat, and teeth should acknowledge the labour as much as the play of mind that issued in such mobility.

I would go further. It is regularly claimed that Moore's pervasive concern for accuracy was a visible sign of her morality. Smudged effects, like simulated flights upward, she regarded as immoral. I agree that moral considerations are implicit in her sense of formal decorum. "Rectitude has a ring that is implicative," she said. A just relation between phenomenon and concept is possible only if each is decently precise, the one well seen and described, the other tested by equity.

But there is much evidence in the *Complete Prose,* as in her poems, that for Marianne Moore the supreme poetic value is beyond morality, while decently attentive to it. The merit of a poem, a novel, a book about landscape gardening, *The Magic Flute,* or a sculpture by Malvina Hoffman consists in the personality it discloses when disclosure is not intended and the artist is minding his proper business. What she asked, in behalf of objects, was that each should be allowed to appear, to shine forth from the surrounding opacity, to disclose its "personality." Personality, the flare of being, is beyond good and evil, though Moore expected to find it issuing from the one and rebuking the other. She often quoted the passage in *The American* where James's Christopher Newman is urged: "Don't try to be anyone else; if you triumph, let it then be all you." But being "all you" was not reducible to the moral exactitude that enabled it.

Moore's common word for the flare of personality, the unity of being in which one's action is true epitome of one's self, was rhythm; "the clue to it all (for me originally)—something built-in as in music." "If I succeeded in embodying a rhythm that preoccupied me," she said, "I was satisfied." She associated it, in poetry, with a tone of voice, "that intonation in which the accents which are responsible for it are so unequivocal as to persist, no matter under what circumstances the syllables are read or by whom they are read." Its informal form is conversation, and "when we impart distinctiveness to ordinary talk," William Archer says, "still keeping it ordinary, we have literature."

Evidence of personality may be come upon suddenly or sensed as conviction over a long stretch. Moore liked to quote Coleridge's remark that "our admiration of a great poet is for a continuous undercurrent of feeling everywhere present, but seldom anywhere a separate excitement." But she loved to find a separate excitement, like a whirlpool, verifying the undercurrent and at last returning to it. Often she found it in English writers of the seventeenth century, Bacon, Donne, Browne, the King James translators of the Bible; later in Defoe, and in Johnson, in whose work she noted "a nicety and point, a pride and pith of utterance, which is in a special way different from the admirableness of Wordsworth or of Hawthorne." When she needed a name for this quality, she called it—using Hazlitt's word for its force—gusto, as in finding Cowper's "The Snail" "a thing of gusto." Alert to it, she didn't bother to mention the most obvious aspects of its setting. In reading Spenser's "The Shepheardes Calender," the passage in which Thomalin tells Willye about the occasion on which he fought against Cupid's arrow, Moore left everything unsaid except that "the impulsive intimacy of the word 'pumies' substituted for a repetition of pumie stones brings the whole thing to life":

> *The pumie stones I hastly hent,*
> *And threwe: but nought availed:*
> *He was so wimble, and so wight,*
> *From bough to bough he lepped light,*
> *And oft the pumies latched.*

In Christopher Smart, Moore found gusto in practice and another name for it, "impression," "the gift of God, by which genius is empowered to throw an emphasis upon a word in such wise that it cannot escape any reader of good sense." The stanza she quoted from Smart's *A Song to David* caught Theodore Roethke's attention, too:

> *But stronger still, in earth and air*
> *And in the sea, the man of pray'r,*

And far beneath the tide;
And in the seat to faith assign'd,
Where ask is to have, where seek is find,
Where knock is open wide.

Gusto, impression, "domination of phrase": under any name it was the sign for which Moore, an undozing reader, stayed vigilant. Tokens of it might be found anywhere, hence distinctions between the constituents of popular culture and high culture didn't preoccupy Moore. She found instances of gusto in a handout from The New York Yugoslav Information Center, the Duke of Windsor's account of his garden, the Central Park Zoo, certain paper knives, strokes in penmanship, the sinuousness of a snake, clothes designed by Worth. Surrounding such gusto, there are the values upon which it thrives: concentration, humility, reserve, reticence, precision, simplicity, equity. Indeed, one feasible way of reading the *Complete Prose* is to look out for references to gusto, and consider the signs of it in the examples she cites.

But Moore's criticism, glorious as it is in quirky detail and things seen in ways no other critic has ever seen them, is more than a *Golden Treasury* or a *Commonplace Book of Ingenuities.* She didn't regard herself as a critic in any systematic sense: for her, Kenneth Burke was superbly enough in that capacity. "I have been accused of substituting appreciation for criticism," she said, "and justly, since there is nothing I dislike more than the exposé or any kind of revenge." She construed criticism as appreciation of the gusto of other people, continuous with that of certain birds, animals, and flowers: some of the favoured people were writers, others baseball players. So a critical essay was an occasion for the display of a personality not her own except that she partook of its life and rejoiced in it. But she thought of criticism as having three obligations: testimony, quotation, and judgement.

In testimony, her aim was to compose sentences as adequate as possible to her sense of the work in hand, and such as to put the reader into a proper frame of mind and sentiment to receive it. I give a few examples. On Emily Dickinson:

A certain buoyancy that creates an effect of inconsequent bravado—a sense of drama with which we may not be quite at home—was for her a part of that expansion of breath necessary to existence, and unless it is conceited for the hummingbird or the osprey to not behave like a chicken, one does not find her conceited.

On Pound's *A Draft of XXX Cantos:*

> "The heart is the form," as is said in the East—in this case the rhythm which is a firm piloting of rebellious fluency; the quality of sustained emphasis, as of a cargo being shrewdly steered to the edge of the quai.

Reviewing *Owl's Clover* and *Ideas of Order,* Moore says that Stevens

> is a delicate apothecary of savors and precipitates, and no hauteurs are violated: his method of hints and disguises should have Mercury as consultant-magician, for in the guise of a "dark rabbi," an ogre, a traveler, a comedian, an old woman, he deceives us as the god misled the aged couple in the myth.

Williams, Moore says, on the reviewed evidence of *Collected Poems, 1921–1931:*

> objects to urbanity—to sleek and natty effects—and this is a good sign if not always a good thing.

Reviewing Elizabeth Bishop's *North & South:*

> With poetry as with homiletics, tentativeness can be more positive than positiveness; and in *North & South* a much instructed persuasiveness is emphasized by uninsistence.

Such testimony is not meant to give the gist of what Moore has already said about the poems at hand: it comes, usually, after the detail, and implies a larger sense of acknowledgement. The face of the poetry is looked at again, as if aslant, its vitality undiminished but gathered up into a consideration of similar and different forms of it. Personality is still the issue, testimony a matter of willing duty, quotation the detailed tribute.

Moore justified her quotations sufficiently by saying that "when a thing has been said so well that it could not be said better, why paraphrase it?" Besides, paraphrase would take the individual flare out of the occasion, and leave the need of it. Comparison of Eliot's quotations with Moore's discloses two different relations to the matter being read. When Eliot quotes a passage from Tourneur's *The Revenger's Tragedy* —

Does the silkworm expend her yellow labours
For thee? For thee does she undo herself?

—his aim is to show that the words hold at bay "a combination of positive and negative emotions" which, arising from the dramatic situation, can't be reduced to it or to the speaker or to Tourneur the man. The words don't entirely issue from a self, or return to a self. "The poet has, not a 'personality' to express, but a particular medium, which is only a medium and not a personality, in which impressions and experiences combine in peculiar and unexpected ways." It follows that "impressions and experiences which are important for the man may take no place in the poetry, and those which become important in the poetry may play quite a negligible part in the man, the personality."

When Moore quotes, she displaces the item quoted so that it may be read, for the time being, as a phenomenon rather than as words compromised by their context. In that removed character, the quotation exerts, like the jerboa and the pangolin in her poetry, the force of irregular detail pulling against a system otherwise in place. She never doubts that the quoted words have a valid adjectival relation to the personality from which they have issued; nor does she concern herself with values embodied in the linguistic medium rather than in a personality deemed to precede it. Many theorists would deny the merit of positing a personality separate from its linguistic form. But Moore resorted to words to assure herself of a personal force as if behind them. "Self flashes off frame and face," Hopkins wrote, an affirmation close to Moore's untheological conviction that a writer's style is his frame and face, domination of phrase being the flash of self. Quotation marks arrest the flash, and hold the writer's *sprezzatura* separate from her own.

Judgement was delicately enforced, for the most part, and often left to be inferred from testimony and quotation. Moore preferred to be an appreciator, a connoisseur, an encomiast. Compelled to report a defect, she chose to make much of the corresponding merit which the defect regrettably postponed or concealed. When she thought Williams wrong about rhetoric, she said that with his wrongness "we are merely poorer by one, of proofs for his accuracy." She made a note of bad writing, but usually as lapses of otherwise admirable tongues. "One wishes that Ellen Glasgow's sanity, moral courage, and contagious spontaneity were not marred by inadvertent triviality." Blame was often removable from one's character to nature or the weather. The critic Elizabeth Drew, who complained that Addison was a "dull writer," has herself "not been proof against the mildew of the stock phrase."

Moore could be, you see, severe. She never indulged herself in gladiatorial vivacities, but the astringency of "Marriage" and other poems was always available to her prose. Admiring Kenneth Burke, she found it necessary to purse her lips. "Complaints? With Rabelais and Joyce to brother him, Mr. Burke is sometimes coarse." Even then, she left the reader free to decide that a little coarseness was a fair price to pay for fraternity with such masters. Appreciative of Robert Frost, she did not approve his "Masque of Reason": "One does not parody the Book of Job." Reviewing *Alexander King Presents Peter Altenberg's Evocations of Love* (1960), Moore indicated that she knew where lines should be drawn:

> That a scene is set in Vienna by no means compensates for an affront dealt one by the courage of too much nudity on the part of waitresses conveying champagne to clothed patrons.

Courage? She is ready to concede that courage, of a kind, may be in evidence, and that timidity would have left the situation unevoked. Again, the reader is free to think that the scene might be redeemed by having the patrons remove their clothes.

But in speaking of testimony, quotation, and judgement, I should not give the impression that Moore's essays are predictably ordained, or that she moved from one duty to the next in a regimental style. Often it is hard to see how she moves from one sentence to the next. Here is a passage from the foreword to *A Marianne Moore Reader*, where the theme is the rhythm of a personality, and the provocation two famous lines from Skelton's "Upon a Dead Man's Head." Moore quoted the lines again in the poem "Sun" and, confessing that she could be enchanted by lines that broke her rules, in her contribution to Mary Brannum's *When I Was Sixteen*:

No man may him hyde
From Deth holow-eyed.

I dislike the reversed order of words; don't like to be impeded by an unnecessary capital at the beginning of every line; I don't like, here, the meaning; the cadence coming close to being the sole reason for all that follows, the accent on "holow" rather than on "eyed," so firmly placed that the most willful reader cannot misplace it. "A fig for thee, O Death!"—meaning the opposite—has for me the same fascination. Appoggiaturas—a charmed subject. A study of trills can be absorbing to the exclusion of everything else—"the open, over-lapping, regular." . . . A London *Times Literary Supplement* reviewer (perforce anonymous), reviewing *The Interpretation of Bach's Keyboard Works* by Erwin Bodky (Oxford University Press) on April 7, 1961, says, "phrasing is rarely marked by Bach . . . except as a warn-ing that something abnormal is intended"—a remark which has a bearing, for prose and verse, on the matter of "ease" alluded to earlier. I like straight writing, end-stopped lines, an effect of flowing continuity, and after 1929—perhaps earlier—wrote no verse that did not (in my opinion) rhyme.

Only a conviction that Moore's trusted and trusty personality is in charge of these details keeps the reader confident that the passage is authoritative rather than distrait. No other critic would step from Skelton's lines straight to appoggiaturas, which the dictionary explains as "a grace-note or passing tone prefixed as a support to an essential note of a melody; from Italian *appoggiare,* to lean or rest upon." It is a shorter step to trills, "a tremulous utterance of a note or notes, as a 'grace' or ornament." The sentences are grace notes adorning a melody Moore knows to be firm. The detour to London, the *T.L.S.,* anonymous reviewing, the book about Bach's keyboard music, the phrase about Bach's phrasing, would in other hands betoken doodling, but Moore knows her way back through phrasings and continuities to the finality—itself suspended by the paren-thetical phrase—of rhyme. It is not a method to be recommended to neophytes, but it produces the "tame excitement" on which Moore claimed to thrive. If personality is the secular word for the soul, with rhythm its audible or suggestive form, we are close to the exalted issues which she chose to weigh in silence.

In her later years Moore too willingly settled into the category of a personage, and colluded with people who wanted to think that poetry is no more of a problem than tricorn hats, black capes, and talk about baseball players. Publishers in search of thrilled endorsements too often found that with a knock her door was open wide. The *Complete Prose* includes the blurbs she emitted, and dismal they are: "I read with reverence anything that Father Berrigan writes." "I find him prepossessing," this of John Ashbery's *The Tennis Court Oath.* Readers of *Harper's Bazaar* discovered at little cost the food the famous poet liked—"honey, Anheuser-Busch high-potency yeast, dehydrated alfalfa, watercress, buckwheat cakes, fruit of all kinds."

There are disagreements about early Moore and late Moore. The early poems seem to me her best work, on the whole, though some of her second thoughts exceed her first. I think World War II forced her into a more expansive style and rotundities which the acting editor of *The Dial* would have expunged. I think the same of her prose, and find most memorable the astringency of the early essays and reviews. I am sorry that she disliked John Crowe Ransom's *Chills and Fever* so immoderately— "mountebank persiflage, mock medieval minstrelsy"—and didn't celebrate his better poems which are as fine as her own and in a manner she might have admired. But that is my sole complaint. For the rest, I am inclined to say of Moore what she said of Samuel Johnson: "In his writings we have so competent a grasp of what was to be said, that we have the effect of italics without the use of them."

From *The New York Review of Books,* Vol. 19, December 4, 1986.

WALLACE STEVENS

Wallace Stevens: A Biography.
The Early Years, 1879–1923, by Joan Richardson.

The first volume of Joan Richardson's life of Wallace Stevens tells the story from his birth in Reading, Pennsylvania, on October 2, 1879, to the publication of his first book of poetry, *Harmonium,* in 1923. *Harmonium* makes a natural break, since Stevens wrote virtually nothing for the next six years. This biography tells as much as can be told of an early life nearly bereft of incident. If Stevens's life was dramatic, its theatre was his mind. There is nothing here to appease a passion for gossip. After his death in 1955, his widow destroyed or erased a lot of his early correspondence and some of the journal entries he made, but it would be wild to imagine that anything disgraceful was suppressed.

By that time she was such a desiccated creature that she could not let him speak for himself, even to posterity. Stevens made few mistakes, in poetry or in life, but he started with an appalling blunder: he pursued Elsie Moll, courted her for five assiduous years, and married her on September 21, 1909. The marriage was, in the event, an unimpassioned thing. There is now no telling what went wrong, except that according to the wisdom of hindsight they should never have married. Elsie had no interest in his poems. Even when he was recognized as a poet, at least by a few qualified intimates, she retained her indifference. In November 1915,

Stevens read some of his finest poems, including "Sunday Morning," "Disillusionment of Ten O'Clock," and "Peter Quince at the Clavier," to a group of friends at Walter and Louise Arensberg's salon in New York. As the company assembled, he introduced his reading by remarking that his wife disliked the poems: "I like Mr. Stevens's things," she said, "when they are not affected, but he writes so much that is affected." Besides, she regarded as her sole property the poems he had written to her in courtship, and resented his publishing them.

Even when Stevens became a successful executive officer in the Hartford Accident and Indemnity Company, and gave her a lavish home and garden, she declined to share his interests. She did not receive company, least of all the company of fellow poets. "Mrs. Stevens and I went out for a walk yesterday afternoon," he told Charles O'Dowd; "we walked to the end of Westerly Terrace, and she turned left and I turned right." Stevens's job (he settled claims for surety bonds) took him away a lot, but he was glad enough to be taken. He had already got into the habit of living a double life.

To be fair to Elsie, the double life was congenial to Stevens long before they were married. When he was at Harvard, he worked hard, read omnivorously, and minded his proper business, but then he would kick over the traces of decorum and drink more than anyone should. By rougher standards, his debauchery was mild; when he confessed his sin, in letters, it turned out to have been a night's drinking and too many cigars. But it introduced a theme that persisted. His daily life in Hartford was bleak, so he enhanced it by epicurean gestures: ordering tea from Ceylon, paintings from Paris, books of Chinese poetry, shirts from Newell's on Park Avenue, dried fruits from California. He had misgivings about such extravagance, but he bore them.

Then there was Florida. Usually his job gave him an excuse for the trip, and his inclination extended it. He was thrilled by the colors, the flowers, the sunshine, the glory of the Keys; and he enjoyed in freedom the company of old cronies, the drink, and the raucous nights. "Since my return," he told Ferdinand Reyher, "I have not cared much for literature." Sex? There is no evidence that he resorted to that extravagance: drink, free talk, and cigars marked his limit. "I live like a turtle under a bush, and when I get away from town, believe me, I don't stay sober any longer than I must."

Not that "the malady of the quotidian" bothered Stevens much. His constitution was far stronger than, say, Eliot's. Pound made arrangements to rescue Eliot from the grind of a job at Lloyds Bank: the effort was a help, but it didn't protect Eliot from nervous collapse or the inevitable recourse to a Swiss clinic. William Carlos Williams found it tolerable to earn his living as a doctor, and to scribble poems every free moment. But Stevens mastered the technique of the double life, and found satisfaction in both parts of it. The evidence assembled in Peter Brazeau's *Parts of a World: Wallace Stevens Remembered,* published a few years ago, suggests that daily life in Hartford presented Stevens as a strong and reserved man, uncordial as if on principle. Such people are often described as shy, especially when their social demeanour seems to a disinterested observer to be abrupt or rude. More often than not, Stevens disliked people, and saw no compelling reason for discovering merit beneath their appearance. His own mind interested him more than anyone else's.

It is regularly assumed that one of the aims of modern literature is to escape from middle-class preoccupations, or indeed, as Lionel Trilling argued, to enable readers and writers to stand "beyond culture," as if in an unconditioned state. Stevens's aim seems to have been to live the high bourgeois life, and to fill it with objects as elegant as his choice of them. His taste in art was of the advanced kind. The paintings he liked didn't offer what he called "the realistic satisfactions," but at this distance what strikes us most clearly about them is the ease with which their incorporation into high bourgeois culture was achieved. Such culture may or may not feature nudes descending staircases, but it has no problem with *Nude Descending a Staircase.*

Richardson believes that the Armory show, held in New York from February 17 to March 15, 1913, was for Stevens, "no less than for America, the most important single exhibition ever held." There is no hard evidence that he attended it, though it would have been bizarre of him to have stayed away. He attended art exhibitions so regularly that in later years he thought his collection of catalogues worth giving to a library. Assuming that he went to the Armory, we are free to take the event as gathering into one occasion Stevens's interest in formally vivacious works of art and in the fellowship he enjoyed with a few men who shared such pleasures—Arensberg, Walter Pach, Donald Evans, Carl Van Vechten. His friendship with Arensberg collapsed after a few years, for reasons not entirely clear, but while it lasted it gave him access to exquisitenesses of form and style that he retained for the emptier years in Hartford. Cézanne,

Picasso, Matisse, Braque, Brancusi, Jacques Villon: it is not fanciful to suppose that Stevens, walking to the bus or strolling in Elizabeth Park, brooded upon the afterimages of their works. He was a modern poet, after all, and construed his modernity from the evidence offered by certain sculptures, paintings, and poems.

Even in poetry he lived a double life. I accept the idea, first put forward (so far as I know) by J. V. Cunningham, that Stevens's entire body of work issued from a single predicament: What is a person of religious sensibility to do, in the absence of a doctrine in which he may believe? What is he to believe? How is he to act, to live? Stevens's poems imply an answer that is straightforward if seen in one light, desperate if seen in another: "In the absence of a belief in God, the mind turns to its own creations and examines them." Instead of meditating upon the three cardinal terms God, Nature, and Man, as in the English tradition from Milton to Wordsworth, Stevens conceived God as Major Man, Nature as the world, and Man as the poetic imagination. The trouble with this device, if it feels like trouble, is that God becomes just another name for Wallace Stevens, for the poet's sense of himself at the furthest reach of his invention.

The result was one of Stevens's two common styles. The first was ruminative, soliloquizing, issuing from one theme and many variations, such that it is common to see Stevens as a philosophic poet, if not as a philosopher. "Sunday Morning" exemplifies this style in its sostenuto mood, and it goes all the way to his final book, *The Rock*. It is a major part of Stevens's world, and Wordsworth is the man in the middle of it, however regularly the Wordsworthian mode is displaced or moved a little aside by more immediate recognitions of Keats, Emerson, Whitman, Arnold, and Pater. We find this style, too, in Stevens's readings of his own poetry: the large voice, unvaried, undramatic, the pace so deliberate that only one's complete confidence in the delivery keeps one in attendance. He sounds as if he were comparing sad notes with Lucretius.

But Stevens had a second style. If your mind turns to its own creations, you do well to make sure that the creations are lively, lighter on their feet than you are. Richardson makes much of Stevens's comic spirit, and of a theory of comedy derived from Bergson. Of course it is hard to think of the author of "The Comedian as the Letter C" as constitutionally a comedian. Did he ever tell a joke? But he found, within the English or American language, the razzmatazz and high jinks of "Le Monocle de

Mon Oncle" and several of the early poems in *Harmonium:* "Chieftain Iffucan of Azcan in caftan / Of tan with henna hackles, halt!" No mere meaning waiting to be released required such lines: they were found in someone's head, rolled on the tongue, and sent prancing on the grass in nude abandon.

The two styles, like the two parts of Stevens's world, rub along well enough together. Staring upon a world God-bereft and therefore blank, you are not helpless. Verbal murmuring upon lack and absence and poverty adds up to time acceptably passed and post-Wordsworthian poems heartbreakingly made. "The Rock" is such a murmur. If you are in Hartford, you can make the best of it: in writing "Of Hartford in a Purple Light" you can think of "lights masculine and lights feminine" and end with "the irised hunks, the stone bouquet." That is to say: things are possible in language that are never otherwise visible even in a purple light. You can go to Florida. You can repair to big dictionaries, and find there words to entice feelings to appear.

Only one part of Stevens, only one mood, is a Nonsense poet. Most of his poems are in endlessly weaving blank verse, as if composed in a long New England evening of fears and memories. But Stevens is no more a philosopher than he is a comedian. When I first read his poems, I thought that their force and coherence must come from the grand philosophic themes, that he was book brother to Plato, Descartes, Kant, Nietzsche, Santayana, Vaihinger, and any other philosopher invited to his salon. He liked reading philosophy, as a pastime and sometimes as an inspiration: he liked to read high sentences, and to compose other sentences continuous with their spirit. Still, now it seems to me that his ponderings of reality and imagination, and the diverse relations he prescribed between those terms, were merely devices to get his mind started, and to keep it circulating. His ruminations are not essays in the theory and practice of cognition. They are articulations of desire. Pleasure, not knowledge, is Stevens's category. The conclusions he appears to reach are not aspects of reality adequately described but provisional appeasings of his desire. And inconsistencies between one apparently philosophical position and another are merely expressions of different moods, moods that, as in Emerson's "Circles," "do not believe in each other."

I do not mean that Stevens was merely an epicure, a dandy, a connoisseur of savours and bouquets. The problem in understanding his life, as in interpreting his letters, is to divine how such grandeurs as

"Notes Toward a Supreme Fiction" and "The Rock" emerged from the ephemera he mostly chose to display. Richardson's biography puts these ephemera on show, and ponders both what they mean and what they conceal. I am sure she is right to emphasize Stevens's early fear that he had suppressed the "natural and easy flow of feelings." In a passage from an early journal he wrote: "I still scoff too much, analyze too much and see, perhaps, too many sides of a thing—but not always the true sides." He was "too cold," he confessed, "to feel deeply the human destitution." Often he found himself more responsive to places, landscapes, and horizons than to the people who lived in his vicinity. Tender to his wife, he displayed most tenderness in urging her, when away, to enjoy her vacation a little longer.

Richardson doesn't blame Stevens for anything. Should he have tried harder, tried differently, with his wife? Swayed more willingly to the rhythm of his daughter Holly's life? Elsie remains where she chose to confine herself, in shadow: it is extraordinary that anyone would be willing to have so little life, and that little so niggardly. The biography allows us to think well of Stevens but to be pleased, on the whole, that we know him chiefly through his poems. Reading the poems with the biography at hand, and flicking the pages of the *Collected Poems* ahead of the early years, I find myself underlining passages that the life seems to annotate. The last lines of "The Novel," for instance: "And one trembles to be so understood and, at last, / To understand, as if to know became / The fatality of seeing things too well." That's worth making a note of.

Many little episodes in the early years, as Richardson narrates them, show Stevens backing away from being too completely understood, even by himself. His sense of "the fatality of seeing things too well" explains his aesthetic of glimpses, his veering from the commitment of a too steady "act of the mind," his recourse to "the pleasures of merely circulating." It is not that he became a major poet by inadvertence. On the contrary: he knew precisely what he was doing, and we find him distancing himself from Hopkins, Yeats, and Eliot so that he can choose the company he needs. The desolation of reality was as deeply his trouble as it was Yeats's. Still, he wrote his greatest poems by trying to evade it, making sure not to see it too well, and by trying to make up for it with gaieties as wonderful as they are desperate.

Richardson's method is to produce the early Stevens from his letters, journals, and poems. This biography is addressed to the common reader as directly as it is to the scholar. Opulently written, it is occasionally so suffused with Stevens's phrases that it conceals Richardson's voice behind his. Two references to Stevens "displaying his muzzy belly" may be thought indelicate by a reader who doesn't know that "A High-Toned Old Christian Woman" has certain "disaffected flagellants . . . smacking their muzzy bellies in parade." A glum passage about the death of Queen Victoria ends with a sentence that British readers are likely to resent—"If her horny feet protruded, they only showed how cold she was, and dumb"—unless they know that Stevens's "The Emperor of Ice-Cream" includes, with no queen in view, these lines: "If her horny feet protrude, they come / To show how cold she is, and dumb." The common reader may wonder, too, why Richardson says of Stevens that, in New York in June 1900, "his starker, barer self in this starker, barer world began to see with an ignorant eye." But these abrupt phrases may be found in "The Comedian as the Letter C."

I should not make too much of this. Everyone who writes about Stevens is susceptible to his finery. It is hard to preserve, in his presence, a mind of one's own. Joan Richardson sometimes yields her style to his, but she soon recovers her poise. Her book is continuously vivid, accurately evidenced, and—when imagination must fill a vacancy—richly imagined.

From *The New Republic,* November 17, 1986.

RANSOM

I spoke with Ransom only once, at Harvard several years ago, so I cannot offer to recite the merits of the man if they are held distinct from the merits of the poet: that there is no dreadful distinction between the several merits in his case, I am pleased to assume. He seemed a gentleman. I had letters from him occasionally, mostly in the line of his duty as editor of *The Kenyon Review,* but the correspondence did not aspire to anything more than an exchange of messages and decency.

Ransom the critic reached me sooner than Ransom the poet, but that was by chance. It so happened that as a student I came upon Ransom and the American critics and preferred them to their English colleagues. *The Kenyon Review* under Ransom's persuasion sounded more engaging to me than *Scrutiny.* I did not think I needed to be told how to live: indeed, I resented the implication, clear enough in Dr. Leavis's prose, that *Scrutiny* presented the only relevant questions. I did not resort to magazines for rough stuff, but for elegance, grace, style. I now think the question of *Scrutiny* more complex than it appeared then, but I still revel in Ransom's critical prose. His arguments are probably fallible and certainly inconsistent, but his style is true. "The object of a proper society is to instruct its members how to transform instinctive experience into aesthetic experience." I am pleased with that. Hence the significance of aesthetic forms which are "a technique of restraint, not of efficiency"; they discourage us from laying violent hands upon the objects of our experience. Literature speaks to our second nature and makes us somewhat sceptical about our first since it is likely to be rough and predatory. A poem is like a code of manners. And so forth: there is more of it in *The World's Body* and it is superb.

As a critic, Ransom sponsored the idea that poets maintain a natural piety, the poet's gift is "for finding the natural world not merely mechanical but hospitable to the moral Universals." "A natural object or confirmation strikes our attention because it seems significant of more than mechanical effect, and we proceed to equate it metaphorically with the appropriate human Universal." But in his poetry Ransom often shows this piety outraged by the turn and fall of events. Providence and Nature are not happy twins. I can still hear that appalling scream issuing from one of the white throats in "Vision by Sweetwater" and, in "Two in August," see the man walking in "the long ditch of darkness." I assume that the critic offers an official view of the relation between poetry and the moral life; the unofficial view, and the turbulence of containing it, are the concern of the poems. The poems look so secure as they move down the page, the stanzas nicely ordained, but there are monsters between the lines. It is my understanding that Ransom made up his mind, in the early poems, that monsters could not be approached directly but must be treated with the precaution of form. He converted mysteries into problems. Metaphysical evils were confronted not directly but obliquely, as though the poet could not look them in the eye but only aslant or askew. However Ransom dealt with the dangerous questions as a man, he handled them as a poet by converting them into problems of form. So he liked his poems to wear a tidy look especially when their occasions and substances were fierce. He admired Hardy for the same reason, because Hardy's poems, many of them heartrending, rend the heart and maintain the decencies at the same time. I mean the formal decencies, signs of a second nature which does not utterly yield to the terrors of the first. Ransom is one of the few critics of poetry who bother about the metres; his reason is, I think, that the metres are the great means of reconciling, where it counts, the possibilities and the resistances involved in formal movement. Certain movements are possible; obstacles are inevitable. It is the tension between these forces that makes the lines vibrate. You could hardly imagine a more oblique way of dealing with a moral problem than the way of prosody, but precisely for that reason it is the way to do it, at once precise and fabulous. Ransom took pleasure in his metres, the kind if not the degree of pleasure he took in the metres of Shakespeare, Donne, Milton, and Hardy; because he could prove upon his ear a movement in the words which he could not prove in any other way. He could not prove the words in any way persuasive to philosophers. Ransom loved philosophy, especially if it took its bearings from Aristotle and complicated them nearly beyond reason by recourse to Kant and Hegel. He liked one or two of his own professional pieces which employed the dialect of the philosophers while not rising in themselves to the formal condition of philosophy. But philosophy was merely his homework to keep the mind in good order so that it could wait upon the visit of poetry. Since he wrote only a modest number of poems and was silent for many years, it is necessary to say that he was a poet by nature as well as by desire.

I do not recall when I first read "The Equilibrists." No matter; it is one of the supreme Ransom poems, a magnificent performance, the Grand Style recovered:

> *In Heaven you have heard no marriage is,*
> *No white flesh tinder to your lecheries,*
> *Your male and female tissue sweetly shaped*
> *Sublimed away, and furious blood escaped.*

> *Great lovers lie in Hell, the stubborn ones*
> *Infatuate of the flesh upon the bones;*
> *Stuprate, they rend each other when they kiss,*
> *The pieces kiss again, no end to this.*

I shall gloss the poem by bringing forward one or two sentences from Ransom's introductory essay to a *Selected Poems of Thomas Hardy* (1961). The human community lives, according to Ransom, under two sovereignties. "There is a natural order within which events go according to a natural law; we have acknowledged the law, and laboured to understand it, and learned to use it often to our own advantage; we did not institute it." There is also a moral order, "whose law is Justice and Pity;

we mean to deal justly and charitably, and to enforce the law against our rebel members." But if the two laws clash, and the natural law prevails? Ransom says that we are always unprepared for that event. "When it is most unexpected we wonder if the moral order is anything more than what we legislated into being, not absolute at all as a sovereignty must be, but choose not to concede the point at once, and are willing to seem slightly ridiculous if we must, while we think and wait." So it is in "The Equilibrists." Ransom is bringing his second nature to bear upon a situation at once beautiful and outrageous to his first. The lovers, "rigid as two painful stars," are imprisoned in the contradiction of two laws, the natural law and the moral law. It is the contradiction that makes the lovers beautiful and their predicament dreadful; without it they would not have a claim upon our feeling. It is a theme congenial to a reader of Donne; the lovers are, like Donne's, planetary, fixed stars whirled about "the clustered night." But there is in "The Equilibrists" a fatality of cadence which establishes between Ransom, Hardy, and Donne a propinquity rather than a dependence. I hear it in the rhymes of the second stanza quoted. Wimsatt and other critics have told us that the best rhymes come when the rhyming words are two different parts of speech; a noun set off against a verb, for instance. "Kiss" and "this" make a good rhyme according to that prescription. It is also good, though I do not recall Wimsatt or other critics saying so, when one rhyming word is held forth prominently and the other one is subdued; as here "bones" is prominent because it is the third and last of the important words in the line, and "ones" is subdued by the greater force of "stubborn" and by the fact that except for "in" it is the mildest word in the line. For similar reasons, "this" is subordinate to "kiss."

Ransom, like the girl in his "Vaunting Oak," was "instructed of much mortality." Most of his poems show a moral order, of whatever kind (love, beauty, grace), doing the best it can with restrictions set by a natural law which is definitively represented by death. That is to say: the poems straddle the long ditch of darkness between morality and nature, with death at the end. It is a minor poetry, Ransom never attempted the big forms, he liked to keep his ambition respectable and neat. If you compare his poems with, say, Empson's, Empson's seem to score in their daring and reverberation, and Ransom's in that company seem too shy for their own good. But after a while Empson's insolence begins to sound theatrical, a bit shrill, and the strength in Ransom's demeanour begins to establish itself. As he wrote in "Survey of Literature," poetry is composed of "consonants and vowels." A lover of words, he was pleased by that consideration. It must be something, dying, to leave behind a body of work, small perhaps but accomplished and secure; keeping open the lines of grace in a churlish time.

From *The New Review,* October 1974.

ALLEN TATE

Collected Poems, 1919–1976, by Allen Tate.

Allen Tate was born on November 19, 1899, in Winchester, Kentucky. To be a Tate in Kentucky, according to Wallace Stevens, is like being a Ransom in Tennessee, except that there are even more Ransoms in Tennessee than Tates in Kentucky. In both cases the conditions of birth, time, and place are felt as privilege and responsibility. On a strict accounting, John Crowe Ransom probably enjoyed his conditions mostly as privilege, if the wit and nicety of his poems are true indications of their author. Terrible events are recited in Ransom's poetry but they are held in poise by his diction and syntax. In Tate's poems a sense of burden and responsibility comes through the lines more clearly than the privilege of being a Tate in Kentucky or the different privilege of being inordinately gifted. Three years ago, at a party held in Sewanee, Tennessee, to celebrate Tate's seventy-fifth birthday, the poet acknowledged the greetings of his friends by reciting a sequence of stanzas he had compiled with a proper sense of the occasion. The stanzas and Tate's commentary are published in his recent *Memories and Essays;* but I mostly recall the dignity with which Tate spoke. In his novel *The Fathers,* Tate wrote of a man "acting upon his dignity which he did not know he had because he had it so perfectly." Tate's own dignity is similarly innocent, and perfect in that quality. But his work gives the impression that he insists upon sustaining the responsibility of his language and his vocation before resorting to their pleasures. This impression is verified in the new *Collected Poems*.

Tate's first independent book of poetry, *Mr. Pope and Other Poems*, was published in 1928, but he was already seasoned in poetry by that date. He started writing poems in 1919, and was ready to defend them in the winter of 1921 when he was invited to join a group of poets who were in the habit of meeting to read their verses at Dr. Sidney Hirsch's home in Nashville. Ransom was the undisputed leader of those young poets at Vanderbilt, but Donald Davidson and Tate made a closer fellowship, it appears, than Ransom and Tate. Ransom and Tate stayed friends, undivided except in opinion, but their opinions came near to dividing them when *The Waste Land* was published in 1922. Ransom was hostile to the poem, and perhaps jealous of its effect upon Tate. In a note to *The Swimmers, and Other Selected Poems* (1970), Tate said of his early poems that by "early" he meant any poem he wrote before reading Eliot in 1922. "My early verses now seem to be a conventional and anonymous mixture," he said, "of Baudelaire (via Arthur Symons), Corbière, James Thomson, E. A. Robinson, Ernest Dowson, and a little of Ezra Pound, whom I had read before I read Eliot." But in the last few years he has evidently become tender toward those early poems, and is not disposed to abandon them. In *The Swimmers, and Other Selected Poems,* only thirteen early poems were retained; in the new edition the number is forty-six, many of them drawn from *The Fugitive* and the years 1922–25. It would be surprising if the recovered poems, including two or three hitherto unpublished pieces, were to include anything remarkable. Tate has gone through this material several times in preparing the several editions of his poetry. I think he has recovered those *Fugitive* poems now for a particular reason. There is a passage in *The Fathers* in which the narrator reports that "in my feelings of that time there is a new element—my feelings now about that time." "There is not an old man living," he continues, "who can recover the emotions of the past; he can only bring back the objects around which, secretly, the emotions have ordered themselves in memory." The *Fugitive* poems are such objects, according to my understanding, and they should be read with the *Memories and Essays* close at hand.

The new poem, "Farewell Rehearsed," was written last year, a love poem in three parts addressed to the poet's wife Helen and their sons Benjamin and John.

I have referred to Tate's sense of responsibility, with an implication that it makes for difficulty in the poet as in the reader. Henry James wrote of Flaubert as being a votary of literature, and said of him that "no life was long enough, no courage great enough, no fortune kind enough to support a man under the burden of this character when once such a doom had been laid upon him." It was a doom because "he felt of his vocation almost nothing but the difficulty." James went on to speak of his missing, when reading Flaubert, "the consecration supposedly given to a work of art by its having been conceived in joy." If I were asked to name a modern poem which sounds as if it were conceived in joy and enchantment, I would say: Eliot's "Marina," on no evidence but its style. I would have a problem in selecting a poem of Tate's to satisfy this requirement. Poems of high spirit, yes, Tate wrote several poems in that mood, especially satires sent with a flourish to colleagues of liberal persuasion in the thirties. But when we read his entire work in poetry, fiction, and criticism, we are moved by his sense of craft and vocation, and by the air of difficulty which surrounds his scruple. Think of Tate's preoccupations; with time, history, belief, the "antique courtesy" of myth, the family, the South, tradition, "the strain of fore and after," and the general failure of the human personality "to function objectively in nature and society." Think of his poems and essays which brood upon "the angelic imagination," that form of pride which insists upon direct access to essence without the mediation of existence. Let us suppose a possible state of harmony among the three classical faculties: feeling, will, and intellect. Tate describes a hypertrophy of the first as "the incapacity to represent the human condition in the central tradition of natural feeling." The second excess is "the thrust of the will beyond the human scale of action." And the third is "the intellect moving in isolation from both love and the moral will, whereby it declares itself independent of the human situation in the quest of essential knowledge." I have quoted these phrases not to comment upon them or to do them justice but to suggest the sources of Tate's difficulty in his own sense of them.

No wonder, then, that Tate sought aid from his masters and nearly lost himself in his fervour. Hardy's mastery was intermittent and there-fore innocent, Yeats's more insidious because it tempted Tate to ride the high horse, and Eliot's mastery nearly suppressed Tate's individual talent altogether. Not the Eliot of *The Waste Land,* incidentally. I surmise that it was the Eliot of "Gerontion" who captured Tate's imagination and took possession of his voice. Even in major poems written several years after his first addiction to "Gerontion," Tate was still enthralled; as in "Ode to the Confederate Dead":

> The hound bitch
> *Toothless and dying, in a musty cellar*
> *Hears the wind only.*

And in "To the Lacedemonians" the old soldier recalling Cedar Run and Malvern Hill has Gerontion's voice rather than his own:

> *Yet I, hollow head, do see but little;*
> *Old man: no memory: aimless distractions.*

I assume that Tate had recourse to Eliot not only because he recognized in Eliot's poems one of the few available ways of setting the imagination to work in the modern world but because he sensed, beneath those poems, the drudgery they had to cope with before they could come to their own possibility and release their voice. Eliot's drudgery was much the same as Tate's: the bother and grit of politics, religion, history, one thing after another, mostly wretched. But Eliot's early poems took up the drudgery and somehow made music of it at last. Tate's early poems took up the drudgery and stayed with it so long and so passionately that the music had to be postponed. At Sewanee three years ago Tate's little speech ended with a word of thanks to George Seferis for lines in praise of simplicity:

> *All I want is to speak simply;*
> *For we have loaded even the song with so many kinds of music*
> *That gradually it sinks.*

This is the defect of Tate's early poems, if it is a defect and not a necessity: so many kinds of music resorted to in the hope of turning drudgery into one's own.

It may be true that Eliot helped Tate to find his voice, though I think it more accurate to say that Eliot held him back from the discovery until he was ready for it. These are questions worth disputing. My own notion is that Eliot's poems told Tate that the responsibility of a man of letters in the twentieth century was likely to be endless, and that it should be taken up at once. How vigorously, and with what degree of conscientiousness Tate took it up: that is not only his own story but "the story of the night," essentially the moral history of America in the past fifty years. The public significance of Tate's work amounts to nothing less than such a narrative; and those who revere him revere him for that reason. It would be monstrous to present the moral history of America in this century without admitting the challenge of everything Tate has written about religion, tradition, the relation between the imagination and the conditions it has to face; admitting it as a challenge, not necessarily as a definition or a conclusion.

I share these reasons for revering Tate, but I choose to find cause for them in the history of his style; how he found his own voice after loading his song with so many dangerous kinds of music. Unless I err, he found it by recourse to other languages, French and Greek but mostly Virgil's Latin and Dante's Italian. The crucial year is 1933, when Tate wrote "The Mediterranean," the first of his perfections. Circumstance, and a casual remark by Ford Madox Ford, sent Tate back to the *Aeneid*. A poet, American at heart as well as on principle, happens to be in Europe, on a picnic at Cassis: a remark about the refugees from Troy sets him thinking of possibilities and discoveries, the sea, the land, the relation between blood and land, worlds Old and New. If responsibilities begin in dreams, they are appeased in a style answerable to their occasions:

Now, from the Gates of Hercules we flood

Westward, westward till the barbarous brine
Whelms us to the tired land where tasseling corn,

Fat beans, grapes sweeter than muscadine
Rot on the vine: in that land were we born.

This is Tate's first achieved style, his own music. There are notes of it already in "Mother and Son," written in 1930, but without the resonance which Tate gained from themes at once personal and historical. Twenty years later he composed a different music, but equally his own, by attending upon the *terza rima* of Dante. In "The Swimmers" and "The Buried Lake," he resorted again to the literal event, a gift of chance, an incident from his own early life recalled now with a new element, his feelings about it. If we place these poems beside Tate's essay on Dante, published in 1952, we see that the poems issue from Tate's renewed sense of "the symbolic imagination" which "conducts an action through analogy, of the human to the divine, of the natural to the supernatural, of the low to the high, of time to eternity." The symbolic poet, according to Tate, returns "to the order of temporal sequence—to action." But the action comes first. Tate does not imply that the way of analogy is easy or that finality of success in that way is possible, except in principle. But he maintains that the symbolic poet, Dante if you will, begins with the common thing, and continues with it, "until at the end we come by disarming stages to a scene that no man has ever looked upon before": the end, the *Paradiso,* is achieved not by transcending the natural world or the human scale of action but by committing the imagination to the natural images. No formula is proposed: to speak of analogy is to accept human limits and to be patient in their shadow. This is not an adequate description of "The Swimmers" or of the note of consecration heard at last in the great invocation to Santa Lucia near the end of "The Buried Lake": it is merely a remark about the probable source of the feeling which issued in those poems.

Of Tate as a presence in modern American poetry, I would make only this comment, and it is mainly apology. I cannot account for my failure to sense that presence where it now seems to me inescapable, as in Robert Lowell's early poems of drudgery and torsion. Lowell once wrote of Tate's poems: "out of splutter and shambling comes a killing eloquence; perhaps this is the resonance of desperation, or rather the formal resonance of desperation." I am satisfied with that, in general, but I am not sure what is killing in Tate's eloquence and I take it as hyperbole going somewhat beyond the desperate conditions in which the eloquence was at last achieved. Lowell's phrases refer as closely to his own early poems as to Tate's, I think; to the best part of Lowell and to the most difficult part of Tate. The relation between splutter and eloquence is one way of putting it, one way of registering the marvellous flame and flare of the *Collected Poems*.

From *The New York Times Book Review,* December 11, 1977.

H.D.

H.D.: The Life and Work of an American Poet,
by Janice S. Robinson.

In August 1912, Ezra Pound, Richard Aldington, and Hilda Doolittle were together in London, reading *The Greek Anthology* in the British Museum and discussing literary matters in the museum's tearoom. On the spur of those experiences Doolittle wrote two poems, "Priapus" and "Hermes of the Ways," which she presented to Pound. "This is poetry," he reported, while slashing at the texts with his improving pencil. At the bottom of the page he scribbled "H.D. Imagiste." Two months later, having created Imagism from nothing more than a few such poems, Pound sent Doolittle's verses to Harriet Monroe, the editor of *Poetry* magazine, praising them: " . . . no excessive use of adjectives, no metaphors that won't permit examination. It's straight talk, straight as the Greek!"

H.D. was born on September 10, 1886, in Bethlehem, Pennsylvania, to Helen and Charles Leander Doolittle. The family moved to Philadelphia in 1895 when her father, a noted astronomer, was appointed director of the Flower Observatory at the University of Pennsylvania. In 1901 Hilda met Ezra Pound. Four years later they decided to marry. But the marriage never took place. Pound's first job ended in dismissal, and he set off for Europe; for Venice first and then London. In 1910 he persuaded her to join him in London. The engagement was "equivocally renewed," despite the opposition of Hilda's parents. But Pound was already involved with other women, especially with Dorothy Shakespear. It seemed reasonable to him that he would take Dorothy as his wife and Hilda as his muse. He was a troubadour and regarded such felicities as the proper reward of his craft.

Janice Robinson's biography of H.D., an extremely interesting and informative book, narrates these matters with due severity. She underlines the indisputable fact that H.D.'s men treated her disgracefully, but she does not fully explain why the poet made herself available to cads and scoundrels. Being geniuses together is not a full explanation. When H.D. found that she had been dislodged by Dorothy Shakespear, she turned to Aldington and in 1913 married him. He was a lecher and a liar. In the spring of 1915, Hilda had a stillborn child. Aldington was the father, but he had lost interest in Hilda and turned his sexual attention to Brigit Patmore. The marriage ended, in every respect but formally, in 1917. Aldington accused Hilda of frigidity, a charge that may have been true, because by 1915 she had fallen in love with D. H. Lawrence. The Lawrentian years are obscure. In 1919 Hilda gave birth to a child, Perdita. The father may have been Lawrence or, as alternative gossip had it, the composer Cecil Gray, with whom Hilda spent some months in the spring of 1918. In a rather graceless sentence Robinson says that "there is some reason to believe that Gray covered for Lawrence by not denying that he might be the father." In any case, Lawrence had brought the relation to an end by the time Hilda told him she was pregnant.

In 1918 she began a new phase of her life. Discovering that geniuses were inclined to conduct themselves like gangsters, she turned to a safer affiliation. Winifred Ellerman, daughter of an extraordinarily wealthy shipowner, sought H.D. out because she liked her poems. She fell in love with H.D. and they lived together. Winifred dressed like a man, called herself Bryher, and enjoyed being referred to as "he." Robinson reports that Bryher and H.D. had a sexual relation for a while, but that H.D. was not sexually attracted to Bryher. In 1921, Bryher entered upon an unconsummated marriage with the writer Robert McAlmon. In 1926 Hilda had an affair with the film director Kenneth Macpherson. Bryher put a stop to it by offering to marry him, an offer he had the effrontery to accept. The marriage was not consummated. In 1930 Bryher starred with

Paul Robeson in Macpherson's film *Borderline,* in which she was cast as a cigar-smoking innkeeper.

There is no reason to think that the loss of Macpherson broke H.D.'s heart. In May 1927 she came upon a new interest; she met Freud. Five years later, Bryher paid the fee to enable Hilda to have analysis, over a period of several months, with the Professor, as H.D. called him in her *Tribute to Freud.* He was then advancing penis envy rather than mother fixation as a theory of woman. Hilda approved the new idea and explained to Bryher that it was important, "as book means penis evidently and as a 'writer' only I am an equal, in the right way, with men." Bryher was not impressed. In any event, Freud stayed with mother fixation as the main explanation of Hilda's case. On one occasion, angered by something or other, he said: "The trouble is—I am an old man—you do not think it is worth your while to love me." On her sessions with Freud, Pound commented: "You got into the wrong pig stye, ma chérie."

The truth is that Hilda's sessions with Freud, whatever effect they had on her immediate case, gave her metaphors for her poetry that kept her working for the rest of her life. The notebooks she filled in 1933 provided her not only with "Advent" and "Writing on the Wall," which together make up the *Tribute to Freud,* but with the poetry of the trilogy she wrote in London during World War II: "The Walls Do Not Fall," "Tribute to the Angels," and "The Flowering of the Rod"—her finest work, in fact.

Robinson maintains that H.D.'s deepest and most passionate relation was to Lawrence. The main evidence is in her "Helen in Egypt," a version of her lives and loves in which Lawrence is Achilles, Freud is several people including Stesichorus, Aldington is Paris, Havelock Ellis is Chiron, and Hilda is of course Helen. The evidence is persuasive, and it is supported by a beautiful late poem, "Winter Love," in which H.D. writes that she found Spirit to match her Spirit only when she met Achilles "in a trance, a dream."

Robinson also argues that *Lady Chatterley's Lover* "is essentially the story of H.D.'s life from 1914 to 1918"; this would mean that Lawrence's Connie is more Hilda than Lady Cynthia Asquith, and that his Clifford is more Aldington than Sir Osbert Sitwell or any other candidate for that unhappy honor. Certainly, H.D. has provoked many writers to construe her as if she were, what she often seems to be, a character in fiction. She is a presence in her own *Bid Me to Live* —a novel about herself and Lawrence—

and also in John Cournos's *Miranda Masters,* Aldington's *Life for Life's Sake,* Bryher's *The Heart to Artemis,* Brigit Patmore's *My Friends When Young,* William Carlos Williams's *Autobiography,* and, most glowingly, in Pound's Canto 79, "O lynx, guard my vineyard."

Her work is nearly all autobiographical, though she never removes more than four or five of the seven veils. She didn't stay an Imagist for long. Indeed, Pound did her reputation more harm than good by sticking that label on her. Even now, she is still regarded as the most complete Imagist, with the result that she is assumed to be the most incomplete poet in every respect that counts. Imagism is the Minimalism of poetry; its prescriptions are: no this, no that, no ideas, no comments, no adjectives, write the poem as if you were carving a piece of wood, cut away the excess, leave only the tensions and rhythms. But H.D.'s early poems are superior to other Imagist work in one respect: they don't dawdle or hang about waiting to have their lines admired. They have momentum and, what many Imagist poems lack, urgency:

> *O wind, rend open the heat,*
> *cut apart the heat,*
> *rend it to tatters.*
>
> *Fruit cannot drop*
> *through this thick air—*
> *fruit cannot fall into heat*
> *that presses up and blunts*
> *the points of pears*
> *and rounds the grapes.*

The later poems largely abandon the pedantry of Imagism in favour of more liberal metres and the freedom of discursiveness:

> *Why did you come*
>
> *to trouble my decline,*
> *I am old,*
> *(I was old till you came).*

The limitation of H.D.'s poetry, early and late, arises from her habit of making premature equations. Her mind was infatuated with coincidences, loose etymologies, conjunctions that seemed to connect anything with anything. Lawrence and H.D. were the same age for one day every year, September 10; she thought that significant enough for pages of twinning daydreams. She ransacked the cultures of Greece, Rome, and Egypt for identifications. Mary Magdalene was equated with "Attis-Adonis-Tammuz and his mother who was myrrh," Myrrha, in Ovid's *Metamorphoses,* who turned into a myrrh tree. And so on. She resorted to landscapes, dreams, and mythologies, the most concessive courts to which a poet can appeal against the abrasions of personal and social life. It may be argued that she suffered enough shocks in her daily life to send her all over world and time seeking a poetry of mercurial transitions and communications. Hermes, god of (among other things) messages, was her poetic man. True: I refer to a limitation, not a fatal disability.

What I love in her later poems is their voice, sign of self-possession often in fear of losing itself, in fear but not in despair:

> *There was a Helen before there was a War,*
> *but who remembers her?*

The Hilda we remember, like the Helen, had much to do with love and war; love from the beginning, war in her London years, and the twinning of love and war in virtually all her memories. In the poems, Troy is her name for marriage. But it would not be right to ask of her, as Yeats asked of Maud Gonne: "Was there another Troy for her to burn?" H.D. did not burn her Troy; men started the fire, and she watched it run through the town. It is my impression that her early experiences of love with Pound, Aldington, and Lawrence imposed upon her a paradigm, a set of expectations and frustrations, which constricted her poetry. Freud helped her, but not enough and too late. As a poet, she was thrown into her official theme too soon, and never had quite enough determination to enlarge it or qualify it. Giving her a theme, men held her back from developing it to its largest reach, or from finding another. The theme was all she had, except for a small rare talent and a pale Greek face.

She died on September 28, 1961.

From *The New York Times Book Review,* February 14, 1982.

HART CRANE

I

The Poetry of Hart Crane, by R. W. B. Lewis.

In August 1928 William Carlos Williams wrote to Ezra Pound:

> As to the Hart Crane–Josephson group—to hell with them all. There is good there but it's not for me. As it stands, Crane is supposed to be the man that puts me on the shelf. But not only do I find him just as thick-headed as I am myself and quite as helplessly verbose at times but that he comes up into clarity far less often. If what he puts on the page is related to design, or thought, or emotion—or anything but disguised sentimentality and sloppy feeling—then I am licked.

Crane at that stage had published his first book of poems, *White Buildings. The Bridge* came in 1930, the *Collected Verse* in 1933, but they made no difference to Williams. In July 1939 he wrote to Horace Gregory:

> I liked the man but I stuck on his verse. We were too far apart there. . . . I was stumped by his verse. I suppose the thing was that he

was searching for something inside, while I was all for a sharp use of the materials.

This is the gist of the case against Hart Crane. More elaborately conceived strictures are merely variations on Williams's theme.

But it is well to keep the theme in mind while reading Mr. Lewis's study of the poet. The book starts where a more exacting account might hope to end, with Crane as "one of the finest modern poets in our language, and one of the dozen-odd major poets in American history." Lewis takes this estimate for granted, the case closed. He does not foster critical debate, quotes other critics only when they bring Crane gifts of praise. Blackmur, for instance, wrote the most damaging study of Crane's language, as well as the most illuminating. Lewis quotes him when the opinion is golden, but only then. F. R. Leavis was not alone in finding *The Bridge* "a wordy chaos, both locally and in sum," the poet devoid of "any relevant gift." John Peale Bishop said of Thomas Wolfe that he "achieved probably the utmost intensity of which incoherent writing is capable," and thought of Crane in the same way, a poetic achievement similarly disabled. Allen Tate, Yvor Winters, and other qualified readers have written of Crane's genius in terms which imply that an imputation of genius, in this case, does not settle the critical question. The debate continues.

The most serious charge against Mr. Lewis is that he does not take up the challenge, he elects not to see the gauntlet. Indeed, as the book proceeds, the praise becomes more extreme. At one point Crane is "the most immediately communicative of twentieth-century American poets." Later, taking Crane's will for the deed, Lewis calls him "the religious poet *par excellence* in his generation," *The Bridge* "the only large-scale work of literature in its generation which . . . is finally concerned not with the death of God but with the birth of God." This reminds me of Yvor Winters's remark, with which I agree, that "nothing save confusion can result from our mistaking the Mississippi Valley for God."

I am not convinced that Lewis has gone the best way to establish Crane in these terms. Encomiastic criticism is a fine thing, but it must be attended by scruple. To read Crane again with Lewis's book at hand is extremely rewarding, but it leaves me with the feeling that if Crane had been somewhat harder upon himself his encomiast would not now be compelled to sing everything *fortissimo*. Lewis often glosses the poems with great subtlety, and I am grateful to him for clearing up many difficulties, but he rarely looks hard at the language, the way the words are put to work. So the difference between bad work and good work is often ignored, unless it obtrudes too violently. Even then, Lewis is resourceful. Most readers, I fancy, find Crane's "Cape Hatteras" very bad. Lewis, determined to save it, calls it "a very deliberate and conscious self-parody." If this goes, anything goes. There is an impression, throughout the book, that rhetorical verve is running ahead of criticism; the effect is often to discourage close attention to the words on the page. So it is hardly surprising that Lewis's book is full of misprints, errors of transcription which regularly make nonsense of Crane's texts and disfigure those of Shakespeare, Shelley, Keats, William James, Henry Adams, Stevens, and Eliot. Marianne Moore said of Crane that "a writer is unfair to himself when he is unable to be hard on himself." Crane and his critic are frequently easy on themselves.

Lewis places Crane in a psychological landscape inhabited by Virgil, Emerson, Whitman, Melville, Laforgue, Eliot, Stevens, Cummings, and Hemingway. This is proper if a writer is defined by the company he keeps, but the present company is not allowed to exert critical pressure on Crane, on the nature and range of his art. The effect is, at best, picturesque; at worst, misleading. No critical point is made.

Lewis gives an elaborate account of Crane's poem "Chaplinesque," but he does not encourage the reader to think of other poems that might measure that poem's achievement. William Empson's poem "This Last Pain," for instance, is demonstrably a better poem on a similar theme. So the argument against Crane must be fleshed out a little before Lewis's version is endorsed.

It may be said that Crane could do anything in poetry so long as it required nothing more than genius, an excited sensibility, and the English language. Reading him, one is reminded of Eliot's comment on Hardy, that "at times his style touches sublimity without ever having passed through the stage of being good." Certainly it is true that Crane cultivated intensity at the expense of every other poetic value, as if he numbered only the hectic hours. Even in his most controlled poems the experience is promoted rather than defined; or it is defined in the loose sense of setting an outer limit of possibility within which the reader's sensibility is urged to roam at will. Mr. Lewis's sensibility is ready. The first stanza of "The Wine Menagerie" reads:

> *Invariably when wine redeems the sight,*
> *Narrowing the mustard scansions of the eyes,*
> *A leopard ranging always in the brow*
> *Asserts a vision in the slumbering gaze.*

Presumably the mustard scansions are the sharp divisions between one thing and another, imposed by the eyes, and in the redeemed sight these are narrowed. Lewis comments:

> And in the narrowing glance, eyes become capable of "mustard scansions." This is a fine and impudent phrase that I can imagine no other modern poet devising. It combines the notion of extreme sharpness, like mustard, with that of scanning, as eyes are said to scan a situation; and then it pulls both notions under the control of scansion, or the art of appraising the meter of a poem.

Lewis does not remark that, according to the grammar, the "scansions" themselves are narrowed. Instead, he insinuates a meaning of scansion, equivalent to "scanning," for which the dictionaries give no warrant. The fact that "scan" is common to both is not enough. Lewis is prompted to this critical osmosis by the presence of "sight" and "eyes" nearby, but the prompt should not be taken. I concede that in Crane's agglutinative style we are encouraged to make anything stick. Ostensibly, Lewis is offering a close reading, but in fact he is trying to fill the empty spaces that stretch beyond the natural boundary of the words to that outer limit which, almost independently of the words, marks the reach of Crane's will. In this reading it is essential that a word with three loosely related meanings be deemed three times better than a word which makes sharp use of the materials.

It should be acknowledged that Crane asks to be read in this way, according to a "logic of metaphor" which is permissive enough to include a great deal of bad writing. Lewis speaks of the poet's vision penetrating "through the junkheap of the actual toward the ideal." Several times he invokes "the visionary and loving transfiguration of the actual world." Part of the justification for this emphasis is a letter Crane wrote to Gorham Munson in June 1922. Reporting the "higher consciousness" he sensed while in a dentist's chair, a celebrated illumination, "I felt the two worlds," Crane said, "and at once." In *The Bridge,* according to Lewis, the "old and fallen world" failed Crane, and his art was now grounded in the nature and power of the imagination itself. But until this failure was complete, the world was capable of transfiguration. There is a remarkable letter in which Crane explained to Allen Tate:

> Having absorbed [Eliot] enough we can trust ourselves as never before, in the air or on the sea. I, for instance, would like to leave a few of his "negations" behind me, risk the realm of the obvious more, in quest of new sensations, *humeurs*.

But Crane did not commit himself to the realm of the obvious: nor did he ascribe any value to its obviousness. So he found it all too easy to move from the junkheap, as Lewis calls it, to the ideal. Because his poems are assertions, they make the trip by will; a trip facilitated by the presumptive logic of metaphor and a vague sense of cosmic evolution. "We are all going on in the regular course of things toward a higher consciousness of life and what it means," he writes. There is no need to fast and pray and strive for a relation to the realm of the obvious. When readers say that Crane never found a theme, they mean that he found, too easily, something that took the place of a theme: hints and guesses of relation, too diffuse to be demanding. Anything is a relation if you say it is.

Predictably, Crane was fascinated by bridges. The exemplary gesture of his poems is that of arching, straddling, crossing, swinging, stretching, spanning. Brooklyn Bridge "vaults" the sea. In "Atlantis," Crane invokes "arching strands of song." In "Sunday Morning Apples," "A boy runs with a dog before the sun, straddling / Spontaneities . . . " In "The River," the train "straddles" the hill, "iron strides the dew." But you do not find a relation to something merely by swinging across it; nor do you transfigure the world by transcending it. "The imagination spans beyond despair," Crane says in "For the Marriage of Faustus and Helen," "Outpacing bargain, vocable and prayer." This is true of Crane's imagination, which insists on going "beyond" without going "through." Thoroughfare is closed to his will and therefore to his style. Blackmur said of him:

> He wrote in a language of which it was the virtue to accrete, modify, and interrelate moments of emotional vision—moments at which the sense of being gains its greatest access—moments at

which, by the felt nature of knowledge, the revealed thing is its own meaning; and he attempted to apply his language, in his major effort, to a theme that required a sweeping, discrete, indicative, anecdotal language, a language in which, by force of movement, mere cataloguing can replace and often surpass representation.

This reminds us, incidentally, that Crane is not at all like Whitman, despite his own insistence and "Cape Hatteras." An indicative style was available to Whitman because he was at home in the realm of the obvious and trusted its relations. Crane was not at home there and had only the vaguest grasp of any relations. Whitman could place one obvious thing beside another and indicate a relation between them because a relation was certified by his whole sense of life. He did not need to insist. Crane had to insist, for the same reason that people whistle in the dark. In his poems, therefore, words which testify to relations are doomed to exaggerate them. His "Elizabethan" style is implicated in this predicament. In "The Wine Menagerie," he writes:

> *Wine talons*
> *Build freedom up about me and distill*
> *This competence . . .*

In "The Harbor Dawn":

> *The sky,*
> *Cool feathery fold, suspends, distills*
> *This wavering slumber . . .*

In "The Dance," a star "bled into the dawn."

Now and again, Crane had misgivings about the exemplary figure of his poetry. In 1926, after reading Spengler's *Decline of the West*, he wrote a rueful letter to Waldo Frank about *The Bridge*. "The very idea of a bridge," he said, depends upon certain "spiritual convictions." In this age of disbelief "the bridge as a symbol today has no significance beyond an economical approach to shorter hours, quicker lunches, behaviorism and toothpicks." I am not sure, one exaggeration stirring another, that those who use Brooklyn Bridge as a mere instrument to these daily ends are not wiser, after all, than the arching poet, on the grounds that a feasible use is better than an impossibly sublime demand. Mediating between exaggerations, Marianne Moore's poem "Granite and Steel" praises the "enfranchising cable" of the same bridge, sings John Roebling's harmony of the eye and the eye of the mind, and leaves the bridge as it is, "an actuality," as it is, subject only to the flick of Miss Moore's imagination. It seems clear to me that Miss Moore has chosen the better way, the more poetic as well as the more religious way. The "force of movement" which Blackmur describes is, in Miss Moore's poem, a quality in the syntax which, moving things along, keeps each in its proper place. It is an achievement of luminous intelligence; call it, in Williams's word, measure. Perhaps it is worth remarking now that the resplendent things in Crane's poetry are marvels of diction. Where the poems fail, normally, they fail in syntax, force of movement, indication.

This brings us back to *The Bridge.* Lewis, trying hard to enforce the unity of the poem against those readers who find it a heap of gorgeous fragments, grounds everything in "the visionary imagination." This means, in cooler terms, that the unity of the poem is totally dependent upon the sensibility of the poet, its "plot" the graph of his interests.

Lewis speaks of "the gradual permeation of an entire culture by the power of poetic vision," but in fact he defeats argument by making the poem an idealist assertion, Crane's Supreme Fiction. It may be necessary to settle for this, since no other mode of unity seems to apply. Kenneth Burke once observed, reviewing G. H. Mead's *Philosophy of the Act,* that "the strategy of romantic philosophy [which Mead likens to the beginnings of self-consciousness in adolescence] was to identify the individual Self metaphysically with an Absolute Self, thereby making the reflexive act the very essence of the universe, a state of affairs that is open to lewd caricature." This gives Crane's poetry, and especially *The Bridge,* the right connotations. It also glosses Lewis's tendency, inevitable if you begin where he begins, to read Crane's poems as parables of the poetic imagination. Even "The Air Plant" is turned in this direction. The trouble with the argument is that Crane's poems soon begin to sound like "The Man with the Blue Guitar," Stevens's "Tom-tom, c'est moi." I am not sure that Lewis intends to go as far as this, but I think he must, to be consistent.

A few details, local disagreements. Dealing with those superb lines in "Chaplinesque":

> *We will sidestep, and to the final smirk*
> *Dally the doom of that inevitable thumb . . .*

Lewis cites a passage from *Moby-Dick* where the whale "dallied with the doomed craft." But Crane's verb is transitive, closer to Marlowe's in *Faustus:* "But wherefore do I dally my revenge?" Lewis thinks that "puckered index" in the same poem refers to the Catholic Index; an interpretation no more persuasive than the later notion that the "twelve" in "The Tunnel" are the Twelve Apostles. He quotes a passage from "The Wine Menagerie":

> *This competence — to travel in a tear*
> *Sparkling alone, within another's will.*

Then he comments:

> On his journey toward fuller vision, the poet will "travel in a tear," and he will sparkle alone, submissive to the will of another. That "other" is of course the wind; and the reference to it is equivalent to the phrase about joining "the entrainments of the wind" in "Passage."

I may be missing the point, but I can make nothing of this. Crane's words seem to me to claim a new poetic power, new to Crane, that of dramatic apprehension; the power that Keats and Hazlitt ascribed to Shakespeare as distinct from Wordsworth's "egotistical sublime." "He was nothing in himself," Hazlitt said of Shakespeare, "but he was all that others were, or that they could become," set off against those modern poets who surround "the meanest objects with the morbid feelings and devouring egotism of the writers' own minds." Crane's claim, if my reading is just, arises from his discovered ability, in the first part of the poem, to enter imaginatively into the lives of other people, the quarreling couple and the "urchin who has left the snow."

These are details. If, on the whole, I disagree with Lewis's presentation of Crane and think that he has pitched his estimate too high, this is not to deny that his reading of particular poems is always lively and often definitive. Perhaps what I miss in his book is a sense of scale: the poems that count are not sufficiently distinguished from poorer work. I would prefer to display the major achievement (such as "The Broken Tower,"

"Repose of Rivers," "Voyages" I, II, V, and VI, "The River," "To Brooklyn Bridge," "The Harbor Dawn," "Legend," "Paraphrase," and "Passage") rather than make large claims for everything. Even within the best work, discrimination is necessary. Very few of the poems are perfectly accomplished. Indeed, Crane still seems to me, even after reading Lewis's study and going back over the poems, a poet whose reach far exceeded his grasp: greater in short poems than in long poems: greater in stanza than in poem, in line than in stanza. Perhaps it is significant that his poems stay in the mind as phrases, often drawing away from their setting: "Moidores of spent grace": "I dream the too-keen cider — the too-soft snow": "the eye / That shrines the quiet lake and swells a tower"; these to stand for many. There are short passages in Crane which for rhetorical grandeur are as conclusive as anything in Yeats, Eliot, Pound, or Stevens. What he lacks, in this company, is the force of continuity and development. His work is not, finally, greater than the sum of its parts. At this point I am afraid my disagreement with Lewis is complete.

From *The New York Review of Books,* November 9, 1967.

II

Hart Crane and Yvor Winters: Their Literary Correspondence, by Thomas Parkinson.

The title of this volume is somewhat misleading. Crane's letters to Winters are available, but not Winters's to Crane. Crane probably destroyed them, enraged by Winters's review of *The Bridge* in 1930; and even if they had survived that occasion, they could not be published, under the terms of Winters's will, until 1993. But Thomas Parkinson's book is extremely valuable. Only one of Crane's letters to Winters is published in Brom Weber's *The Letters of Hart Crane, 1916–1932* (1952). Nearly fifty are printed in Mr. Parkinson's book, with judiciously informative comment and elucidation. We are also given a pretty clear indication of Winters's response to Crane's letters, sometimes by reading between Crane's lines, sometimes by reference to Winters's letters to Allen Tate.

Hart Crane (1899–1932) and Yvor Winters (1900–68) were associates rather than friends. The relation was mutually useful rather than warm. During Christmas week 1927, they had several conversations, but that was their only meeting, so we are not dealing with the sort of warm and turbulent friendship that Crane had with Waldo Frank, Gorham Munson, Slater Brown, Malcolm Cowley, Allen Tate, and Kenneth Burke. The correspondence was hectic while it lasted. Between October 25, 1926, and December 10, 1928, Crane wrote more than forty letters to Winters. Then there was a break for more than a year, until January 14, 1930, when Crane sent Winters the final text of *The Bridge.* After Winters reviewed the poem, Crane wrote him a letter so rough, apparently, that Winters destroyed it. That was the end. But the episode is a lively moment in American literary history, and is of great intrinsic interest. Crane was sufficiently stimulated or provoked by Winters to mail him his views on sundry themes: notably the poetry of William Carlos Williams, Donne, literary form, Indian symbolism, science, Imagism, Whitman, Cummings, Joyce, Edmund Wilson, Hardy, Fielding, Hopkins, Eliot, Marlowe—even his recently discovered cure for hay fever.

The relation began sweetly, with Winters praising Crane in letters to Harriet Monroe, the editor of *Poetry* magazine. When *White Buildings* was published in 1926, Winters not only agreed with Allen Tate's high assessment of it but listed five poems from the volume that he felt placed Crane "among the five or six greatest poets writing in English." These poems—"Repose of Rivers," "For the Marriage of Faustus and Helen," "Recitative," and the second and fifth of the "Voyages"—provided the criteria by which, in reviewing *The Bridge* four years later, Winters pronounced Crane a ruined man and a defeated poet. Crane was understandably desolate when he read the review: understandably, because he had sent Winters several parts of *The Bridge* as soon as they were written, and he had no reason to anticipate that Winters would take such a dim view of the whole poem. In the event, Winters maintained that Crane, on the evidence of *The Bridge,* was a naïve genius dazzled by Whitman, and therefore a lost soul. His poetry was now diffuse, loosely emotional, lenient toward its vices. Structurally incoherent, *The Bridge* achieved the condition of true poetry only in single lines and phrases.

Winters never retracted or modified this judgement. He repeated it in 1947, when he wrote "The Significance of *The Bridge* by Hart Crane or What Are We to Think of Professor X?" The only difference made by the lapse of seventeen years was that instead of blaming Whitman for Crane's degeneration, Winters now blamed Emerson for both Whitman's mindlessness and Crane's suicide. "We have," he wrote, "a poet of great genius, who ruined his life and his talent by living and writing as the two greatest teachers of our nation recommended." But there was even more to the story than that. Winters's own poetry was in question. In 1927 and 1928, the years of the main correspondence with Crane, he was ridding himself of one style and taking on another. The aesthetic of free verse that produced most of the poems in *The Immobile Wind* (1921), *The Magpie's Shadow* (1922), and *The Bare Hills* (1927) struck Winters now as too fluid for his good. The change to a far more conceptual style was begun in the years between *The Bare Hills* and *The Proof* (1930). It was a change that could not be rushed; it required time, patience, and determination.

Winters never confused Crane's style with his own, but he saw that there were vices common to both: a misunderstanding of the nature of imagery, a failure of discrimination. Crane was an important cause of the long war that Winters started in 1928 against formlessness, fluidity, Romanticism, the asserted primacy of feeling over judgement. I suspect Crane was the poet Winters had chiefly in mind when he wrote the "Statement of Purpose" for *Gyroscope* in 1929, attacking "all doctrines of liberation and emotional expansionism, since they deprecate and tend to eliminate the intellect, the core of conscious existence."

Again in 1929, Winters proclaimed the doctrine of good and evil that animated his criticism for the rest of his life. "The basis of Evil is in emotion," he declared, "and Good rests in the power of rational selection in action, as a preliminary to which emotion in any situation must be as far as possible eliminated, and, in so far as it cannot be eliminated, understood." The function of poetry was to understand emotion, as a second best to eliminating it. Only a besotted Whitmanian would culti-vate emotion as a good in itself. Stylistic precision, Winters maintained, "is merely the ultimate manifestation of spiritual precision and strength." The way to achieve this precision, this strength, was by studying the masters: in Renaissance poetry, Ben Jonson, Fulke Greville, George Herbert; in the modern poets, Baudelaire, Valéry, Hardy, Bridges, a few poems by Wallace Stevens.

In the years of his correspondence with Crane, Winters was setting his mind upon a monastic discipline, practising the fierce schedules of a recent convert. His new poems were not quite as stern as his critical imperatives, they were content to achieve a state of poise between Wilderness and Wisdom. Wilderness was allowed to instigate experience, provided Wisdom was at hand to curb it. The object was certitude, known by the finality of its tone. So the correspondence with Crane had to end, for many reasons. Parkinson allows us to guess that Winters offered Crane some heavy-handed advice about alcohol and homosexuality. I can well believe it. Both men were despots, in their different ways. Winters was a despot of order, knowledge, concept, restraint. Crane's despotism luxuriated in passion, instinct, genius. Winters believed that he could keep evil at bay only by sentencing himself to the hard labour of knowledge, and by the rational imitation of his peers. Crane seems to have believed that daily life enforced a sufficient degree of penance and that a man had the right to make the best of it, taking his pleasures where he found them. He does not appear to have felt guilt, unless it took the form of dissatisfaction with his poetry. In the end, I don't think Winters had any real influence on Crane; they veered too far from each other too soon. Crane remained for Winters a cautionary instance, a text from some terrible Old Testament of his own devising. Still, I keep thinking of one moment in the relationship between them: Winters's review of *The Bridge.* If Winters had been more equably settled in his convictions when he read it, he would have avoided reviewing it, made up an excuse. A lesser man would have dodged the occasion. Of course, that would have only postponed the breach; it was inevitable. Winters could not have listened to Crane's Orphic voice much longer; nor could Crane have borne Winters's righteousness.

From *The New York Times Book Review,* February 4, 1979.

AUDEN

I

Early Auden, by Edward Mendelson.

The life of W. H. Auden is conveniently divisible into two unequal parts. Early Auden, born in York in 1907, went to school and university in England and stayed there, except for frequent travels, till January 19, 1939, when he sailed for New York. Late Auden made himself a New Yorker if not entirely an American: he liked to keep up his relation to Europe by spending some months of the year there, and he returned to Oxford in his last few years, but he remained a New Yorker on principle. He died in 1974.

Auden's decision to leave England and settle in America caused a flurry among his English friends. It was easy to represent his departure as a run for safety from war and bombs, which he and nearly everybody knew were inevitable. In January 1938, Auden went with Christopher Isherwood to China and Japan. They spent three months there and came back through Canada and America. In New York they decided that America would be their next place. Isherwood thought of an extended stay, short of permanence, but Auden felt that the move should have such permanence as the human condition would allow. But the decision had been made, by intention if not yet in effect, in 1936. Auden was lonely and rather miserable. He identified England with the drab thirties, the "low dishonest decade" he attacked in "September 1, 1939." Disillusioned by his brief experience of the Spanish Civil War, he thought Europe a hopeless mess. His writings during those years were doom-laden and noisy, a combination many of his English friends found tiresome. In 1938, William Empson parodied him in the poem "Just a Smack at Auden," presenting him as a poseur, a dandy of the apocalypse:

> *Shall I turn a sire, boys? Shall I choose a friend?*
> *The fat is in the pyre, boys, waiting for the end.*

Edward Mendelson's book is a history and interpretation of Auden's writings during the years 1927–39. It is not a biography. There was a plan, a few years ago, that he and Stephen Spender would write the authorized life of Auden, but the difficulties raised by considerations of delicacy and tact proved insurmountable. Many of Auden's lovers are living unruffled lives, some of them enjoying marital satisfaction. It would be a wretched business to disturb them. So the biographical plan has been dropped. Mendelson has now directed his attention to the writings, the poems, plays, and essays which he edited and published in 1977 as *The English Auden.* These are, mainly, *Paid on Both Sides* (1928), *The Dance of Death* (1933), *The Dog Beneath the Skin* (1935), *Letter to Lord Byron* and *The Ascent of F6* (both 1936), *Letters from Iceland* (1937), *On the Frontier* (1938), and *Journey to a War* (1939).

It is an odd book. Mendelson claims that Auden "became the most inclusive poet of the twentieth century, its most technically skilled, and its most truthful." The claim is loosely worded: before it could make sense, virtually every adjective would have to be expounded, the necessary qualifications taken into account, judicious comparisons made. But in any case the claim is effectively refuted by the book itself. The dominant impression enforced by Mendelson is that Auden's moral and intellectual vanity kept him at every moment of his early life excited and bewildered, able to talk loud but not to think straight. Going through the early poems and plays, Mendelson finds, mostly, incoherence, contradiction, extravagance. Indeed, while he mocks those critics who thought of Auden as a permanent undergraduate, a glittering adolescent, he goes far toward proving them right. F. R. Leavis spoke of Auden achieving his early success in a context "in which the natural appetite for kudos is not chastened by contact with mature standards, and in which fixed immaturity can take itself for something else." Mendelson adverts to this assessment, without quoting it, but his account of Early Auden has the effect of confirming it.

In fact, he has little good to say about Early Auden. Most of his commentaries are impatient with what he regards as Auden's pretension. Virtually nothing elicits his approval or stirs him to warmth, except for "A Summer Night" (1933), a poem whose values were gained only to be lost again before the ink was dry. At one point Mendelson refers with capitalized irony to "critics for whom the young Auden is the One True Auden," and he makes it clear that he is not among them. But there is more, if not more good, to be said about Early Auden. His imagery has not worn well. Helmeted airmen, spies, groups of initiates crossing frontiers with doubtful passports, these have receded into the early cinema, Garbo-land, the stuff of revivals on Bleecker Street. Auden did a lot of loose thinking under the guise of a meditation on History. For a man who wrote so much about this abstraction, his span of attention was remarkably short; he was mostly to be found twitching from one enthusiasm to another. Momentary vibrations were enthralling to him, so long as they were intense. He expressed passing opinions with the assertiveness, but not the authority, of convictions. When people are both unhappy and discerning, as Kenneth Burke has said, they tend to believe that their unhappiness is derived from their discernment. So in Auden's early poems and plays; but the belief did not assure him that he would make for himself a future consistent with his merit. Nevertheless, Auden's early work is more forceful than Mendelson's account of it suggests. Bewildered as he often was, and unduly receptive to casual notions, he had a voice distinct from the other, fainter voices which issued from much the same experiences. Empson has praised Auden's "curl of the lip," and it is worth a critic's while to ask how the lip got curled and what its curl meant. Besides, years were not wasted which yielded such poems as "This Lunar Beauty," "That Night When Joy Began," "What Siren Zooming," "Lay Your Sleeping Head, My Love," "Miss Gee," "The Watershed," "Paysage Moralisé," and "A Summer Night." The plays are interesting because they were written by the author of these poems, but not for any other reason.

Mendelson is informative on the early influences: mainly T. S. Eliot,

Yeats, Freud, John Layard, Homer Lane, D. H. Lawrence, Trigant Burrow, T. E. Lawrence, Marx, Edward Upward. But these are standard issues by now. Sometimes he gets himself into such a hurry that he gets things wrong. A glance at Eliot's *Criterion* or at Perry Meisel's *Twentieth Century Views on Freud* would have saved him from the error of saying that "Auden was the first imaginative writer in English to take Freud seriously—Lawrence dismissed him, Joyce derided him, everyone else ignored him." He makes a fuss about Auden's theory of the origin of language, but it is clear that the theory was Malinowski's rather than Auden's. These lapses issue, I think, from Mendelson's impatience: he is anxious to move along to what really engages him, Later Auden. The implication of the present book is that the best thing about Early Auden was that he eventually thought straight enough to make himself Later Auden.

The change began, for Professor Mendelson, in the months between Auden's final decision to leave England, July 1938, and his departure for New York in January 1939. During that period, Mendelson says in an arresting sentence, Auden "sought poetic subjects in knowledge that he could share, rather than in knowledge that set him apart." At this point Mendelson's book is nearly finished, but the best pages in it are the last; nothing becomes him so much as the warmth with which he points beyond this book to his next, a study of Later Auden. If it takes up where the vivacity of these last pages leaves off, it will be splendid. At the end, Mendelson gives what I assume is the plot of the next volume:

> Without pomp or melodrama Auden has made the one discovery that can release him from his private island. All his daring projects for changes of heart and history led to contradiction and defeat. But his small private hopes, which he had scarcely noticed, brought lasting rewards. For a young poet, praised by the crowd and conscious of his genius, this realization was both unsettling and exhilarating: if he was not so special as he hoped, then he need not be so isolated as he feared.

Well said. There is clearly a relation between Auden's later styles and the decision to settle for minor recognitions in the absence of grand unity. The later work has much to do with the middle style, music, opera, Christianity, the gratifications of weather and landscape. But these are matters for another book, Professor Mendelson's next.

From *The New York Times Book Review,* August 9, 1981.

II

Epistle to a Godson, and Other Poems, by W. H. Auden.
Forewords and Afterwords, by W. H. Auden.
Man's Place: An Essay on Auden, by Richard Johnson.
W. H. Auden as a Social Poet, by Frederick Buell.

"For Valéry," W. H. Auden has remarked, "a poem ought to be a festival of the intellect, that is, a game, but a solemn, ordered, and significant game, and a poet is someone to whom arbitrary difficulties suggest ideas." For Valéry, and now for Auden, especially in *About the House, City Without Walls,* and *Epistle to a Godson,* books written according to the principle that, whatever life is, poetry is a carnival. The poet begins with language, delighting in the exercise of its possibilities, and he stops short of Mardi Gras only by requiring his language to recognize the existence of the primary world in which we live.

The poem makes a secondary world, according to prescriptions as congenial as they are ingenious. In *Epistle to a Godson* the primary world contains for the most part certain grand maladies of daily living: age, loss, grief, loneliness, violence, nuances of damage, bloody-minded monsters at large. The secondary world is still managed with the most charming intention, and a prosody of good humour, good taste, good luck. The dominant tone implies that the quest is now too perilous to be undertaken directly, better wait till morning and the possibility of "cleansed occasions." Meanwhile the poet writes short, brisk poems, a few smacks administered to the world's bottom for its good. There is a lot of grousing, but no harm is meant, the poet is merely telling young people to mind their manners, speak decent English, and wash.

Mr. Auden has become a crusty old fellow somewhat before his time; by my reckoning he is only sixty-six but he talks in this book like something carved on Mount Rushmore. The familiar ghost of T. S. Eliot's "Little Gidding" disclosed three gifts reserved for age: first, "the cold friction of expiring sense / Without enchantment"; second, "the conscious impotence of rage / At human folly"; and finally, "the rending pain of re-enactment / Of all that you have done, and been."

Epistle to a Godson takes a milder view of its gifts. There is still a touch of enchantment, there are good friends, there is music. Human folly is inescapable, but Auden does whatever poetry can to turn the impotence of rage into irony, keeping his temper as sweet as possible. "Our world rapidly worsens": well, perhaps it does, but I don't propose to worry too much if the only evidence produced in the poem is the fact that Auden at Schwechat Flughafen was frisked by a cop for weapons. Methinks he protests too much. As for Eliot's last gift to the aged, Auden does not trouble himself too much or spend his spirit fruitlessly re-enacting what he has done or been. He takes Yeats's line on that, forgives himself a lot, casts out remorse.

Leaving the blues aside, Auden tells us something of the world as it would be if God had consulted the poet before making it. It would be a sweet world, ruled by the laws of prosody, a lot of rhymes, "a stunning display of concinnity and elegance," a lot of freedom, short of anarchy. From an earlier poem: "A sentence uttered makes a world appear / Where all things happen as it says they do." Such a world would be a gentle place, "nothing obscene or unpleasant," since "only the unscarred overfed enjoy Calvary / as a verbal event." Things would be easy on the senses, there would be plenty of time for love and wit. No excess though: against Blake, Auden says that the road of excess leads, more often than not, to the Slough of Despond.

Sometimes, in such a mood, Auden is inclined to say to his juniors: listen, kiddos, I've had my life, why should you whine about yours? Or words to that effect. In one poem he tells those who may be curious about Circe's charms that they can take his word for them, they're overrated. Free love is discouraged, like free verse, and for similar reasons, apparently. In "Moon Landing," reversing Johnson's famous remark to Boswell about the Giant's Causeway, Auden says of the moon that it was probably worth going to see, but not worth seeing. The gist of the rhetoric is that the primary world should be modeled on the best of the available secondary worlds: our institutions like our symphonies. State occasions would be featured like proper names, which are "*an-sich* poetic," as amenable as limestone.

Auden's images of value are those now familiar to us from his poems of the last decade. He praises "a watered / lively garden" and remains uncharmed by deserts. He much prefers nature when she's courteous than when she's throwing a tantrum: "earthquakes, floods, eruptions, / seem a bit vulgar." It is my impression that animals get a better press in *Epistle to a Godson* than in earlier books, mainly because their inability to listen to a story is now felt as a minor defect in view of their instinctual certainties, lucidities apparently superior to those of men, officially "their lonely betters."

Insects are still separated from our affections by "a prohibitive fracture empathy cannot transgress." Mice are addressed with a certain fellow feeling I cannot share. I could not love even a white one. Auden is tender to dogs, bacteria, and many other instances of life, though he reserves the right to be selective and to play favourites. He thinks well of plants, mainly because their response to a gardener's handling shows that they "like to be given the chance to get more than a self-education." Of minerals in this book he has little to say, having said so much and so warmly in earlier poems of great celebrity; but he has a wonderful line about the regime of minerals "where what is not forbidden is compulsory." Naturally, most of the grousing poems are about man, presented as a nuisance, with rare exceptions. Still, he's all we have: besides, he's a miracle, God knows, "for who is not certain that he was meant to be?"

But the trouble is that man, this miraculous fellow, is a bore and, increasingly nowadays, a dangerous clown. He ought to live with joy and laughter, good food, good music. His books ought to be delightful, not "plain cooking made still plainer by plain cooks," to recite an earlier version of the poet's plaint. If "the truest poetry is the most feigning," poets should feign like mad, but take care not to go crazy. So Auden, it is well known and in part approved, has been making merry with the dictionaries in recent years. I suppose he thinks of them as pure poetry, containing thousands of words virtually untouched by human hands; marvellous words now archaic, obsolete, and for that very reason waiting to be resuscitated by a poet addicted to that pleasure.

In this book he uses "faith" as a verb, its object someone you trust. "Conster" is used instead of its current form, "construe." "Annoy" is a noun, "odd" a verb, "decent," "false" are verbs. "In tift" is Anglo-Saxon for "in good order." "Blithe" is used as a transitive verb; "librate" instead of "oscillate," so to librate between a glum and a frolic, in the poem "Talking to Myself," is presumably to give the movement a moony touch, the libration of the moon being the only sense in which the word is still recalled.

Again, Auden runs to the dialect dictionaries. Instead of asking what the moon landing means or portends, he asks: "What does it osse?"—a Cumberland verb recently deceased and therefore in need of Auden's attention. In "Talking to Mice" the sight of a dead mouse "obumbated a week." At first I suspected a misprint for "obumbrated," a word well represented in the great O.E.D., meaning "overshadowed." Perhaps it is a misprint, like Yeats's "soldier" for "solider"; unless Auden wanted to touch the word with "abate" as an even darker shadow falling upon the first. In any case, the verb stands for the formal acknowledgement of grief, and its archaic air takes some of the harm out of the occasion by observing the decencies with a particular mark of attention, a Latin mark more plangent than the Saxon version which has survived.

The only point I want to make is that Auden, who likes a lark as well as anybody, is not merely larking with the dictionary: in nearly every novelty he has a sound reason, but also a sense reason. "*O Happy Grief!* is all sad verse can say": a motto from an earlier book, practised in this one so that the grief, redeemed by the poet's language, becomes good without losing its other attributes. A grudging reader, faced with Auden's novelties, might refuse to acknowledge a serious purpose being pursued, might declare in anger that he writes thus not because it is necessary but because it is possible. Such people remind me of a passage in Henry Adams's *Democracy* where envy is the topic and Madeleine the occasion: "People who envied her smile said that she cultivated a sense of humor in order to show her teeth." My own view is that for such a cause any reason is good enough. If Auden starts with language rather than with big thoughts, good luck to him; one judges by results.

Epistle to a Godson is Auden's first collection of new poems since *City Without Walls* (1969). It begins with a godfather's advice, not Marlon Brando's "Make him an offer he can't refuse" but the Red Knight's admonition, somewhat modified to take account of the fact that its object is Philip Spender not Alice: "Turn out your toes when you walk—and remember who you are." The book ends with a soul's address to its body, pleading for the boon of a quick death when the time comes:

> *Remember: when* Le Bon Dieu *says to* You Leave Him!
> *please, please, for His sake and mine, pay no attention*
> *to my piteous* Dont's, *but bugger off quickly.*

Between these good counsels there are poems about doctors, illness, "my sad flesh," the distinction between persons and animals, the superiority of sight to hearing (all sensory things considered), photography, music (notably that of the first cuckoo in spring), the weather, William Empson (in praise), and "eucatastrophe," "regeneration beyond waters." Auden welcomes a theme only when it has given him some sign, however demurely, that if properly appreciated it will respond with affection. Courtship, thereafter, is a matter of style, and if it seems easy the appearance is deceptive: it takes a rich mixture of grace and luck to win, even with a smiling theme. If the theme keeps its distance, refuses to meet the poet's eye, then Auden leaves it alone: why should the aging eagle stretch his wings, he is not trying to write *Paradise Lost.* He has certainly done enough, in *Epistle to a Godson,* to please me.

Foreword and Afterwords* is a collection of Auden's essays and reviews, chosen from his occasional writings between 1943 and 1972. Not as formally organized as *The Dyer's Hand,* it retains many of the same themes, the nature of civilization, the hero, religion, beauty, and so forth. Most of the essays are literary, the rest are musical, mainly operatic. In prose, Auden is happiest with minor writers, because he can make the most of them: with major writers he seems to feel that only a miraculous leap of imagination would come at all close to them, and it is too late to go in for such athletics. I list his official topics: Shakespeare, Luther, Pope, Goethe, Kierkegaard, Poe, Tennyson, Mayhew, Wagner, Verdi, Trollope, Leontiev, Lewis Carroll, Van Gogh, Wilde, A. E. Housman, Cavafy, Kipling, Valéry, Max Beerbohm, Walter de la Mare, Chesterton, Mann, Virginia Woolf, Stravinsky, Hammarskjöld, J. R. Ackerley; I may have dropped a few.

Auden is splendid on Beerbohm, and on Wilde: he needs a good deal of space if he is to engage with his themes, he is cramped by the short review and can do nothing much with it except offer a few small deliberations and sign off.

Some of the essays are autobiographically revealing. We now know that among the Greek writers Auden dislikes Lucian, that among Pope's poems he could live without the *Essay on Man,* that he dislikes behaviorists, Lord Alfred Douglas, Carlyle, the Action Française people, the theory of random Creation, and dreams, "nocturnal manias." He particularly likes Irenaeus, Ronald Firbank's novels, Pope (on the whole), Horace, Bonhoeffer, and nearly every minor writer who has settled gracefully for minority status and therefore lives at peace with himself.

In the longer essays, as in *The Dyer's Hand,* Auden likes to set his mind working upon the distinctions between two rival forces often equally compelling: Eros and Agape, Body and Soul, Catholic and Protestant, Prospero and Ariel, Petrarch and Shakespeare (as sonneteers), humans and animals, France and England. Many of his grandest perceptions come from the practice of looking now upon this picture, now upon that: he is gifted in comparison and contrast, for the energy they release. He mentions playing a parlor game in which each player names two persons "of such different temperaments that on meeting they would dislike each other intensely, and they are condemned to live together in Purgatory until they come to understand and love each other." T. S. Eliot and Walt Whitman, he offers for a start, then Tolstoy and Wilde. I have never played the game, though I am not too old to learn, I suppose.

Prompted by *Forewords and Afterwords,* I would prefer the game of Who-Said-It? Here is a set to begin with, culled from Auden's book. Name the author of each of the following:

> "If the Gospels omitted all mention of Christ's resurrection, faith would be easier for me, the Cross itself suffices."
>
> "There is a great difference between believing something *still* and believing it *again.*"
>
> "True love is like seeing ghosts, we all talk about it but few of us have ever seen one."
>
> "Art exists to be seen, not to be talked about, except perhaps in its presence."
>
> "Nothing knits man to man like the frequent passage from hand to hand of cash."
>
> "It is worth living if only to make absolute demands on life."
>
> "It is impossible to put a distance between oneself and an object without turning around to see if one is succeeding."
>
> "If Satan were to promise me all the kingdoms of the earth on condition that I bowed down and worshipped him, I should laugh because I should know that, given my limited capacities, he could not fulfill his promise."
>
> "However hard Tolstoy tried, he could never think of a peasant as an equal; he could only, partly out of a sense

of guilt at his own moral shortcomings, admire him as
his superior."

"Under Kipling's will, the vulgarest words learn to wash
behind their ears and to execute complicated movements at the word of command, but they can hardly
be said to learn to think for themselves."

"Poe's 'The Raven' strikes the reader as 'contrived' in a bad
way, which means that it is not contrived enough."

Now here are the answers: Simone Weil, Lichtenberg, La Rochefoucauld,
Goethe, Walter Sickert, Alexander Blok, Valéry, Auden, Auden, Auden,
and Auden. So *Forewords and Afterwords* is a commonplace book, and a
good one. Auden is not primarily interested in the *bricolage* of a man's life
but in ideas which become experience when they are interrogated: the
interrogation must be conducted with zest but also with a sense of
propriety, the mind should not resort to assault and battery. It is easy to
understand, when one reads these two books, why Auden so much
admires the writings of Marianne Moore.

Of the two critical studies of Auden's verse, Mr. Johnson's is chiefly
concerned with the later Auden, and he begins with *New Year Letter*
(1941) as making a new departure. I am not sure that his chosen idiom has
proved itself as instructive as he had hoped: his reliance upon the concept
of "humanism" seems to me excessive. But his book is useful as a guide to
the later work. Mr. Buell is concerned rather with the early Auden than
the later, he places his main stress on the poet of the thirties, making the
air dense with references to Freud, D. H. Lawrence, Georg Groddeck.
He gives a lot of background, but the background has a way of
obumbrating his foreground, so that the poetry has trouble in declaring
itself. Still, each of these books complements the other, and their differing
emphases remind us of the range and diversity of Auden's work; all those
toads, all those gardens.

From *The New York Review of Books,* July 19, 1973.

KENNETH BURKE

Attitudes Toward History, by Kenneth Burke.
Permanence and Change: An Anatomy of Purpose,
by Kenneth Burke.

With these two books, the University of California Press has brought all of Kenneth Burke's books—eleven to date—back into print. What are we to make of them? It is still not clear what kind of writer Burke is: it doesn't seem adequate to call him a literary critic, a poet, a novelist, a short-story writer, a sociologist, or a philosopher of history. Perhaps we should simply call him a sage, and think of the latitude traditionally taken by such a mind. In a certain light his work resembles Emerson's, especially in its zest to provoke the perceptions that a mind attains by sufficiently trusting itself, but Burke's takes account of far more evidence and requires his vision to make its way against far keener objection. No comparison nearer home suggests itself.

Where to begin? Burke's first literary problem, in the early 1920s, was clear enough: how to make a living, a bare one of necessity, and effect the swiftest transition from a dispiriting suburb of Pittsburgh to Greenwich Village. The solution was to live on a run-down farm in New Jersey and spend many talkative evenings at John Squarcialupi's restaurant on Perry Street or loitering with the Provincetown Players in Macdougal Street. Burke soon involved himself in various little magazines:

Secession, Broom, the *Little Review, Hound and Horn, Pagany,* and especially *The Dial,* "the deep and dirgeful *Dial,*" as Hart Crane called it in 1923. Burke's closest friend was Malcolm Cowley, but he was also on discursive and argumentative terms with Gilbert Seldes, Scofield Thayer, Marianne Moore, E. E. Cummings, Crane, Slater Brown, Matthew Josephson. *The Dial* published his stories, poems, musical criticism—he still composes a little music—and parts of what was eventually published as *Towards a Better Life,* his novel about a man under great stress, in which especially resourceful sentences are presented as medicine.

I see Burke's interests as having developed in three phases, with plenty of continuity to complicate the narrative of change. He found in himself enough evidence that new affiliations never entirely suppress old ones. The first phase is appropriate to a man who pursued bohemian and avant-garde sentiments in Greenwich Village, and rented for a spell Hart Crane's apartment on Grove Street, while writing poetry and fiction acceptable only to fugitive magazines. Burke's interests chimed with those of writers who thought of themselves as modern—Joyce and Eliot, especially. His first book, *The White Oxen,* a collection of fifteen short stories, was published in 1924. His early fiction is heavily if ingeniously indebted to Thomas Mann's—he was the first American translator of *Der Tod in Venedig*—and it features twisted, lonely characters like John Neal, the morbidly inventive hero of *Towards a Better Life.*

This phase may be called aestheticism, since it proposes the bohemian life as a response to the social conditions otherwise imposed by bureaucracy, the corporations, banks, and government at large. Literature and art are presented as counterstatements to the statements made by the rough magicians in power. Burke's motto, in this phase, was: "When in Rome, do as the Greeks," a program consistent with his somewhat desperate belief that "an art may be of value purely through preventing a society from becoming too assertively, too hopelessly, itself." Art could not be expected to defeat science and positivism in the streets, but it might modify the rampancy of their success.

To give his morbid heroes some encouragement, lest they fall into the despair of thinking that they must merely put up with the actions of others, Burke urged them to regard their own thinking as an action. In this spirit he invented what he called dramatism, "a technique of analysis of language and thought as basically modes of action rather than as means of conveying information." This he presented in his first and most influen-

tial work of literary criticism, *Counter-Statement* (1931). He showed, in
the chapter on Mann and Gide, that one may become skilful in the
management of vacillation, experimentally fastidious in nuances of doubt:

> Irony, novelty, experimentalism, vacillation, the cult of conflict —
> are not these men trying to make us at home in indecision, are they
> not trying to humanize the state of doubt?... Could action be
> destroyed by such an art, this art would be disastrous. But art can at
> best serve to make action more labored.... Why could one not
> come to accept [one's] social wilderness without anguish, utilizing
> for [one's] self-respect either the irony and melancholy of Mann, or
> the curiosity of Gide?

In the chapter on Flaubert, Pater, and Rémy de Gourmont in
Counter-Statement, Burke argued that a writer's style should be understood
as the property that can't be taken from him. Should style then be
cultivated for its own sake? "Decidedly, not at all," Burke answered in the
essays collected in *The Philosophy of Literary Form* (1941). Rather, we
should understand "style solely as the beneath-which-not, as the admoni-
tory and hortatory act, as the example that would prod continually for its
completion in all aspects of life, and so, in Eliot's phrase, 'keep something
alive,' tiding us over a lean season." In a bad time, as Burke suggested, one
should have the decency to compose good sentences. No particular style
was prescribed. It was understood that a writer would somehow turn his
predicament to aesthetic advantage, and guard his style against encroach-
ment, as Pater in *Marius the Epicurean* used ideology "for its flavor of
beauty, rather than of argument," and treated ideas "not for their value as
statements, but as horizons, situations, developments of plot, in short, as
any other element of fiction."

I would make much of Burke's first phase, and give it shamelessly the
character of aestheticism, against those who too neatly regard him as a
man of the thirties, fully in league with that Marxizing decade. It is true
that Burke aligned his interests with those of the American Left, and
wrote essays in Marxist cultural analysis in the hope of hastening the
collapse of capitalism. But he made himself a nuisance to his colleagues, as
at the American Writers' Congress in April 1935, by uttering sentiments
in keeping with his aestheticist, formal, and musical temper.

Briefly, I would regard Burke's progress much as he defined William

Empson's development from *Seven Types of Ambiguity* to *Some Versions of Pastoral:*

> Here the balloons of Empson's earlier pure aestheticism are effectively tied to a social basis of reference; the later work has a kind of "gravitational pull" in which the former is lacking. Yet he has by no means abandoned the liquidity of his previous volume—the happy result being that there is here no sociological simplism.

It seems clear, however, that the Depression forced Burke to acknowledge his own version of the gravitational pull, and to develop his work beyond aestheticism. He proposed, in this second phase, to read literature "as equipment for living." His idea of regarding thinking as action was put to more specific uses. Poems, plays, and novels were approached as strategies for dealing with particular situations. One might find in a poem "the dancing of an attitude." A novel could deal with a situation not by disposing of it but by naming it:

> A work like *Madame Bovary* (or its homely American translation, *Babbitt*) is the strategic naming of a situation. It singles out a pattern of experience that is sufficiently representative of our social structure, that recurs sufficiently often *mutandis mutatis,* for people to "need a word for it" and to adopt an attitude towards it.

In *The Philosophy of Literary Form* Burke proposed "a sociological criticism of literature" which would codify the various strategies that artists have developed to name situations. But he made the point that many of these would be "timeless," "for many of the 'typical, recurrent situations' are not peculiar to our own civilization at all." Aesop's Fables, for instance, still name situations familiar to any modern reader. Burke would compare particular books on the basis of some strategic element common to them, rather than on considerations of genre or quality. The works examined in *The Philosophy of Literary Form* include, for the elucidation of the diverse situations they name, Hitler's *Mein Kampf,* Shakespeare's *Julius Caesar* and *Twelfth Night,* Clifford Odets's *Golden Boy,* and various writings of Marx, Freud, Mann, and Coleridge. Burke was inclined to use anything that came to hand, and he gave up worrying about neat distinctions between literary and subliterary works. Anything can be read as a strategy for dealing with a situation.

Mein Kampf, for instance, explained Hitler's proposed medicine for the illness of confusion, the parliamentary Babel, and general muddlement: it showed one man's plan to gain certitude by projecting his woes upon a scapegoat — the Jews — ennobling himself by recourse to Aryan purity, and offering a spiritual explanation for economic catastrophe. As Burke said,

> A people in collapse, suffering under economic frustration and the defeat of nationalistic aspirations, with the very midrib of their integrative efforts (the army) in a state of dispersion, have little other than some "spiritual" basis to which they could refer their nationalistic dignity. Hence, the categorical dignity of superior race was a perfect recipe for the situation. It was "spiritual" in so far as it was "above" crude economic "interests," but it was "materialized" at the psychologically "right" spot in that "the enemy" was something you could *see.*

In this second phase, Burke developed a far more elaborate system than any required in the first. Start, he suggested, with the fact that we are bodies: many of my motives are attributable to the interests attendant upon my being a physical organism. Hence the need of a metabiology, as it appears to Burke, rather than a metaphysic. We have to understand the central nervous system even if the divine logos remains obscure. Burke seems to me to invoke biological considerations where someone else would invoke "human nature," in pointing to the continuity and repetition of fundamental human responses. In *The Philosophy of Literary Form* he refers to "the permanent forms that underlie changing historical emphases." These permanent forms are stirred by symbols: symbolism is our knowledge of them, and of the degree to which we share them with others.

Burke's dramatism is not, therefore, a philosophy of Cartesian consciousness; it is not an idealism or an essentialism. Grounded upon a metabiology, it resorts to Aristotle's *Poetics* and *Rhetoric* for their endorsement of action as the central term to concentrate on, and to Aristotle's *Metaphysics* as main authority for the scholastic definition of God as "pure act." Keeping his argument cool, and taking precaution against the eruption of idealism, Burke calls upon American pragmatism, and especially upon William James, to set reasonable limits upon an Aristotelian or Thomist affiliation.

I have in view, documenting this second phase, not only *Permanence and Change* and *Attitudes Toward History*, but *The Philosophy of Literary Form*, the *Grammar* and the *Rhetoric of Motives*. Dramatism is fully worked out in the two books on motives, though Burke has long felt that a third volume, "Symbolic of Motives," would be necessary to complete the project. "Motive" is indeed an embarrassing word, because its ordinary usage disturbs the distinction that Burke makes between action and motion, a distinction he has to enforce since his system is predicated upon drama as its ideal form. "The man who designs a computer is acting. The computer that he designs can but move." Things move—the waves in the sea, for instance—but people act. Presumably the distinction would enable us to throw into the bin marked "motion" any "action" that is spurious. If I think I am playing a role I have composed for myself, and the role then turns out to have been already enforced or inscribed, I would remove it from action, understand it as motion, and discount it accordingly.

The key words of dramatism are five: act, scene, agent, agency, and purpose. The act is what took place, in thought or deed. It may be prepared for by a corresponding attitude, which Burke thinks of as an incipient act, a head of steam worked up to bring the act into play. The scene is the setting in which the act is performed. The agent is the performer, the role-player, the central nervous system, which in the case in point is his and not mine. The agency is the means, the instrument employed by the agent, as a poet resorts to available formal procedures and the body to its metabolism. Purpose is the chosen end.

How does the scheme work? Mainly by alerting us to privileged relations between one term and another. But Burke starts by considering each term in itself, or as if it were removed for the moment from any further complications. He adverts, for instance, to the fact that idealism in philosophy features properties belonging to the word "agent." Then he notes that "in his preface to *The Portrait of a Lady*, Henry James gives us a characteristically idealistic statement when referring to the artist's prime sensibility as the soil out of which his subject springs and which grows the work of art":

Here a book is treated as an act grounded in the author's mind as its motivating scene. The same idealistic pattern is carried into his methods as a novelist, when he selects some "sensibility" who will serve as the appreciative "centre" of his story, and lets the reader follow the story *in terms of* this single consciousness.

In this instance, you could go further by considering possible relations between James's sensibility as agent and the other terms in Burke's pentad.

Or suppose you were thinking of pragmatism, you would regard it as featuring *agency* rather than any of the other four terms. William James called pragmatism "a method only." You would consider the implications of this stress on agency, and the resultant adjustment of the values denoted by the other four. You might then alert yourself to the *stressing* of agency where you would not expect to find it; as in Emerson's early essay "Nature," which ponders at one point the "uses" of Nature, and the natural things that "serve" in Nature's "ministry to man." One of the boons of the *Grammar of Motives,* not at all incidentally, is that the reader moves through the various philosophic schools without feeling intimidated by any of them. Were he to align himself with any one school, he would, if he were to follow Burke's method of analysis, have to retain the thought that the choice features six of one and half a dozen of its rivals. This is not the worst of sentiments, given the virulence with which each of the rivals tries to enforce its authority.

The five terms also permit various ratios, as Burke calls them in the books on motives, various relations between one term and another. Take, for instance, the ratio between scene and act. There is, Burke argues, a qualitative kinship between what is done and the scene in which it is done, both in life and in literature. Suppose you are reading Keats's "Ode on a Grecian Urn." On the prompting of the first stanza ("What men or gods are these?") you distinguish two levels on which action may take place. You relate these to two aspects of Keats's distraught state—on one side, there is a "breathing human passion" that leaves a heart "high-sorrowful and cloyed, / A burning forehead, and a parching tongue." On the other, a purified spiritual act is being evoked, as if "forever young." What would this spiritual or transcendent act require to complete it? It would require, Burke says in *A Grammar of Motives,* "a scene of the same quality as itself," because an act and a scene "belong together," and the nature of the one must fit the nature of the other. The act, having transcended its bodily setting, "will require, as its new setting, a transcendent scene." And lo, in the fourth stanza, we read:

> *Who are these coming to the sacrifice?*
> *To what green altar, O mysterious priest,*

and so spiritually forth.

Has Burke himself a position, in this second phase, if only such a position as arises from a method?

Much edified by Rémy de Gourmont's essay on the dissociation of ideas, Burke argued in these middle books that instead of basing our conduct upon long-congealed prejudices, we should cultivate "perspective by incongruity." We should look at situations aslant, putting like with unlike. This policy would keep us alert to the fact that our differences are differences of interpretation. We are not moved by the reality of a cause but by our interpretation of it. As in *Attitudes Toward History:*

> In men as different as Malraux and Whitehead, we see the essentially religious attempt to socialize one's loneliness, though Whitehead stresses purely idealistic strategies in the accomplishment of this, whereas Malraux seeks the corrective "dialectically" in collective action, in according with Marx's formula for the socialization of losses, to the effect that "I am not alone as a victim; I am in a class of victims." Swift, being essentially religious, was essentially tragic; but overindividualistic emphases turned the tragic scapegoat into a satiric scapegoat, thereby turning a device for solace into a device for indictment.

Once we recognize that our enemy is just as muddled as we are, we are likely to act upon an ethic that mitigates what is offensive in his position. We are likely to construe his ostensibly evil acts as foibles, his vices as errors not much worse than our own.

What Burke is offering is both a poetics of social life and a way of reading as an epitome of a way of living. Like William James, he is willing to admit any recourse that enables him to have the sense of making things a little bit better: he prefers a philosophy of betterment to one that insists on having the best or nothing. "Towards a better life": he claims no more than that.

The literary form that takes care of this sense of life is comedy: so the comic approach, the bundle of congenial attitudes that sustains at least one tradition of comedy—Shakespearean rather than Jonsonian—is "the most serviceable for the handling of human relationships." Specifically, the comic attitude avoids the euphemism that goes with the more heroic modes of epic and tragedy—the euphemism that enables rotting corpses to turn into noble remains; and equally the debunking that paralyzes human relationships "by discovering too constantly the purely materialistic ingredients in human effort." The programme does not involve learning a style from a despair—Empson's advice in one of his poems—but trying to reach an attitude undisdainfully beyond the specific conflict of interpretations.

Indeed, I recall that in *A Rhetoric of Motives* Burke praised Empson's book on pastoral for drawing attention to the ways in which pastoral sentiments and forms were felt to imply a beautiful relation between rich and poor:

> True, whereas the "proletarian" critic's emphasis upon "class consciousness" would bring out the elements of class *conflict,* Empson is concerned with a kind of expression which, while thoroughly conscious of class differences, aims rather at a stylistic transcending of conflict.

You can see how incongruous it would be to try to enlist Burke in a rhetoric in favor of either Left or Right.

E. M. Forster's *A Passage to India* is a work especially fitting to Burke's recommendations in favour of the comic attitude; and it is so treated in an essay of 1966, reprinted in *Language as Symbolic Action.* Burke takes the book as social comedy: "The story is told from a novelistic point of view that transcends the perspective of any one character, and that is designed to evoke in the reader a mood of ironically sympathetic contemplation." That last phrase is specifically designed to replace the words "through pity and fear effecting the catharsis of such emotions" in Aristotle's recipe for Athenian tragedy. Burke then points out such details as these: in Forster's novel there is no villain; the embarrassments of the "Bridge Party" in which the British and the natives are expected to "bridge" their "gulf" are an instance of improvised protocol. The incidents of personal separation on which the story closes—between Fielding and Aziz—take place during a Hindu ritual proclaiming the principle of

universal unity. One is left respecting all the more both the novel and
Burke's use of it as illuminating the power of the comic.

I can be brief about Burke's third phase, and think of it as the third
act of a play, an intellectual comedy. Act I: Aestheticism. Act II:
Communication. Act III: call it Entelechy, Aristotle's word for the complete expression of some function, or the condition in which a potentiality becomes an actuality, or, for Burke, the rounding out of a vocabulary
partly for the pleasure of seeing it rounded. Suppose you were to discover,
while ardently engaged on communications in the spirit of fellowship
and comedy, certain possibilities intrinsic to your medium but not strictly
relevant to your undertaking: as Joyce came upon certain heady possibilities in writing the later chapters of *Ulysses.* You might be impelled to
pursue those possibilities to the end of the line, even if they surpassed
communication and threatened to undermine it, as they did in *Finnegans
Wake.*

Such a motive predominates in Burke's third phase, especially in *The
Rhetoric of Religion* and some of the essays in *Language as Symbolic Action.*
Burke speaks of it as "tracking down the implications," and we may think
of it as the critic's version of entelechy or completeness, the determination
to leave no linguistic resource untried. Burke's strivings in this spirit are
provoked, in *The Rhetoric of Religion,* by the *Confessions* of St. Augustine
and the first chapters of Genesis. It is not a book about God but about
man's relation to the word "God" and the ultimate linguistic strategies
that the word entails. Burke calls this inquiry "logology," the secular
cousin of theology:

> If we defined "theology" as "words about God," then by "logology"
> we should mean "words about words. . . . " Our purpose is simply to
> ask how theological principles can be shown to have usable secular
> analogues that throw light upon the nature of language.

So he is concerned, in *The Rhetoric of Religion,* with secular ana-
logues and correspondences to such matters as these: God, Creation,
original sin, conversion, eternity, sacrifice, providence, predestination,
salvation. No debunking is intended: the question of religious belief is
put in parenthesis, where a believer is free to find it at any time. Statements within an avowedly religious literature (Genesis, Paul, Augustine,
Bunyan, Pascal) are studied "in their sheer formality" as if they were

observations about the nature of language. Perspective by incongruity indeed; and to be judged only on its results.

During the past year or two, as in the new afterword to *Permanence and Change,* Burke has compressed his "definition of man" into a phrase: we are "bodies that learn language." Not a bad formula, if a formula is required.

Burke is now revered, however belatedly, as literary critic, sage, expounder of symbolic actions. I know of no dissenters on that issue. He seems to me unique in the range and resourcefulness with which his mind engages its evidence. The mobility of his work makes it hard to assimilate, but I can't regret that he remains a maverick, his mind running free and sometimes wild. Better that way than that he stand in line. I expect to see his work haggled over, and appropriated for one cause or another, as in Frank Lentricchia's *Criticism and Social Change* (1983). Or attacked for not being as Marxist as a Marxist—Fredric Jameson, for instance—would like it to be. No matter. Burke's books seem to me wonderfully intelligent, strange, often bizarre, and unfailingly vivid.

From *The New York Review of Books,* Vol. XXXII, No. 14 (September 26, 1985).

JOHN BERRYMAN

The Life of John Berryman, by John Haffenden.

On January 7, 1972, the poet John Berryman committed suicide by jumping off the Washington Avenue Bridge between St. Paul and Minneapolis. It was the second time that week he had resolved to kill himself. On January 5 he left a note for his wife, Kate—"I am a nuisance"—and went off to do the deed. But he came back and wrote a poem about the episode, beginning: "I didn't. And I didn't," and ending, after a dismal account of his life and job: "Kitticat, they can't fire me."

Berryman was born October 25, 1914, in McAlester, Oklahoma. His father, John Allyn Smith, was a shadowy figure, working betimes as a game warden, a banker, or whatever, until he turned shadow into dire substance in 1926 by killing himself. "I spit upon this dreadful banker's grave / who shot his heart out in a Florida dawn," Berryman wrote many years and torments later. A few weeks after Smith's death, his widow, Martha, married John Angus McAlpin Berryman; her sons, John and Robert, took their stepfather's name. The poet's mother did not go in for shadows; she was all substance from the start. John remained, for the rest of his perturbed life, a mother's boy. John Haffenden's splendidly just and well-tempered biography plays fair by Berryman's mother and is patient even with her meddlesomeness. She relentlessly interfered in her son's life, haranguing him in the diverse tones of mother, father, and—you would almost think—lover. Berryman remained dependent on her and hated his dependence. It may be the case, though Haffenden leaves the reader free to make it or not, that Berryman's obsessive womanizing was his way of getting rid of his mother or punishing her for being so much to him. His stepfather was another shadow but kind enough and materially helpful.

Indeed, Berryman was lucky in his friends. At Columbia, Mark Van Doren went miles out of his way to rescue him. Delmore Schwartz was crucial to him: being geniuses together answered one of Berryman's many needs. But the good company of friends is impressive: Blackmur, Saul Bellow, Allen Tate (though Berryman came to distrust and resent him), Randall Jarrell (though he was severe in an early review), Robert Giroux (who fostered and published Berryman), and Robert Lowell (the only poet Berryman acknowledged as his peer). Haffenden quotes several of Lowell's letters to Berryman, and they are noble things, extraordinarily warmhearted when warmth and heart were the only blessings Berryman could receive. Lowell, too, reviewed Berryman severely, but in public one is on oath; in private there are other considerations. As for women, Berryman was fortunate in his wives and often, according to Haffenden's book, in his lovers. He had a weakness for falling in love, but he was so tempestuously attractive that the women he desired came to him, it appears, almost before they were sent for. Besides, the poetry scene was more hectic then. Those, more than now, were the years of readings, presences, images, performances. To have seen a Ginsberg plain, a Ferlinghetti high, a Lowell careworn was to be young and easy, even though the public times were monstrous. Berryman was never, or never for long, in Ferlinghetti's league for big occasions, but he was an unforgettable presence, bearded, shortsighted, offering his audiences the marks of his suffering and a little knowledge of it.

Haffenden's biography is an appalling story of love and drink. Some people maintain that Berryman was a good drinker, that drink, like Guinness according to the Guinnesses, was good for him, especially for his eloquence and cordiality. I doubt it. I had only one evening with him, in his house in Dublin, where he came to spend a year for the worst possible reason, to confront Yeats—"I have moved to Dublin to have it out with you / majestic Shade." In the event, he met many unmajestic characters, Dublin drinkers, the most dangerous kind. The evening, night, and early hours of the morning I spent with him were a mess, exorbitant in every remembered respect, the brew too rich for me, every opinion delivered as if it were Custer's last stand. Too much of everything: drink, noise, waste of spirit.

A few years after Berryman's death, Lowell wrote a mediocre poem in which he mused: "Yet really we had the same life, / the generic one / our generation offered." There is indeed something to be explained, the extravagantly untidy lives of Lowell, Berryman, Jarrell, Schwartz, and many more in their generation. But Lowell's poem turns several contingencies, choices, and chances into a mythology and removes from poets the responsibility—not, however, the blame; there is no question of that—other people have to take. These several poets did not have the same life; only an ennobling mythology makes them seem to have had a life in common. It is certainly true that for a man of Berryman's precarious constitution, the times were wrong. Heroes were required, because the continuous possibility of heroism had to be maintained in the face of a public world in nearly every respect corrupt. What "our generation" offered to poets was the heroic role and the fame that attended it. Poets could assume the role, accept the offer, because they worked in language, a spiritual medium free, at least in principle, from the sordidness nearly inevitable in political office and the direct exercise of power. Poetry had its own power, but it was occult, magical; it spoke an ancient tongue, true in the long run and, even in the short, truer than anything audible on Capitol Hill. Even if a poet "failed," his failure could readily be construed as a constituent of tragedy, the most exalted and exalting artistic form, according to the Western assessment of art.

Berryman was impatient to assume the heroic burden, as if to represent his time by being defeated in the end. He wanted of the tragic form only its suffering, not the acts and responsibilities which cause the suffering and in the end, if the form is sound, transfigure it. Pathos was his most opulent emotion. Like many another hero of a bourgeois time, he couldn't find a world fit for his consciousness to live in. He was often magnanimous, but in his dog days he gave in to petty sentiments: envy, the bourgeois passion; rage if a rival poet were praised; obsession with "the thriving gangs."

Long before the end he wanted to die. Always more than half in love with easeful death, he fondled its images. If a poem could be turned toward sleep and death, he turned it; as, in a superb essay on Shakespeare, he has Prospero in *The Tempest* longing for his little life to be rounded, rounded off, with sleep, the great globe at last (thank God) dissolved. Haffenden doesn't, perhaps can't, make up his mind about Berryman's grieving—his grieving, for instance, when Dylan Thomas died, a wail so deep and resounding that you would think Thomas must have been to Berryman what he was not, his closest, most needed, most loved friend. It is easy to be ill-mannered on this theme. Didn't Milton write "Lycidas" when Edward King, hardly next of kin, died? But Haffenden sometimes thinks Berryman's grief literary in a compromising sense and is not quite willing to regard it as justified on every occasion by the representative or generic brunt of the death. In any case, every death for which Berryman grieved—"The high ones die, die. They die. You look up and who's there?"—was a rehearsal for his own.

Suicide was already in the script. Even with this biography at hand, it is still not clear to me whether John Allyn Smith's suicide was the monstrous catastrophe to his twelve-year-old son that it became in Berryman's poetry. Even in the poetry Berryman veered. Sometimes his words are all loss—"I join my father / who dared so long agone leave me"—sometimes spitting rage. In one of the "Dream Songs" the father "did what was needed," though Berryman confesses bewilderment, mainly—"I cannot read that wretched mind, so strong / & so undone"— and puts himself through the motions of forgiveness. But in the last years he seems to have felt that the script of suicide was inescapable. His father willed him a tragedy to play: it might be postponed from one diversion to the next, but finally it would have to be enacted, even if it meant that the hero was heroic only or chiefly in his victimage.

Haffenden's book shows that the relation between Berryman's poetry and the events that provoked it was peculiarly close. The poet went far out of his way to confound the relation, by inventing characters or named shades—Huffy Henry, Mr. Bones—and by giving them minstrel-show voices in preference to his own. But taking on someone else's voice was always Berryman's way of claiming that, deep down, he had one of his own—like Hamlet, who, according to William Empson, kept his secret by telling everybody he had one. In the early poems the conspirator in Berryman's ventriloquism was Yeats. In some of the poems of *The Dispossessed* and throughout *Homage to Mistress Bradstreet,* it was Hopkins. Even in the 77 *Dream Songs,* a demented buffoonery sanctioned by the title of the book, Hopkins is still audible in a demotic form. But something in Berryman ensured that he would talk straight only by talking out of the side of his mouth. He sounds most completely himself when he takes the risk of sounding like someone else.

The *Selected Poems, 1938–1968,* a selection Berryman made a few months before his death, is as much of the poetry as time will probably retain. It has *Bradstreet* and the best of the *Dream Songs,* with enough of *The Dispossessed,* and "Canto Amor" too, which I find staying in my head as two lines: "the flowing ceremony of trouble and light, / all Loves becoming, none to flag upon." But I would want to add, making up an ideal *Portable Berryman* or *Berryman Reader,* three stories, "The Imaginary Jew," "Wash Far Away," and "The Lovers," along with the essays on Shakespeare, Hardy, and Eliot's "Prufrock," and I would end with the interpretation of Lowell's "Skunk Hour."

The poetry of Berryman's last years was a mess. He seemed to think that all he had to do to write a poem was to transcribe minor contingencies, report his daily doings as if he were taking dictation from the weather. Many of the poems Haffenden quotes as evidence of those years are already dead to themselves, sullen in every purported gesture. It was as if the lurid determinism that Berryman fulfilled in suicide made him kill the language before he killed himself. T. S. Eliot once remarked that "the really fine rhetoric of Shakespeare occurs in situations where a character in the play sees himself in a dramatic light." The remark would have to be modified to take account of situations like Berryman's, in which a character is congealed in the sense of himself as victim, "a huddle of need" and nothing more. The rhetoric, as in Berryman's *Love & Fame,* is numbed.

Given a few years, it will be easier than it is now to read Berryman's work in a disinterested spirit. John Haffenden's book lights up the subject, but the light is necessarily lurid: such waste, such despondency, such madness. Berryman was clearly a genuine poet—a minor one by any serious standards and more limited than he seemed a few crazed years ago, but still the real thing. The mythology of his generation has waned; for this relief much thanks. One of the many merits of Haffenden's book is that it tells a story, not a legend.

From *The New York Times Book Review,* October 24, 1982.

ROBERT LOWELL

I

History, by Robert Lowell.
For Lizzie and Harriet, by Robert Lowell.
The Dolphin, by Robert Lowell.

Everybody knows that Robert Lowell has been changing his mind again. His poetry has never relied for its continuity upon the exercise of a mind set in its ways, but the recent changes testify to a grand intention and a spirit spectacularly busy. Not content with a *Notebook* published in three versions, Lowell has been running over the same notes again, adding marginalia, putting asunder phrases joined together by a younger god, multiplying implications by nuances, raising selected quotations to the power of x; he cannot leave those wells of loneliness alone. Some of the love notes, changed, make *For Lizzie and Harriet,* hundreds of old woes new wailed make *History,* and even *The Dolphin,* presented as entirely new, has three or four old poems, including "Dream," which appeared in *Notebook* as "The Hunt" in a form which only a determined hunter or a clairvoyant dreamer would want to change. Three books for the price of six? Not at all.

One of the poems in *History,* "Rilke Self-Portrait," ends thus:

> *As a thing that hangs together, the picture fails;*
> *nothing is worked through yet or alive,*
> *carried to enduring culmination—*
> *as if hidden in accidents and stray things,*
> *something unassailable were planned.*

Forget Rilke, keep Lowell in view, because nearly thirty years ago Blackmur said much of the same thing of Lowell's first book, *Land of Unlikeness,* and I fancy that Lowell has kept the occasion green in his memory. The book showed, according to Blackmur,

> not examples of high formal organisation achieved, but poems that are deliberately moving in that direction and that have things put in to give the appearance of the movement of form when the movement itself was not secured.

Recall too what Lowell said of the first *Notebook,* that "accident threw up subjects, and the plot swallowed them—famished for human chances," a figure repeated in *History* with John Berryman in mind:

> *Luck threw up the coin and the plot swallowed,*
> *monster yawning for its mess of pottage.*

It is my guess that Blackmur's critique, which Lowell remembered clearly enough to make a poem of it, struck a nerve. *History* is Lowell's latest plot to give his poetic life not mere existence in separate poems, which it already has, but the movement and the momentum of form, to produce something unassailable, epic in proportion and grandeur, from the accidents that incited earlier notes and the stray things those notes became. "I stand face to face with lost ages," Lowell reports, but some of them may still be recovered by a poet with a classical education and a dissatisfied memory, and the recovery may constitute form. In time, the movement of form is history, events being merely its partial appearances. In words, the movement is poetry, provided it has been achieved. So the poet has been plundering his own life, assailing stray poems, planning to change the appearance of movement into its reality. Never short of accidents, since he has put himself in their way, he has lacked a design, a moving plot, a grand action. Now he thinks he has found one good enough to make *History.*

At least that is the general intention. The author of *History* is not merely a poet secreting poems, he is the Poet ordaining poetry. There is no question of personal vanity, Lowell is only doing what Milton, Gray, Whitman, Yeats, and many other poets have done, he is speaking ostensibly in his own person but in fact as the spirit of poetry, its custodian. His mere life does not matter, it has no privilege over any other, the usual wrestling of chances and choices, accidents and what we make of them. It is the spirit of the enterprise that matters, and the letter in which it issues: "I am Whitman, I am Berkeley, all men." Lowell is speaking as one of Emerson's representative men, the poet, his pride a function of his role rather than of his character. I compare his new intention with the movement, described in Lukács's *History and Class Consciousness* and *Theory of the Novel,* from "description" toward "narration." Description is merely the subject's encounter with objects as an essay in subjectivity, and the objects are merely stimulants. Narration is the subject's acknowledgement of objects in their significant properties, a transaction in which the subject tries to discover a meaning implicit in historical events: to discover is not to impose. In narration, the subject's engagement with history becomes, without his making an issue of it, the form of his vitality. The comparison is only provisional, it marks in Lowell a direction rather than an end. Besides, Lowell's spirit is too wilful to hand itself over to any authority, Church, State, or History, even if it presented itself as the imperative truth of doctrine. Lizzie had a point in saying to him, "Why don't you lose yourself / and write a play about the fall of Japan?"

Still, the material of *History* is history, including the poet's own accidents and contingencies. The immediate scene is preoccupied by old affections still vivid, promises broken but not rescinded, remorse, pain, wives, children, friends. The difference between the new and the old notes is that the range of Lowell's attention is now far wider than before, and there is a corresponding sense of individual events as moments in a more articulate chronology. The view from Boston Common now includes Israel, Greece, Rome, Canterbury, Versailles, Waterloo, Paris. The New England poet gives his attention to Adam, Eve, Clytemnestra, Sappho, Xerxes, Alexander, Diogenes, Hannibal, Horace, Dante, Eloise, Abelard, Coleridge, Rembrandt, Milton, Rimbaud, Mallarmé, Rilke, and many other purple patches of significance. The principle of choice is Lowell's sense of what his style can handle. But it would be foolish to take the intention in each case for the deed. Lowell has not suppressed himself in favour of these luminaries, he has merely admitted them to his consciousness for a reason and at a price.

There is room for argument about his hospitality. In principle, it is hard to think about yourself if you have promised to spend the time thinking about Hannibal, but it can be done, you can think about Hannibal in such a way that he would regard himself as drawing the short straw, not for the first time. You can bring him to his knees again, drag him behind your chariot of sensibility. Lowell says that his history is "what you cannot touch," but he touches it all the time, never leaves it alone. In general, what he says to history is a stark iambic pentameter: *j'accuse, j'accuse, j'accuse, j'accuse, j'accuse.* The charge sheet reads: treason, bad faith, false witness, calumny, and a pretty universal failure to deliver the goods. The official criminals are mostly big shots of history and legend, and they stand for authority in its diverse forms. Lowell's poems have always been fascinated by authority (family, Church, New England, law) as that which cannot be defeated but must be circumvented if the individual will is to assert itself. In principle, these ostensibly historical poems are Lowell's way of escaping from subjectivity, if only because they say there have been other times; but I suspect he does not really want to escape. He moves three steps toward narration, then two back toward description. He wants to break out, cause a fuss, and then be caught.

This distinguishes his sense of history from Ezra Pound's. Pound was convinced that all we need on earth can be discovered by putting aside our subjectivity and, with open eyes, searching for luminous details in the given world, mostly in the records of literature and power. Distance is no problem: "How is it far if you think of it?" The perceptions gathered and ordered make a civilization. Nothing else matters. Pound ascribed no value to the cackling of feeling unless it resulted in an egg of perception. *Paideuma* was the thing worth caring for. Lowell's research has not been as extensive as Pound's, though he has done a fair amount of homework. The real difference is that he has been looking for meaning as a function of himself, he is not willing to think historical events significant in their own right, apart from his intervention. If he were, would he pester them as he does? Perhaps he has it in for the big shots not because he thinks them insignificant by definition but because he thinks their meaning incomplete, and he torments them with fanatical determination to complete their meaning with his own, by *fiat.* Or, another possibility, since he cares so deeply for a few people (Lizzie, Harriet, Caroline, Elizabeth, Mary, Randall, Allen, John, Ivor), he needs history as a directory of personages whom he is not obliged to love, it is enough that they are available as sparring partners. In any event the enterprise, so far as its intention goes, has indisputable if somewhat perverse grandeur: even failure in such a case would be majestic. Some readers may be shocked by the thought that the whole fabric of human history culminates in a thrice-married Bostonian now resident in England. They are too easily shocked. Besides, Lowell does not claim that the story ends with him or that its interest will not survive his departure from the scene: a future is assumed, though not necessarily a good one.

So there is no theoretical scandal. Lowell is only trying to make sense and spirit of what would otherwise remain, he thinks, the lost properties and dead letters of time. Theorists of history may dispute his assumptions and the representative value of his emblems; that is their business. As between Pound's sense of history and Lowell's, I favour Pound's in principle and only quarrel occasionally with its practice. Lowell's sense of history is, in that comparison, inordinate. He has a way of torturing facts to make them confess and even when they tell everything he never thinks it enough, they are liars and thieves: many of them die at his hands. This would not matter if the poetry stayed pure of heart, but Lowell has got into the habit of being rough with language, too often offering not genuine power but a show of force, as if he planned to scare words into submission. I cannot separate his roughness, when he is rough, from the accusing eye he turns upon most of the productions of time: nearly everything is seen in a form in which he does not want it. The poet takes little pleasure, apparently, in the diverse histories which presumably offered themselves to him for pleasure as much as profit. He has gone for a quick profit.

I think this marks the fact that the memorable things in these three books, as in the *Notebook,* are more often single lines than complete poems. Most of the poems, except in *The Dolphin,* read like essays in willpower; the will is set to do the work of imagination and mostly runs to torture and excruciation. But every now and again it relents and for a moment the air is filled with ease and light. I treasure these moments more than the torture, though I concede that Lowell knows his job, too, when a Cosa Nostra muse tells him to give a theme a bit of rough stuff. Mostly the free and easy lines are aphoristic. "Rome, if built at all, must be built in a day." "A man running for his life will never tire." "Old age is all right, but it has no future." "*Praise,* the last drink for the road, last welcome friend." "I have my place . . . if one is put in his place / enough times, he becomes his place." "Age is nice . . . if that's your age . . . thirteen." "Some meaning never has a use for words." Aphorisms, often floating free from their contexts: or, in other poems, sentences which bear to history or legend the relation an aphorism bears to wisdom; as in a Clytemnestra poem, "In one night, boys fell senile in her arms." Or, in a love poem, "like God, I almost doubt if you exist."

If I make much of these grace notes it is not because I want Lowell to write the kind of songs one can whistle, or sonnets to be inscribed as mottoes on a sundial, it is because much of the surrounding verse is the work of will and insistence. There are exceptions to this harsh rule, poems here and there which give the impression of moving by their own sweet will rather than by Lowell's determination that by God they will move when he tells them to move. In the love poems especially Lowell is more concerned to do justice to those he loves and hurts than to make a dreadful pother with himself; the concern makes a broken music of its own. What the poet does when he merely sets his will to it is formidable enough: what he does when he packs his will off on vacation is even more memorable, and I don't need to consult my notes to recall those occasions from "Night Sweat" to "Monkeys," "Returning Turtle," "The Mermaid Children," and "In the Mail."

This is recent work, so Lowell has not lost his touch: there are poems here, though not many, "to set the woods on fire and warm the glacier," poems fit to keep company with the classic poems, "The Drunken Fisherman," "Mr. Edwards and the Spider," "The Quaker Graveyard in Nantucket," "The Ghost," "Skunk Hour." Lowell has not lost any accomplishment, but he forgets from time to time that the only alternative to his special *virtu* is his special vice. Blackmur described it in that extraordinary review when he said that in Lowell "logic lacerates the vision and vision turns logic to zealotry." Lowell's zealotry takes a secular rather than a Roman Catholic form these days but it is still vindictive when allowed to run wild. So a reader may well ask: what has life done to this man that he has not done to life? Every *dies* is *irae.* I am not saying that Lowell's recent poetry is merely *Land of Unlikeness* revisited with a bigger cast for a wider screen. Lowell's virtues are more diverse than his vices, the vices being few and mostly sour. But I think he has been having a lover's quarrel with his characteristic talent, and I welcome *The Dolphin* especially as an indication that the quarrel is nearly over. I find the mood of these latter poems, following a hint of John Crowe Ransom's poetry, *agitato*, yes, *ma non troppo*. Which is good. Indeed, proposing a motto for Lowell's classic poems, I think of Ransom, Lowell's *cher maître*, saying for his own good reason:

> *Assuredly I know my grief,*
> *And I am shaken; but not as a leaf.*

From *The New Statesman*, August 31, 1973.

II

I cannot be the only reader whom Robert Lowell's last few books disappointed; the books, I mean, since *Near the Ocean* (1967). Disappointed; I don't mean bored. Books as revealing as *History*, say, could hardly fail to "interest" or even to provoke concern. These books raised again the old question about the use of one's experience, what a poet makes of his life when he wants to make poetry of it. David Kalstone has been pondering this theme in his recent *Five Temperaments;* the five are Elizabeth Bishop, James Merrill, Adrienne Rich, John Ashbery, and Lowell. So the question is in season. But I want to think of it in terms somewhat different from Kalstone's for the moment: why is the relation between personal experience and the produced poem, in Lowell's case, somehow less fruitful in *Day by Day* than in, say, *Life Studies*?

The question is raised specifically in the "Epilogue" to *Day by Day*, though the answer which Lowell enforces seems to me disingenuous:

> *Those blessèd structures, plot and rhyme—*
> *why are they no help to me now*
> *I want to make*
> *something imagined, not recalled?*
> *I hear the noise of my own voice:*
> The painter's vision is not a lens,

it trembles to caress the light.
But sometimes everything I write
with the threadbare art of my eye
seems a snapshot,
lurid, rapid, garish, grouped,
heightened from life,
yet paralyzed by fact.
All's misalliance.
Yet why not say what happened?
Pray for the grace of accuracy
Vermeer gave to the sun's illumination
stealing like the tide across a map
to his girl solid with yearning.
We are poor passing facts,
warned by that to give
each figure in the photograph
his living name.

Disingenuous, however touching: the question ("something imagined, not recalled") is too important to be dissolved in the rhetoric of "fact" and appeal to Vermeer. "Yet why not say what happened" is not the point: the gap between "what happened" and the "saying" is precisely the point. Call it the question of Memory and Imagination. Recall, too, the quarrel between Wordsworth and Blake on that ground; how Wordsworth thought memory and imagination compatible forms of energy, but Blake thought memory a nuisance, alien to the original and originating power of imagination.

The question is not only genuine; it is inevitable. An honest poet who has turned his entire life, with whatever degree of definition and success, into an *oeuvre* is bound to resent the aesthetic habit which has enabled him to do such a thing. Or at least to resent it on occasion. He is bound to feel, from time to time, that he has merely taken dictation from the circumstances of his life, that he is, in Yeats's term, a naturalist, helpless before the contents of his mind. A secretary, or a dictaphone, at best a telephone. There is evidence that Lowell often felt his poetry a mere function of his life. This feeling would not matter, if his spirit were truly Wordsworthian: it would then be easy for him to persuade himself that memory is a form of imagination, that it is not a machine for transcribing facts. But I think he was of Blake's party, at bottom: or, the same thing in other words, he became sceptical of fact and event, perhaps bored by the poverty of his recollections at the end.

I have to offer some evidence for these assertions. One: Lowell regularly writes of poetry and of the poetic spirit in terms of the neo-Platonic tradition in which the originating experience is inspiration. "I would write only in response to the gods," he protests in *Day by Day*, "like Mallarmé who had the good fortune / to find a style that made writing impossible." Again:

> *Can poetry get away with murder,*
> *its terror a seizure of the imagination*
> *foreign to our stubborn common health?*
> *It's the authentic will to spoil,*
> *the voice,*
> *haunted not lost,*
> *that lives by breaking in*
> *berserk with inspiration.*

That's clear enough, surely. Only one tradition authenticates the diction of terror, seizure, illness, divine frenzy. In that tradition, even one's mistakes hit the right mark; as Lowell says in "Unwanted":

> *I was surer, wasn't I, once . . .*
> *and had flashes when I first found*
> *a humor for myself in images,*
> *farfetched misalliance*
> *that made evasion a revelation?*

Once; in *Life Studies* certainly. A further piece of evidence that Lowell was of Blake's party, in principle:

> *Coleridge,*
> *the author of* Dejection,
> *thought*
> *genius is the discovery*
> *of subjects remote*
> *from my life.*

Not exactly: what Coleridge said, commenting in Chapter 15 of *Biographia Literaria* on Shakespeare's "Venus and Adonis," was that a proof of Shakespeare's genius in that poem was his use of a subject remote from his own "private interests and circumstances." A point common to Keats, Coleridge, and Hazlitt is that Shakespeare's imagination is dramatic rather than egotistical, he gives things a life of their own, he does not merely lend them his life or force them to receive it. But note, too, Lowell's irony in describing Coleridge as the author of the "Dejection" ode, a poem as close to Coleridge's own personal interests and circumstances as anything in Lowell. Coleridge thought Shakespeare's way the highest and greatest, but in his own poetry he had to do the best he could with the poor device of turning his moods into verse. If that way's good enough for Coleridge, why should Lowell feel abashed? And so forth.

What am I saying, then? Just this: that according to the aesthetic principle which he avowed, Lowell was a Romantic, a visionary, a Blake man; the problem he set himself was that of transfiguring his experience, making it not merely his own but Everyman's. Not by generalizing—"to generalize is to be an idiot"—Lowell's method, in *Life Studies* and *For the Union Dead,* was to trust his sense of the continuity between his own nature and that of others. His sickness was merely a particular instance of a general sickness. There is a passage in René Char's *Hypnos Waking* which describes the imagination:

> L'imagination consiste à expulser de la réalité plusieurs personnes incomplètes pour, mettant à contribution les puissances magiques et subversives du désir, obtenir leur retour sous la forme d'une présence entièrement satisfaisante. C'est alors l'inextinguible réel incréé.

Lowell's fully achieved poems exemplify this process: think of "Memories of West Street and Lepke," "Skunk Hour," "Eye and Tooth," "Myopia: A Night," "Night Sweat," and the two "No Hearing" poems from *For Lizzie and Harriet.* In these, the "presence" is not a transcription or, in the spirit of the "Epilogue" to *Day by Day,* a "fact": in Char's terms, we feel that many experiences, persons, events were indeed expelled for their incompleteness, and were redeemed for the poems by the poet's desire: the particular conjunction of absence and desire makes them, in the poems, the "entirely satisfying presences" they are. Clearly, in this formulation, desire is a crucial stage in the action of the imagination: I am not sure how otherwise it may be characterized. It is not, to use another of Yeats's phrases, the will trying to do the work of the imagination; it is the imagination itself in the phase of its need, desiring to transform absence into presence. If someone says that memory is the same desire, I deny it, because the transformation is not active in its character: the "plusieurs personnes" are "incomplètes," hence their expulsion, and if memory is content to recall them in their incompleteness, the imagination is not. Presence is completeness; the figures in Lowell's achieved poems make a presence for themselves, they constitute presence for the poet and for his reader, the poem is their presentation, their immediacy to the language. In the fully achieved poems, Lowell's imagination acts by a process similar to that described by Char; or rather, it earns the right to turn absences into presences. That is why the personages in those poems give the impression of having been expelled, kept out of the place, and that they came back, came into the poems because Lowell's desire could not be appeased without them. The summer millionaire in "Skunk Hour" is not recalled by memory. Nor was he dragged in for some portentous symbolic reason. The poetic truth is that, kept out of the poem, he pressed upon it and demanded to be admitted. I speak of an impression, but with an implication of the language sustaining it, the transforming style at work.

There is very little transformation in *Day by Day.* The themes are the old congenital ones, brought up to date: loss, end, suicide, the way we were in Baton Rouge, Peter Taylor, "Red" Warren, the good days, dreams, Jean Stafford, Auden, Elizabeth Hardwick, rural England, "my unhealthy generation," Caroline, Sheridan Lowell, turtles, ants, a dolphin. Nothing wrong with these, as themes. But Lowell can do little or nothing with them; or nothing beyond what he has already done. And he writes with the low spirits of a poet who knows that he cannot transform them any more. In one poem he complains that his words no longer "sound": and it is true, the reverberation of *Life Studies,* the "hum and buzz of implication," is suppressed. The book has an air of weariness, as if the personal troubles behind the poems never got to the point of transpiring in the lines and made, therefore, only a dead weight upon them:

> *We only live between*
> *before we are and what we were.*

. . .

In the lost negative
you exist,
a smile, a cypher,
an old-fashioned face
in an old-fashioned hat.

Three ages in a flash:
the same child in the same picture,
he, I, you,
chockablock, one stamp
like mother's wedding silver—

gnome, fish, brute cherubic force.

We could see clearly
and all the same things
before the glass was hurt.
Past fifty, we learn with surprise and a sense
of suicidal absolution
that what we intended and failed
could never have happened—
and must be done better.

This poem, "For Sheridan," is full of good intentions, but they are allowed to drift away in a tired, elegiac manner. The perceptions are not remarkable, except for their lassitude, their air of not having enough energy left to bring them to fulfilment or even to test their value. The enervated, offhand style is trading on a stronger past. Nothing in the poem is earned: the details which call attention to themselves are exorbitant, usurious. "Before the glass was hurt": "hurt" is offensive, blatantly in excess of anything worked for or earned in the poem. And the elegant weariness of "Past fifty, we learn with surprise . . ." makes a claim upon the reader's sympathy which the perception itself, banal as it is, does nothing to justify.

　　Is there an easy, dreadful explanation for this? That Lowell never had anything to write about but himself, and that in the last few years he had used himself up, there was nothing more or new to say, nothing but the same daily round? But what about those plays, and the translations, imitations, versions, and what about *History*? Were they not about other things? In *The Dolphin*, Elizabeth Hardwick is quoted as saying to Lowell, "Why don't you lose yourself / and write a play about the fall of Japan?" I take this as meaning: "Why don't you forget about yourself for a while, suppress yourself, and write something 'objective,' remote from your private interests and circumstances?" Or, in Char's terms, why don't you expel yourself, in all your incompleteness, from the scene, and expel all the other people whom you are in the habit of dragging into your poems as functions of yourself; and wait, trust in the Lord, until you will all be ready, combining in genuine presence? I think Lowell was willing, at any time, to take up the task, observe a Lenten self-discipline; but that his language did not let him. Or rather: certain habits of his language, mostly bad habits indulged in his later books. The language of *Day by Day* is mostly sullen, surely, as if all the joy of words had leaked away or gone sour. This is probably bound to happen when a poetry of seizure, like Lowell's in the early books, tires of itself, gets bored with its repetitions. It is the price a poet has to pay for a hair-raising art when his energy falls off: he lapses into poses, the gestures of habit, going through the motions.

It is sad. It would be wonderful to report that *Day by Day* is a superb book, the ripest fruit of Lowell's art; but it is not. What I particularly miss is Lowell's patience: he could be patient, when he was at ease in his language. We do not think patience his character, or his most visible sign, but, looking back over the *Selected Poems* (1976), I find myself stopping not at the famous dramatic things but at the quieter moments, when every force came together and the words sounded with ease. I am thinking of one such moment which tells against the drift of my argument and says that, when the going was good, Lowell could indeed lose himself for a while. Here is "Death of Anne Boleyn," a poem from *History* which didn't touch me very much when I first read it, but it touches me now:

> *Summer hail flings crystals on the window—*
> *they wrapped the Lady Anne's head in a white handkerchief.*
> *To Wolsey, the nightcrow, but to Anthony Froude,*
> *stoic virtue spoke from her stubborn lips and chin—*

five adulteries in three years of marriage;
the game was hotly charged. "I hear say I'll
not die till noon; I am very sorry therefore,
I thought to be dead this hour and past my pain."
Her jailer told her that beheading was no pain—
"It is subtle." "I have a little neck,"
she said, and put her hands about it laughing.
They guessed she had much pleasure and joy in death—
no foreigners admitted. By the King's abundance
the scene was open to any Englishman.

The poem exists in at least three versions: there may be even more. I count only the revised and enlarged *Notebook* and the *History* and now the *Selected Poems,* different texts in each case. The differences are interesting, but they make another day's work. Most of the narrative is taken from the second volume of James Anthony Froude's *History of England from the Fall of Wolsey to the Defeat of the Spanish Armada,* but there is a striking detail which I have not seen in Froude. In the first published version of the poem the reference to the spectators in the last line was introduced by a weak phrase: "But thanks to her husband . . . " In the second version this was replaced by: "though by the king's abundance." The change is a stroke of patience, a superb invention:

Her Husband hoped she'd have small displeasure in her death—
no foreigners, though by the King's abundance
the scene was open to any Englishman.

In the final version Lowell brought the King in only once, as in Froude, where it is the chaplain Mr. Kingston who says, "I have seen many men, and also women, executed, and they have been in great sorrow; and to my knowledge this lady hath much joy and pleasure in death." But "abundance" is retained, thank God.

This is the Lowell I most admire. Not the most typical Lowell, I concede: that man is probably the moody, violent poet who took every occasion to present himself in that spirit. What troubles me about him is not that he was so vexed with himself and others and with circumstance but that he was so vexed with the English language; so often used its gifts as if they were insults. Patience came slow and hard to such a poet; so I warm to it when it comes through the turbulence and flows into the rhythm. "Death of Anne Boleyn" is much indebted to Froude for fact, but the rhythm of the poem is pure, patient Lowell.

From *The Hudson Review,* Vol. XXXI, No. 1 (Spring 1978).

SYLVIA PLATH

The facts of the case are easily reported. Sylvia Plath was born on October 27, 1932, daughter of Otto and Aurelia Plath. Her father taught German at Boston University and in 1934 published a study of bees. He died on November 2, 1940. Sylvia had a scholarship to Smith College, where she won the prizes, including a Fulbright to Cambridge University. In 1956 she married the poet Ted Hughes; their first child, Frieda, was born on April 1, 1960, their second, Nicholas, on January 17, 1962. In October 1962 the marriage fell apart, and they separated. A girl who lived mostly and terribly on her nerves, Sylvia made several attempts to kill herself, the first apparently in 1953. She died by her own hand on February 11, 1963.

Plath's first important book, *The Colossus,* was published in 1960, and her novel, *The Bell Jar,* appeared a few weeks before she died. But most of her work was published after her death: *Ariel* (1965), *Three Women* (1968), *Crossing the Water* and *Winter Trees* (1971), and a book of stories, *Johnny Panic and the Bible of Dreams* (1977). To a few readers Plath was already a legend before her death, but the publication of *Ariel* made the legend common if not universal property.

It is not an insult to Plath to say that her death was widely used to serve a wretched rhetorical purpose. It was already volubly assumed that the only valid experience was an experience of the abyss: risk was suffused with an aura entirely heroic. The ideal death was supposed to fulfil the appalling logic of being forced to live in such a world at such a time. Suicide was the sign of authenticity. Sanity was supposed to feel ashamed of itself. R. D. Laing and other writers made this sentiment popular and encouraged people to believe, or at least to assert, that divinest sense is indeed constituted by much madness. The jargon of authenticity, heightened with the vocabulary of sacrifice, provided the context in which Plath's poems were first widely read; and, before we knew where we were turning, Plath was accompanied in suicide by other gifted poets, Randall Jarrell in 1965, John Berryman in 1972, Anne Sexton in 1974.

Plath's early poems, many of them, offered themselves for sacrifice, transmuting agony, "heart's waste," into gestures and styles. In a short and often commonplace life, Plath's experience was not extensive. The fact that it was extraordinarily intense does not mean that it was in other respects remarkable. Self-absorbed, she shows what self-absorption makes possible in art, and the price that must be paid for it, in the art as clearly as in the death. Even in her famous poems she resented experience for not being enough or for not suiting her well enough or disposing itself warmly in her favour. The truth is that there was much in life, even in those bad years, which she prematurely rejected, despised even when it was not despicable. Probably the world is never worthy of us, but this is a conclusion we should reach later rather than sooner and never as a matter of theory or principle. The intensity of Plath's poems is beyond dispute, but not the justice of their complaint. Famous poems, including "Tulips" and "Lady Lazarus," now seem petulant to me, their self-regard understandable but still, when all is said, a pity:

> *Dying*
> *Is an art, like everything else.*
> *I do it exceptionally well.*
>
> *I do it so it feels like hell.*
> *I do it so it feels real.*
> *I guess you could say I've a call.*

You could also say, I guess, that self-absorption has turned into self-satisfaction and that the reader is unjustly taken for one of the "peanut-crunching crowd" pushing forward to see the big striptease, Lady doing her number and singing the blues.

The moral claims enforced by these poems now seem outlandish. It requires an indecently grandiose rhetoric to make a cut finger, in the poem "Cut," bleed global agony. The same rhetoric, in such poems as "The Tour" and "Eavesdropper," sends the poet's rage over the edge into spleen. Reading *The Bell Jar* again, I find blatant rather than just Plath's comparison between the electric-shock treatment administered to the heroine and the execution of the Rosenbergs. Even in Plath's most admired poem, "Daddy," the poet's conceit of herself as an imaginary Jew, "a Jew to Dachau, Auschwitz, Belsen," is far less convincing, by which I mean far less earned and imagined, than Berryman's in his story "The Imaginary Jew." The thrill we get from such poems is something we have no good cause to admire in ourselves. It is true, as Eliot wrote in "The Dry Salvages," that moments of agony are permanent, "with such permanence as time has," and that the torment of others remains an experience "unqualified, unworn by subsequent attrition." That is what we resent in the torment of others, that we cannot see it, as we see our own, wearing away. I recognize that this is a factor in my recent experience of going through Plath's poems again.

But there is something else. I cannot recall feeling, in 1963, that Plath's death proved her life authentic or indeed that proof was required. As a Christian, I acknowledge one sacrificial hero, and one is enough. But I recall that *Ariel* was received as if it were a bracelet of bright hair about the bone, a relic more than a book. Even if I wanted to have that feeling today, reading the *Collected Poems,* I would find it impossible. For one thing, the times have changed. The elaborate mixture of rage, guilt, frustration, and hysteria does not seem a mark of the present years. About death, evidently, there is much to be said; ignorance of the experience is not a constraint. Many of Plath's poems say on that subject as much as can be decently said, and more. In one of William Empson's coolest poems, "Ignorance of Death," the poet says that death, though an important subject, is one most people "should be prepared to be blank upon." I agree with him; also when he says that liberal hopefulness regards death "as a mere border to an improving picture," and that Freudians, regarding the death wish as fundamental, "though the clamour of life proceeds from its rival Eros," don't say "whether you are to admire a given case for making less clamour." Let me quote him:

> *Because we have neither hereditary nor direct knowledge of death*
> *It is the trigger of the literary man's biggest gun*
> *And we are happy to equate it to any conceived calm.*

We seem to have come back now, forty years after Empson's poem, to something like its tone: poised, not indifferent, but unwilling to provoke appalling ends.

I am not saying that our first reading of Plath was wrong, or even naïve, but that it seized upon an element in her poetry which spoke the hectic, uncontrolled things our conscience needed, or thought it needed. By being real, the poems made us real, certain that we existed. We accepted their violence as the true form of our own and were grateful. But in some respects we were naïve. I don't recall thinking, for instance, how derivative so many of Plath's poems are, how they hang upon poems by Blake, Ransom, Hopkins, Robert Lowell, and especially Theodore Roethke. "Bucolics" is an exercise in Ransom's way with language, "Pursuit" clings to Blake, "Ode to Ted" is a nice compliment to Hughes and weak only by comparison with his strength, "Point Shirley" is, as Hughes remarks, "a deliberate exercise in Robert Lowell's early style," and "Poem for a Birthday" is just as deliberate in its relation to Roethke. Debts don't matter, but the limiting factor in Plath's debts is that they begin and end by miming their originals, their relation to their masters is never more than adhesion.

What we should have noticed, though, in our first reading of Plath's poems was the distrust she turned upon communication. Not that her poetry is obscure. Part of its appeal is its directness. But her sense of language and her sense of other people were equally untrusting. Like many modern poets, she felt herself shortchanged by words:

> *The word, defining, muzzles; the drawn line*
> *Ousts mistier peers and thrives, murderous,*
> *In establishments which imagined lines*
> *Can only haunt.*

"Establishments" is a wonderful perception, especially as Plath wanted nothing established but a free range, open to ambrosial revelations. She never trusted words or trusted to luck with them or believed that words sometimes give, by grace and favour and courtship, more than they are importuned to give. She often took to language as if to revenge.

But I have to be more specific. Many of Plath's poems speak of words as if they were hooks, twisted with malice, letters twisted into smiles, hooks on which she, poor fish, is hung up to wriggle to her death. In a poem about burning old letters:

> *And here is an end to the writing,*
> *The spry hooks that bend and cringe, and the smiles, the smiles.*
> *And at least it will be a good place now, the attic.*
> *At least I won't be strung just under the surface,*
> *Dumb fish*
> *With one tin eye,*
> *Watching for glints,*
> *Riding my Arctic*
> *Between this wish and that wish.*

In "Daddy":

> *I could never talk to you,*
> *The tongue stuck in my jaw.*
>
> *It stuck in a barb wire snare.*
> *Ich, ich, ich, ich.*
> *I could hardly speak.*

In "The Courage of Shutting Up": " . . . there is that antique billhook, the tongue, / Indefatigable, purple." And in one of the heartbreaking hospital poems, "Tulips":

> *My husband and child smiling out of the family photo;*
> *Their smiles catch onto my skin, little smiling hooks.*

Every inviting gesture falls under the shadow of suspicion; nothing is innocent.

It is my recollection that in our first reading of Plath we thought her best work was that which expressed her talent, which we called her genius, most extremely. The poems were good in proportion to the outrage that provoked them. I read them differently now. In poems like "Wreath for a Bridal," there is a serious disproportion between what is being said and the moral claim enforced by the saying. The best poems now emerge as those that live without fuss, poems in her middle style which eschew willed sublimities, often poems of pure observation, the way something looks, the music it makes by looking so. I'm thinking of "Black Rook in Rainy Weather" or poems that discover something in the world other than Sylvia Plath worth attending to, like "All the Dead Dears" or poems about landscapes "unaltered by eyes" or felt to be so unaltered. Plath once claimed, quite early on, that she had forty unattackable poems. I haven't counted the poems that seem, on this recent reading, indisputable, but they include "Lorelei," "Mussel Hunter at Rock Harbor," "Two Campers in Cloud Country," "Candles," "Insomniac," "Stars over the Dordogne," "The Moon and the Yew Tree," "Mirror," "The Baby-sitters," "Three Women," "Little Fugue," "Poppies in October." As for "Daddy" and "Lady Lazarus," I am unrepentant; they are too pleased with themselves. The last stanza of "The Disquieting Muses" is unforgettable, but what leads to that place is rather slack.

The publishing history of Plath's work has been a mess; random, haphazard, no make or shape to it. The new edition prints 224 poems written after 1956 and set out now in chronological order of composition, or as near as possible to that end. A further 50 poems have been chosen by Ted Hughes from Plath's work prior to 1956. The "complete list of poems composed before 1956" is not, in fact, complete. In many cases, dates for early poems are not given, presumably because they are not reliably known. Still, there are bound to be more poems lying around or buried in improbable magazines. Ted Hughes has added some notes about circumstances in which certain poems were written. What the entire book shows is that Plath's work makes not so much a development but unpredictable explosions. The poems she wrote in October 1962 are the work of a poet possessed by a demon if not by herself, and from then to February 5, 1963, every day, virtually, is a torrent and a torment till the end.

From *The New York Times Book Review,* November 22, 1981.

JOHN ASHBERY

I

As We Know, by John Ashbery.

John Ashbery's new book is a collection of forty-eight poems, most of them fairly short, some as short as one sentence, the title and its completion in two lines. One poem, "Litany," is very long, several thousand lines, a double poem of two monologues running simultaneously down the pages. How you read it is up to you. The poem is divided into three unequal sections. On a first reading I read the left-hand monologue complete, all three sections, without even adverting to what was happening on the right-hand side of the page. Then the same for that side. On a second reading I switched from left to right at the end of each section. I can't report much difference. One can read each page as it appears, but that would be perverse, because the sentences rarely end with the page. The two voices are not as fully differentiated as the "He" and "She" of "Fantasia on 'The Nut-Brown Maid' " in Ashbery's *Houseboat Days* (1977), but the differences are enough to show that B is more ample, more opulent than A, more explicit, more in command of the feelings. A and B are my names, Ashbery doesn't give the speakers any names or differentiating marks. The two speakers could be one, in different moods or phases, but I choose not to think so.

A detour, first, otherwise I have no hope of making sense of *As We Know.* Let us agree, for the sake of such clarity as agreement provides, that a typical poem in one American tradition would be likely to feature a poet, or at least a poetic character, walking alone by the sea and trying to make sense of it. The self, the beach, the sea: constituents adequate to a certain kind of poem, though not to a complete poetry, unless we are content to see poetry discard its civic, social, and political concerns. In any case, think of the poetic character striding there alone, facing out and up to reality in the guise of the sea. Certain possibilities disclose themselves: the poet may, against great odds, find the reality of the sea so satisfying that he is content to apprehend it; or he may find it totally incomprehensible, and turn inland; or he may impose upon it his own vision, mastering it, or feeling that he masters it, answering one fact with a correspondingly imperious fiction, supreme, as Stevens liked to call it. From Emerson's "Sea-shore" to Stevens's "The Idea of Order at Key West" and Ammons's "Corsons Inlet," it has been a question of reality and the poetic imagination: the sea and the imagination, which I construe as the mind in the aspect of the freedom it claims.

John Ashbery's poems belong to this Romantic or post-Romantic tradition, even though his walks are not as marine as Ammons's. His beaches are more often city streets. No matter: it is the same question of reality and imagination. But the first sign of a poem by Ashbery is the misgiving with which conclusions are broached or approached. Stevens wanted to come to conclusions, and to let them differ from one another, according to his mood. In some of his poems, the imagination is baffled; in other poems, baffled for the moment but strong enough to grope toward an integration; and in still other poems, buoyant, triumphant, at least for the place and the time being. But Ashbery's poems post guards against conclusions. He once remarked, in a passage I quote from David Kalstone's *Five Temperaments* (1977):

> It seems to me that my poetry sometimes proceeds as though an argument were suddenly derailed and something that started out clearly suddenly became opaque. It's a kind of mimesis of how experience comes to me: as one is listening to someone else—a lecturer, for instance—who's making perfect sense but suddenly slides into something that eludes one. What I am probably trying to do is to illustrate opacity and how it can suddenly descend over us, rather than trying to be wilfully obscure.

Charming, and accurate enough, except that opacity is not the way
Ashbery's poems have of being difficult. If opacity means something that
is hostile to the transit of light, something defeating the swift translation
of words into sense, his poems are not opaque or even obscure. They are
serpentine, they allow us to follow them but not to know where precisely
we are going, or why. In "Clepsydra," a poem from *Rivers and Mountains*
(1966), Ashbery gives the formula we need, referring to

> *a serpentine*
> *Gesture which hides the truth behind a congruent*
> *Message, the way air hides the sky.*

This explains Ashbery's attitude to congruent messages, otherwise known
as conclusions. He doesn't mind producing them, so long as the reader
knows that they do not make the truth visible.

In "Notes Toward a Supreme Fiction," Stevens writes of revery:

> *He comes,*
>
> *Compact in invincible foils, from reason,*
> *Lighted at midnight by the studious eye,*
> *Swaddled in revery, the object of*
>
> *The hum of thoughts evaded in the mind,*
> *Hidden from other thoughts . . .*

That seems close to Ashbery's own thoughts: if you are shy about
congruent messages, and feel at home only in the misgiving with which
you entertain them, you are likely to feel that something as definite as a
thought is bogus, or at best premature. One of the speakers in "Litany"
speaks of

> *too much direction,*
> *Too many coils*
> *Of remembrance, too much arbitration.*

And the other one reports, in a similar mood:

                              Under
              The intimate light of the lantern
              One really felt rather than saw
              The thin, terrifying edges between things
              And their terrible cold breath.
              And no one longed for the great generalities
              These seemed to preclude.

In Ashbery's poems, what we feel is the hum of thoughts evaded in the mind, great generalities pressing to be heard and, in the event, being eluded.

Hence his procedure: "chronic reverie." Not daydreaming, but mind concentrated upon everything that defeats the logic of premise and conclusion. Ashbery is always willing to see "the evidence of the visual" replaced by "the great shadow of trees falling over life," because shadows have for him the same status as substances, variations the same status as themes. He likes to take his theme to Land's End, and if at that point it is barely visible: no matter. He does not "line phrases with the costly stuff of explanation."

His long poems are like letters to an intimate friend or lover, permitting the usual mixture of news and inconsequence, relying upon the friend's goodwill, knowing that, within reason and cadence, nearly anything goes. He wants "the kind of rhythm that substitutes for 'meaning' " or, as I would say, the kind of rhythm that evades "meaning." So his relation to things and messages offering themselves as congruent is that of a voluntary exile; he chooses to live in another country. The haven of citizenship is premature. Owing so much to Stevens, Ashbery settles his debts without aspiring to anything as grand as a supreme fiction: that, too, must be evaded.

Ashbery's poems turn and twist upon the question of self and the conditions it has to face. Mostly, they trace an elaborate and endlessly inventive circuit of consciousness as it tries to establish itself, working toward its proper tone. Sometimes, for pure relief, he takes pleasure in the otherness of things, "this otherness, this not-being-us" as he calls it in "Self-Portrait in a Convex Mirror," but more generally he approaches the forms of his experience as temptations, and regards their otherness as temptation in its most refined form. Among the available attitudes, he leans toward those that are suspicious of themselves and alive to the tempting positions they eventually disown. So his nouns often denote possible commitments he is not quite prepared to make. The truth is something else, it rarely coincides with the signs that offer to indicate it: it is neither this nor that, though it includes something of both. In "Self-Portrait," he writes of

> *Your gesture which is neither embrace nor warning*
> *But which holds something of both in pure*
> *Affirmation that doesn't affirm anything.*

But the problem is: how much can you disavow before you lose even the desire to avow? There is an unforgettable passage in "Self-Portrait" which begins with an acknowledgement that "the soul establishes itself." But immediately, as if the sentence were enough to draw suspicion upon it, the soul is put in question. How far can it swim out through the eyes and still return safely to its nest? Within a line or two the soul is discovered as a captive, and soon it is feared

> *that the soul is not a soul,*
> *Has no secret, is small, and it fits*
> *Its hollow perfectly: its room, our moment of attention.*

True, Ashbery is glossing a Renaissance painting, Parmigianino's self-portrait painted on a hemisphere of wood in imitation of his reflection in a mirror. But the passage goes far beyond Parmigianino, and brings one stage further the rhetoric of evasion I have been describing. Still, the risk is measurable.

It ceases to be measurable, however, when it threatens to suppress or neutralize the poet's own voice. Most poets who take on the sundry of experience have an interest in modifying the privilege of one part of an experience over another: they don't want to endow with special aura any particular images or symbols. But they make an exception in favour of their own voices. With this privilege, you can do nearly anything: the reader is willing to go along with a dominant voice wherever it leads him. Ashbery is remarkable in treating his voice with the same suspicion he directs upon other things. Taking every precaution against sounding like Stevens, he goes further and avoids sounding like himself. The fact that he does not succeed makes it wonderful that he should even try.

If you think that Ashbery's voice is not vigorous enough to make its suppression a problem, read "The Skaters" and "Self-Portrait" again, and listen to a voice that could not be denied.

> *It is best to remain indoors. Because there is error*
> *In so much precision. As flames are fanned, wishful thinking arises*
> *Bearing its own prophets, its pointed ignoring.*
> *And just as a desire*
> *Settles down at the end of a long spring day, over heather*
> *and watered shoot and dried rush field,*
> *So error is plaited into desires not yet born.*

But generally Ashbery apparently believes that his aesthetic of evasion requires him to include his own voice among the propositions, ideas, thoughts, and other congruent messages he must circumvent. In the short poems of *As We Know,* the voice we hear is what Ashbery could not entirely withhold. In this he is the most un-Yeatsian of poets.

Yet he is a stylist, one of the best. But the style he seeks and, with increasing flair since *Self-Portrait in a Convex Mirror* and *Houseboat Days,* finds is a flexible style in which he can negotiate everything on his own terms: no privileges are offered. There is a nice description of this style in Ashbery's introduction to *The Collected Poems of Frank O'Hara* (1971): " . . . a bag into which anything is dumped and ends up belonging there." Or it is a style consistent with the equable hospitality ascribed to the mind in *Houseboat Days:*

> *The mind*
> *Is so hospitable, taking in everything*
> *Like boarders.*

What Ashbery asks of his style is that it keep him in the space of his themes and, if necessary, let him escape their importunity: going back into style again. In *Three Poems* (1972), he describes, not at all ruefully, a situation in which "the life has gone out of our acts and into the attitudes." Normally, attitudes are preparations for acts, but in some cases, as Kenneth Burke has pointed out, they are substitutes for the corresponding acts. In Ashbery's poems the recession from acts to attitudes is seen as having its uses because it provides "an open field of narrative possibilities" instead of a single story he is no longer disposed to endow with authority. So his long poems do not tell stories as privileged interpretations of what happened; they make spaces to move around in, "which is all that matters."

Ashbery's sense of poetry, it follows, cannot be too severe in what it demands of the poet. In "Self-Portrait," charmed to remark that in French the word for weather is the word for time, Ashbery allows the reader to think that poetry is weather in following a course "wherein changes are merely features of the whole." The whole

> *is stable within*
> *Instability, a globe like ours, resting*
> *On a pedestal of vacuum, a ping-pong ball*
> *Secure on its jet of water.*

Presumably the mind, too, is weather, its veerings and derailings into opacity merely features of the whole. The analogy is common to Ashbery and to Stevens, as in "An Ordinary Evening in New Haven" where "the self, the town, the weather, in a casual litter" together say that "words of the world are the life of the world." Stevens's conclusion is more resolute than anything in Ashbery, who has always wanted to stop short of defining in any terms the life of the world. It is enough for him that poetry, like weather, includes all sorts of vagary without refuting the whole nature of weather.

Style, then, is a way of keeping going in all sorts of weather: but what does it look like on the page, or sound like in those held breaths and withheld voices? On the page it looks trim enough, in the voice or voices it sounds like talk; not talk that draws attention to the speaker, but talk as such, to be attended to mainly for its continuity. Ashbery's long poems keep the talk going until it threatens to denote a resting place, a conviction, a thought as distinct from the mind thinking, and then they circumvent the impulse, diverting it to convey the diffidence their poet feels about such grandeurs. "No sighs like Russian music." Talk, in Ashbery's poetry, denotes not a reference but a need to speak: such stability as he wants is embodied in the circuit of talk and does not luxuriate in the brilliance of any particular aperçu. As in "Litany"

The talk leads nowhere but is
Inside its space.

A long poem is simply a big space, congenially occupied. But of course it fends off other spaces over which the poet has otherwise no control. Within the space of the poem, Ashbery can set his own ostensibly casual decorum in which monsters, like hijackers, are talked down, diverted, or appeased. Ductility is Ashbery's word for this decorum in "Litany," though he has in mind the relation between writing and imagination; it corresponds to the ingenuity of a talker who keeps going lest some terrible fact, temporarily sequestered, invade his space.

As We Know is a difficult book, but not as obscure as, say, *The Tennis Court Oath* was obscure. Ashbery has sometimes believed that poetry should be able to do whatever painting can do; forgetting that a painting does not talk at all. He has also believed, at times, that the painter's freedom can be achieved in poetry by somewhat Surrealist means. None of these beliefs inhabits *As We Know,* and therefore its difficulty is of another kind. Neither of the monologues in "Litany" is difficult, only the relation between them. And in the relatively short poems the reader's mind is often puzzled but rarely brought to a standstill: lucidities come quickly and regularly enough to keep him in a buoyant state, his spirits well kept up. But it would be absurd to maintain that reading *As We Know* is plain sailing, or that the joy of its intermittent gorgeousnesses ("And imagine radiant blue flamingoes against the sacred sky") is enough to keep you going for the rest of a page.

The difficulties are not in local meaning, but in knowing or even sensing how one such meaning bears upon the next. I am reminded of William Empson's account of one of his seven types of ambiguity, which occurs "when a statement says nothing, by tautology, by contradiction, or by irrelevant statements, so that the reader is forced to invent statements of his own and they are liable to conflict with one another." The statements you invent for such poems as "Otherwise" and "There's No Difference" provide the contexts: in these poems the lines predicate a situation, but no particular situation is indicated, so we are forced into guesswork until we realize that a context, precisely established, would force the poem to be at home in it; and this is yet another fixed reference that Ashbery evades.

Still, the poems belong to an apparently human situation which we divine mostly by following the manoeuvrings of "I" and "You." These terms are not as reliable as their grammar, we must be prepared to see them fade out of sight and return as ghosts or shadows, but they give us points of reference, a body of feelings we care about, if not quite a definition. Fixity would be, on the reader's part, a gaucherie equivalent to insistence. Ashbery's time is "a present that is elsewhere," so there is no point in forcing his poems into a present that we insist upon fixing here.

Stevens says in *The Necessary Angel* that "modern reality is a reality of decreation, in which our revelations are not the revelations of belief, but the precious portents of our own powers." Finding the idea of decreation in Simone Weil's *La Pesanteur et la Grâce*, he noted "that decreation is making pass from the created to the uncreated, but that destruction is making pass from the created to nothingness." In Ashbery's version:

> We must first trick the idea
> Into being, then dismantle it,
> Scattering the pieces on the wind.

We must do this, apparently, because we are conscientious, sceptical of our native rhetoric.

Often in *As We Know* we come upon poems in which the weather is so changeable that we can barely recognize the season; and yet the style is so convincing that our assent runs ahead of the demand the poem makes for it. As in "Many Wagons Ago":

> At first it was as though you had passed,
> But then no, I said, he is still here,
> Forehead refreshed. A light is kindled. And
> Another. But no I said
>
> Nothing in this wide berth of lights like weeds
> Stays to listen. Doubled up, fun is inside,
> The lair a surface compact with the night.
> It needs only one intervention,
>
> A stitch, two, three, and then you see
> How it is all false equation planted with

Enchanting blue shrubbery on each terrace
That night produces, and they are backing up.

How easily we could spell if we could follow,
Like thread looped through the eye of a needle,
The grooves of light. It resists. But we stay behind, among them,
The injured, the adored.

I am not sure I understand this title, even with the help of "passed" in the first line. Two lovers, the injured one speaks, the adored one is not reported as even listening. The strongest gesture of the poem is the correction of an entertained hope ("But no I said"). "Forehead refreshed" is the sign of a relation seen with the thrill of hope; only to have its illumination quenched. Several senses conspired to report this disenchantment: "nothing . . . wide berth of lights . . . weeds . . . stays to listen." Presumably the lover's desire finds its history epitomized in passing from "fun" to "lair."

I take the poem to be about the difficulty of spelling, of reading the signs that pass between people, even when we are given bright letters to read, bright lights to negotiate. The equation, the sense we make of the evidence, is false because premature. You don't see this until you start stitching the pieces together. What I find touching in the poem is the evidence of easy conclusions entertained only to be set aside, relegated to the enchanting blue shrubbery; as, in the last stanza, two unusually opulent flourishes are sobered by the steadying force of "It resists." This force removes any suspicion we may have entertained that Ashbery is the Prufrock of American poetry ("It is impossible to say just what I mean!") or that he takes his feelings so seriously that he doesn't risk expressing them. Not so: his feelings do not sink to rest upon commonplaces of certitude and connection, but that is their distinction.

From *The New York Review of Books,* January 24, 1980.

II

Shadow Train, by John Ashbery.

If it were feasible to distinguish between poetry and poems, I would find the distinction handy for *Shadow Train,* John Ashbery's new collection. The book consists of fifty poems, each sixteen lines, four quatrains, unrhymed but variously linked. Of these eight hundred lines, I estimate that I can make sense of about five hundred; or, to put it more delicately, I find negotiable meaning in five hundred. But I believe the unforthcoming remainder is somehow germane to Ashbery's poetry as a whole, part of his enterprise, though it defeats me in every local sense.

The basic assumption of Ashbery's poetry is that everything is equally accessible to contemplation. Some of his poems have brooded upon the otherness of things, in several different tones of wonder, ruefulness, or satisfaction. But more typically he allows his mind to assume that reality is willing to be spiritualized, or spirited away, into poetry. A poem by Ashbery, even when it offers itself as one page and sixteen lines, is really a slice of meditation. At any moment his work is less a particular poem than poetry, or a long poem in progress. He knows "how to get by on what comes along," but his poetry is not dependent on such chances, it could get by nearly as well if nothing came along. The poems in *Shadow Train* get by, many of them, almost without contexts: most of their lines are grammatically clear, but they rarely have a context to which they may be referred, narrative, dramatic, or whatever. Many lines are like fragments of speech overheard in passing, they have the suggestiveness of being contextless, an air of meaning rather than a specific meaning.

Presumably Ashbery distrusts the certitude with which normal sentences point to their context to complete what their diction and grammar have started. In these new poems the only certitude permitted is the mind's confidence that it can somehow keep going. But the mind's power is shown mostly in evading the invitation of a theme, a situation, or a subject. Many of these poems veer from their subjects, thwarting the common satisfaction of a theme engaged in establishing itself. Themes come along, but the poet construes their arrival as effrontery, and with an unspoken appeal to a higher form of taste, he evades their importunity.

The evasion is imaginative and circuitous, and the circuit it describes is poetic; it makes poetry, rather than poems. Many of the new poems have arbitrary endings, and subside with a suggestion that the question will be continued "in our next," overleaf. Finality is not the merit they seek.

The current phase of Ashbery's art is marked by distrust, and by his confidence in getting along without the consolations of trust. His poetry speeds up the process by which a thing (a stone, a tree) becomes, in anyone's mind, a shadow of itself. Matter becomes spirit, and in that phase is indistinguishable from one's own spirit. The objects to which these poems ostensibly refer give the impression that they have never been other than virtual; knowing that they will eventually have to be transformed into spirit, they see no point in postponing the day. Ashbery's mind encounters things which, given his kind of attention, turn into mind with extraordinary speed and retain of themselves only a ghostly presence. The process is mimed, in its subversive character, by surrounding a word with inverted commas, to show that its aspiration toward the thing to which it refers has been deflected or nullified. To do this with words is to make oneself immune to their eloquence, now deemed blatant or banal.

It follows that the reader cannot be trusted: he would be likely to settle for the premature satisfaction that comes with a theme, complete with a beginning, a middle, and an apparently unarbitrary end. Ashbery's current poetry is at once secretive and voluble; secretive, because it does not trust the reader to ascribe the right status to secrets, once disclosed; and voluble, because the process of dislodging a reader from premature satisfactions takes time as well as a rarefied charm. If the poet takes away so much, he has to give much in return, some higher pleasure consistent with scruples and a decent reserve. Mostly, the higher pleasure is that of watching a mind of remarkably sinuous character contriving never to be caught in mere possession of a theme.

The poem "At the Inn" begins:

> *It was me here. Though. And whether this*
> *Be rebus or me now, the way the grass is planted—*
> *Red stretching far out to the horizon—*
> *Surely prevails now.*

I can't think of any other poet who would start by putting such a rebus around his head and yet keep going till he shrugged at last and stood free of it. It is a victory, I grant, but such as King Pyrrhus glossed at Asculum by saying: "One more such victory and we are lost." Eighteen pages later in *Shadow Train* we come to another Asculum called "Corky's Car Keys," beginning:

> *Despite, or because*
> *Of its rambunctiousness, Kevin and Tracy—only appearances*
> *Matter much—lingered in the not-night, red-painted brick*
> > *background*
> *Of festivals.*

About such lines, I find, it is easy not to care, but Ashbery's confidence is catching. I still don't know what the fuss in "Corky's Car Keys" is about, and as a poem it leaves me in the cold outside, but I trust Ashbery enough to believe, on the little evidence he provides, that this alienating poem plays some wild part in the larger effort, the poetry as a whole not yet whole.

It would be easy to say that in *Shadow Train* there is a notable disproportion between manner and matter. The manner is distinctive enough to put the poetry in danger of starting another school of Mannerism. But we can hardly talk of disproportion if the main object of the poetry is to subvert one's preoccupation with matter, or at least to surround its delivery with misgiving and distrust. Why ascribe privilege to matter, or to any particular matter, if it is all going to end up as spirit? If everything is equally accessible to contemplation, why italicize something merely because it happens to come along? The matter is subsumed in contemplation, a spiritual act verified not by an inventory of its deliveries but by the convincing momentum of the act itself.

If Ashbery distrusts what comes along bringing gifts, he distrusts for the same reason the imperiousness of a strong poetic voice. He is not one of the poets we think of as producing an easily recognizable voice; not Dickinson, Hardy, Yeats, Frost, or Larkin. His rhetoric does not draw his experiences toward itself, the voice proclaiming its authority. He is closer to Stevens in this respect, poets who withhold their voices, lying low within a language that can be set astir by a poet gifted in such manoeuvres. Ashbery undermines the authority of a single voice by setting up, within his sixteen lines, the partiality of several disembodied voices. In Frost's poems the speaker can be recognized as such, and the unity of the poem depends upon his conviction that he coincides with himself. Ashbery, offered this satisfaction, demurs, and veers away from any gesture that would herald the unity of a self. If you believe that man does not coincide with himself, you are likely to find the assumption of a single peremptory voice an effrontery.

The three hundred lines I find baffling in *Shadow Train* denote not the several parts of a unitary experience but the disparateness of experiences which refuse a common source or centre. The meditations persist but they evade, mostly, the unity of a single speaker: their force is dispersed as if among several voices, casually rather than causally related. I take it, then, that such accessible poems as "Untilted," "Written in the Dark," "Hard Times," and "Drunken Americans" represent in *Shadow Train* Ashbery's concession not only to the reader but to himself. If you have a voice, it's difficult to keep suppressing its certitude. In "Drunken Americans," Ashbery mocks the habit of thinking that our "god-given assertiveness" can triumph over "the stingy scenario," but there are times when he has to give himself over to the habit rather than to the more severe pleasure of kicking it. But he is never content for long: at any moment he is liable to jeer at himself or snarl at his felicities. Even in one of the more available poems, "Or in My Throat"—though the title is opaque to me—Ashbery catches himself in the act of being sweet and gives sourness the last words:

> *That's why I quit and took up writing poetry instead.*
> *It's clean, it's relaxing, it doesn't squirt juice all over*
> *Something you were certain of a minute ago and now your own face*
> *Is a stranger and no one can tell you it's true. Hey, stupid!*

From *The New York Times Book Review*, September 6, 1981.

III

Selected Poems, by John Ashbery.

John Ashbery has gathered into a remarkably handsome volume his choice poems from ten of the eleven books of poetry he has published in the past thirty years: *Some Trees* (1956), *The Tennis Court Oath* (1962), *Rivers and Mountains* (1966), *The Double Dream of Spring* (1970), *Three Poems* (1972), *Self-Portrait in a Convex Mirror* (1975), *Houseboat Days* (1977), *As We Know* (1979), *Shadow Train* (1981), and *A Wave* (1984). The selection comes, by my glancing impression, to about one-third of his complete work in poetry. His work in fiction and drama is of course another story.

Now that he has long survived his early poems, it is enough to say that they were precocious; which is what we usually say of a talent too clever for its own eventual good or too pleased with its brilliance. Some of Ashbery's earliest poems, including "The Instruction Manual" and "Illustration," were entirely accessible, but most of the work in *The Tennis Court Oath* seemed wilfully hostile to its readers. The poem "Europe," for instance, consisted mostly of phrases cut from *Beryl of the Bi-Planes,* a children's book which Ashbery found in Paris. Respect for Gertrude Stein is a permissible sentiment, but hardly enough to justify the arch configurations *The Tennis Court Oath* presented with an air of self-evident adequacy.

The standard explanation for this phase of Ashbery's work is that he resented the premature commitment of words, and wanted to seize the diverse freedoms of music and painting. Music, because it enacts its presence without offering to mean something: painting, because relations between paint and canvas may be promiscuous, exempted from the contract words have signed to mean, more or less, what they say. The musical analogy doesn't bring us far into Ashbery's early work, but painting is indeed more feasible. How to take Cubist freedoms in a linguistic medium inimical to arbitrary juxtaposition: that, or something like it, seems to have been Ashbery's project in the early years. In "Leaving the Atocha Station," authority is claimed not for experiences real or imagined but for the mind provoking itself to extreme fancies and, as if in the same gesture, mocking its inventions. T. S. Eliot said of Shakespeare's early poems and plays that they were "intractably poetic," and he praised him for putting his precocious language on a thin diet, cooling its blood, so that it might gain flexibility over a far wider range of feelings. The elaborate music of *The Tempest* and *A Winter's Tale* would be impossible but for the disciplined flexing of his style in *Coriolanus* and *Antony and Cleopatra.*

Rivers and Mountains was Ashbery's *Coriolanus.* Or at least it was the book in which he gave up his addiction to "the poet's gibberish"—in Stevens's phrase—and resorted to "the gibberish of the vulgate." Conventions of discourse may be just as arbitrary as snippets from *Beryl of the Bi-Planes,* but Ashbery evidently decided at least to take them into his poetry, like boarders. He was not under obligation to trust them or to expose them to the temptation of stealing the spoons. Besides, he could always hold clichés and common discourse for questioning and let them defend themselves against his gibberish. Ideally, and in much of his poetry from *Rivers and Mountains* to *A Wave,* he could maintain decent relations not only between these two dictions but between corresponding affiliations in his temperament.

The temperament I have in view is found in two forms or moods. One is that of an aesthete, a not distant cousin of Walter Pater and Apollinaire, adept of somewhat contrived elegance, as debonair as he is knowingly doomed. The second is that of a man willing to credit routine with a sort of truthfulness: to such a man, the surface of things is just as valid as the depth we too easily assume it conceals. Willing to sway with the drift of things, he trusts that his presence of mind will be enough to keep him going. Day-by-day vigilance is a better bet than refusals and pedantry.

What common phrases seem to speak of, in Ashbery's later poetry, is the possibility of consent, a form of communication predicated upon nothing more exacting than daily habits and currencies but capable at any moment of being nuanced, as by a flick of the wrist, into more challenging and more challenged forms of itself. In "Clepsydra"—the word, by the way, means a water clock, and the poem is a revery about time—Ashbery has a passage about waterfalls and the way they "drum at different levels." Then this:

> Each moment
> *Of utterance is the true one; likewise none are true,*
> *Only is the bounding from air to air, a serpentine*
> *Gesture which hides the truth behind a congruent*
> *Message, the way air hides the sky, is, in fact,*
> *Tearing it limb from limb this very moment.*

"Tearing it limb from limb" and "this very moment" are not in any disabling sense clichés, they are Ashbery's acknowledgement of congruent messages behind which his nuancing mind is free to go its serpentine way. They are also his unironic acceptance of a shared context, the weather of things as the basis of consent. Truth doesn't inhere in anything separately considered but in the transaction, the bounding, between different elements of speech; public and private, curial and vernacular, studied and demotic. Or if it is pompous to speak of truth, the poetry settles for processes of understanding, which may be enough to be going on with.

It follows that Ashbery's common style in his later poems is the vernacular, turned and tuned toward cadences we soon recognize as his, as in "The One Thing That Can Save America":

> I know that I braid too much my own
> Snapped-off perceptions of things as they come to me.
> They are private and always will be.
> Where then are the private turns of event
> Destined to boom later like golden chimes
> Released over a city from a highest tower?
> The quirky things that happen to me, and I tell you,
> And you instantly know what I mean?
> What remote orchard reached by winding roads
> Hides them? Where are these roots?

I braid, say, a girl's hair by dividing it into three or more strands and interweaving them, making a diagonal pattern along its course: a procedure agreeably but not emphatically ornamental. What the speaker does with his snapped-off perceptions is, he allows, much ado of a structuring kind about nothing much. It is the intimacy of tone in the passage which makes it possible for Ashbery to accommodate not only his self-deprecation but his grandeurs, the booming chimes which we think we hear more regularly in Hart Crane's poems than in Ashbery's. It is his trust in such intimacy that enables him to get by winding roads to the remote orchard.

I concur with the fairly common view that *Self-Portrait in a Convex Mirror* is Ashbery's finest achievement to date, and that "The Skaters," from *Rivers and Mountains,* made the later title poem of *Self-Portrait* possible. Both poems make a poetics of contingency by the device of accepting it and unresentfully living with the acceptance. But I shouldn't give the impression that Ashbery has relaxed into a banal sense of life. His current style is indeed concessive, but it retains enough force of quirkiness to take the harm out of his concessions. It is true that Ashbery's selection for the new book has set aside the really bizarre poems of *The Tennis Court Oath* and retained from that book only the poems which at least pay some tribute to accessibility. But he has not turned his book into a *Golden Treasury* or eliminated the hard poems. I wish he had given more of "The Skaters" and the later "Litany" (1979), but the selection is still so rich that I can't complain. What it makes clearer than ever is that Ashbery's mature poems, circuitous and odd as they often are, are the kind of poetry one cares about. Many descriptions of them make Ashbery sound like a lesser Wallace Stevens, but they are misleading. "Self-Portrait in a Convex Mirror," "The Skaters," "Fantasia on 'The Nut-Brown Maid,'" and twenty other poems nearly as good make up a body of work extraordinarily diverse and winning. I once thought that Ashbery was a poet's poet, and that the pleasure of the poems must be too rarefied to be commonly available. Not so: the formula is obtuse, it doesn't recognize the warmth of Ashbery's engagement with the themes I now see in the *Selected Poems* —loss, grief, the difficulty of making sense, gratitude for such sense as can be made.

From the *Boston Globe,* December 22, 1985.

A NOTE ON THE TYPE

The text of this book was set in film in a typeface called Griffo, a camera version of Bembo, the well-known monotype face. The original cutting of Bembo was made by Francesco Griffo of Bologna only a few years after Columbus discovered America. It was named for Pietro Bembo, the celebrated Renaissance writer and humanist scholar who was made a cardinal and served as secretary to Pope Leo X. Sturdy, well balanced, and finely proportioned, Bembo is a face of rare beauty. It is, at the same time, extremely legible in all of its sizes.

Composition by Superior Type, Champaign, Illinois

Printed and bound by The Maple-Vail Book Manufacturing Group, Binghamton, New York

Designed by Tasha Hall